Service-Learning

Service-Learning

History, Theory, and Issues

EDITED BY BRUCE W. SPECK AND
SHERRY L. HOPPE

Westport, Connecticut
London

5/2005

Library of Congress Cataloging-in-Publication Data

Service-learning : history, theory, and issues / edited by Bruce W. Speck
and Sherry L. Hoppe.
   p.   cm.
   Includes index.
   ISBN 0–89789–852–4
   1. Student service.   I. Speck, Bruce W.   II. Hoppe, Sherry L. (Sherry Lee), 1947–
   LC220.5.S4583   2004
370.11′5—dc22   2004008683

British Library Cataloguing in Publication Data is available.

Library of Congress Catalog Card Number: 2004008683
ISBN: 0–89789–852–4

First published in 2004

Praeger Publishers, 88 Post Road West, Westport, CT 06881
An imprint of Greenwood Publishing Group, Inc.
www.praeger.com

Printed in the United States of America

The paper used in this book complies with the
Permanent Paper Standard issued by the National
Information Standards Organization (Z39.48–1984).

10 9 8 7 6 5 4 3 2 1

Copyright Acknowledgments

The editors and publisher gratefully acknowledge permission to use the following material:

Excerpts from *Personal interviews related to the service-learning program at the University of the
Incarnate Word,* by R. Connelly & P. Lonchar (2003, unpublished manuscript, University of
the Incarnate Word Faculty, San Antonio, TX) used by permission of Dr. Robert Connelly
and Dr. Patricia Lonchar.

Contents

Introduction

Bruce W. Speck and Sherry L. Hoppe

As Barber and Battistoni (1993) noted ten years ago, service-learning "is [in] some ways a rather new pedagogy" (p. ix). (Barber and Battistoni hedge by using [in] *some ways,* and as Rocheleau points out in Chapter One of this volume, the theoretical underpinnings of service-learning can be traced to antiquity.) In fact, the bulk of the literature that has been produced on what has become known as service-learning has been published in the last decade. For example, the earliest source Ikeda (2001) cites in her list of significant resources for service-learning was published in 1996, and as Ikeda notes, the venerable *Michigan Journal of Community Service-Learning* was first published in 1994. Indeed, the literature on service-learning literally began exploding in the mid-1990s and has not abated. If the scholarly writing dedicated to a particular topic is any indication of the topic's interest to scholars, then service-learning has captured the imaginations of many in the academy. Why?

The brief answer to that question is stolen from Chinua Achebe: *Things Fall Apart.* A dominant theme in the literature on service-learning is that American culture has lost a sense of community; socially things have fallen apart, and Robert D. Putnam's *Bowling Alone* is often cited as evidence of the loss of what might be called social capital. Barn raisings are wistfully recollected from bygone days. *Alienation* is a word found often in postmodern criticism, and deconstructionists take delight in showing that a reader can't trust authorial intentions as *appear* on the surface of a text. A text has to be deconstructed so that the import of authorial intentions is revealed, and, in general, that revelation will be the uncovering of an author's attempt to mask a grab for power. Despite the anticommunity approach of deconstructionists, universities should be models of community, but as Astin (1993) has pointed out, "During the past forty or fifty years American universities have come to be dominated by three powerful and interrelated values: *materialism, individualism,* and *competitiveness*" (p. 4), thus demoting community as a vital force within the academy itself. It appears, then, that the academy is implicated in the fracturing of community in America.

Enter service-learning as a remedy for fractured community. By linking theory in the classroom with student participation in some sort of community activity outside the classroom, professors can help remedy the problem of a broken community nationally. And as service and learning became more intimately connected, the literature began using the term *service-learning,* the hyphen being a symbolic nexus that linked inextricably praxis and theory so that they are no longer two separate activities but symbiotic. An intense interest in service-learning throughout the academy has been fueled by the high idealism of service-learning as a way to make a difference nationally by producing a generation of citizens who would restore community. And if that motivation for service-learning explained sufficiently the meteoric rise of service-learning, this book would not be necessary, but the seemingly transparent value of service-learning as a pedagogical initiative to promote community is really not so transparent. Service-learning, it turns out, is not monolithic, relying on one theoretical stance unattended by complex questions about what the teaching-learning enterprise is all about. Indeed, service-learning is quite controversial, even revolutionary.

As Howard (1998) says, "Over time I have come to realize that to create a classroom that is consistent with the goals and values of service-learning, it is absolutely necessary to deprogram or desocialize students and instructors away from traditional classroom roles, relationships, and norms, and then resocialize them around a new set of behaviors" (p. 25). Harkavy and Benson (1998) agree. They say that the goal of service-learning should be to "overthrow the aristocratic Platonic theory of 'liberal education' and institute a democratic Deweyan theory of 'instrumental education'" (p. 19). Morrill (1982) also stresses the importance of dramatic educational change to accommodate service-learning: "The task of civic education is, then, especially difficult and ambitious for it involves the empowerment of persons as well as the cultivation of minds. This is not an undertaking for which contemporary colleges and universities are especially well equipped because many of the well-known features of modern collegiate education create serious barriers to a powerful civic education" (p. 365). In short, service-learning is a revolutionary pedagogy, perhaps even a dangerous pedagogy.

But we reiterate that service-learning is not monolithic, and although one theoretical position that undergirds service-learning can be accurately labeled revolutionary, another theoretical strain that seeks to provide opportunities to service and allows students to serve without requiring them to assume the validity of a particular political position is quite modest in its call for educational reform. The academy can continue to encourage students to think critically, but it should not promote a particular social agenda.

The historical and theoretical tensions in service-learning pedagogy prompted us to create a volume that would forthrightly outline and address those tensions. The purpose of this volume, therefore, is to provide readers with an overview of the issues related to service-learning and to provide a debate format for three theoretical positions. Accordingly, the book is divided into three parts.

Part One deals with historical issues related to service-learning. In Chapter One, Jordy Rocheleau traces the theoretical roots of service-learning to the ancient world but hastens to add that community service is most firmly linked pedagogically to progressive education as expounded by John Dewey. As Rocheleau notes, service-learning is not the vocabulary Dewey used, but service-learning can be traced to his educational theory. One of the objections to Dewey's educational theory, as Rocheleau points out, is that it appears to foster indoctrination and forgoes the value neutrality so admired by proponents of logical positivism, a charge that continues to haunt service-learning based on Dewey's educational theory.

In Chapter Two, Gregory Zieren and Peter Stoddard focus on the history of service-learning in the context of American education in the nineteenth and twentieth centuries. They argue that service-learning is tied closely to the development of professional education in America, the application of learning for those who intended to become engineers and home economists, for example. Zieren and Stoddard also discuss the Progressive Era and Dewey's influence, but they direct their attention to the role social work has taken in promoting the ideals of service-learning. Thus, social work is seen as the prime example of a profession that has promoted democratic participation by aiding the disadvantaged through the integration of theory and praxis, in other words, through service-learning.

Part Two of this book addresses the need for a thorough investigation of three dominant theoretical perspectives that undergird service-learning praxis. In this section of the book, our intention is to allow a proponent of a theoretical perspective to provide a detailed justification for that perspective. Then a critic of that perspective provides a rebuttal. At the close of the section, the three justifications and rebuttals are synthesized. In essence, the second section is the heart of the book. Our desire is to provide informed perspectives on the vital theoretical issues that drive service-learning pedagogy, and we think the authors of the chapters in this section demonstrate quite clearly that they are passionate about the theoretical positions they hold.

In Chapter Three, C. F. Abel provides a justification of the philanthropic model, the position that classroom pedagogy should be designed to nurture students' judicious self-direction sans promoting a particular political stance. In Chapter Four, Arthur Sementelli critiques the philanthropic model and finds it wanting. For Sementelli, the philanthropic model justifies privilege, undermining equality and democratic participation.

In Chapter Five, J. B. Watson, Jr., provides a justification of the civic model, the position that a vital role of American higher education is to socialize the next generation of citizens so that these citizens actively promote democratic ideals such as equality and become agents of social change. In Chapter Six, Robert Exley disputes Watson's claims, including Watson's notion that the civic model is the dominant model of service-learning, pointing out four models of practice in service-learning. In fact, Exley notes that service-learning as explicated by Watson does not allow for the complexity of integrating service and learning.

In Chapter Seven, Frank Codispoti provides a justification of the communitarian model, the position that citizens are social creatures who naturally seek community. Citizens as social creatures perceive that their best interests are served when they renounce a rights-bearing approach to the social order and accept the communitarian approach that fosters a sense of commonality and shared experience among all the members of the community. In Chapter Eight, Christina Murphy takes issue with Codispoti, noting that Codispoti defines communitarianism in such as way as to limit the usefulness of the communitarian approach. In Murphy's view, communitarianism, to be effective, must move away from the liberal ideas of community and autonomy that Codispoti espouses. For Murphy, the most telling problem with Codispoti's argument is that Codispoti is long on theory and short on application.

In Chapter Nine, Sherry L. Hoppe synthesizes the issues in the previous six chapters, showing that theoretical issues related to service-learning are complex and the different schools of thought appear to be irreconcilable.

Part Three of this book addresses other issues related to service-learning. For instance, Chapter Ten tackles the ethics of classroom advocacy. C. F. Abel, J. G. Lacina, and C. D. Abel provide a theoretical matrix for evaluating whether classroom advocacy is ethical and then apply that matrix to the philanthropic and civic models. In Chapter Eleven, Richard Henderson shows how professional programs at a Catholic university fit the philanthropic model of service-learning. Finally, Bruce W. Speck provides an unannotated bibliography of selected service-learning sources for those who wish to delve deeper into the literature on service-learning.

If, as we suspect, service-learning will continue to attract the attention of the academy as a viable pedagogy to address social concerns, then a review of the historical roots of service-learning, a debate about the appropriateness of employing a particular theoretical position to inform the applications of service-learning, and a frank discussion of classroom advocacy and the application of service-learning in a sectarian setting are all topics that merit the attention of the various constituencies of the academy. Indeed, our hope is that this volume will spark increasing debate about a new pedagogy that promises so much for the good of society and concomitantly requires so much of the academy, even the possible overhaul of the academy as we now know it.

REFERENCES

Astin, A. W. (1993). *Higher education and the concept of community*. Fifteenth David Dodds Henry Lecture, University of Illinois at Urbana-Champaign. (ERIC database: No. ED 384 279)

Barber, R. B., & Battistoni, R. (Eds.). (1993). *Education for Democracy*. Dubuque, IA: Kendall/Hunt.

Harkavy, I., & Benson, L. (1998). De-Platonizing and democratizing education as the bases of service-learning. In R. A. Rhoads & J. P. F. Howard (Eds.), *Academic service-learning: A pedagogy of action and reflection* (pp. 11–20). New Directions for Teaching and Learning, no. 73. San Francisco: Jossey-Bass.

Howard, J. P. F. (1998). Academic service-learning: A counternormative pedagogy. In R. A. Rhoads & J. P. F. Howard (Eds.), *Academic service-learning: A pedagogy of action and reflection* (pp. 21–29). New Directions for Teaching and Learning, no. 73. San Francisco: Jossey-Bass.

Ikeda, E. K. (2001). Additional resources. In M. Canada & B. W. Speck (Eds.), *Developing and implementing service-learning programs* (pp. 97–100). New Directions for Higher Education, no. 114. San Francisco: Jossey-Bass.

Morrill, R. L. (1982). Educating for democratic values. *Liberal Education, 68*, 365–376.

PART I

History

CHAPTER 1

Theoretical Roots of Service-Learning: Progressive Education and the Development of Citizenship

Jordy Rocheleau

SERVICE-LEARNING'S ROOTS IN PROGRESSIVE EDUCATION AND THE CONTRIBUTION OF DEWEY

In one sense, the connection of education to community service has venerable theoretical roots. Philosophers of education have repeatedly argued that a central goal of education, and higher education in particular, is the production of citizens prepared to serve the community. The classical theories of Plato (1961) and Aristotle (1997a, 1997b) presented education as intended to produce good persons, a goal that included both knowledge and a disposition to act on that knowledge in pursuit of good ends.

This concern continued into modern philosophies of education. The classic liberal thinkers argued for a central role for values and citizenship in education. John Locke (1997) and Immanuel Kant (1997) argued for character education and John Stuart Mill (1997) for an education for "capable and sensible" civic participation. Even Jean-Jacques Rousseau's romantically individualistic philosophy of education articulated in *Emile* (1979) ultimately involves a plan for sympathetic and civil interaction with other members of society.

In the United States, in his influential program of education for Virginia, Thomas Jefferson (1964) argued in favor of a basic universal education for males on the grounds that this would prepare them for the necessary conditions of citizenship. Furthermore, Jefferson argued that more advanced education should be provided for a select few who would then become civic leaders and civil servants. Criticisms of Jefferson's aristocratic elitism aside, he is clear that the education of the future elite should have the aim of benefiting the state and society. The student would graduate to civil servant, applying the broad information, theories, and principles gathered in his liberal education to practical affairs as he became a lawyer, legislator, business leader, scientist, or engineer.

Thus, classical philosophers of education are in agreement that education should include not only facts and scientific theories but also knowledge of fundamental moral principles and the development of a character with the disposition to act on these principles. With respect to higher education, these philosophers envisioned university graduates prepared to contribute to the alleviation of human suffering, the insurance of human rights, and the development of a productive society. For their own well-being states should provide an education of economic and political leadership and social and ethical concern.

However, although these classic theories delineated community service as a goal of education, the idea unique to service-learning—that community service should be part of the educational curriculum itself—has more recent roots. Whereas in classic educational theory, the application of knowledge to social problems was thought to follow the completion of study, in service-learning, community service is part of the pedagogical method through which theories and facts are learned.

The idea that community service can and should be introduced in the course of education as a means of instruction can be traced to progressive education and its most influential, original, and systematic theorist, John Dewey. Dewey's understanding of the nature of knowledge and society and his corresponding philosophy of education provide theoretical roots for service-learning. His pragmatist, or alternatively instrumentalist or experimentalist, theory of knowledge was central to his philosophy of education (Dewey, 1916, 1963; Giles & Eyler, 1994). He argued against the prevalent epistemological theories from early modern rationalism and empiricism to the twentieth-century analytic philosophy. These theories portrayed knowledge as objective and of two general types: on one hand, empirical knowledge based on the data provided by our senses and on the other hand, a priori, principled knowledge provided by the inherent workings of the mind, in areas such as math, logic, and ethics.

Against this view of objective knowledge, Dewey argued that knowledge is always an active attempt to respond to one's situation in the world. Knowledge does not mirror the world but is rather a tool for getting around in it. In fact, Dewey suggested that the purpose of reasoning is to solve the problems that confront us. When one feels no difficulty or challenge—when one is moving freely, easily, and comfortably about in the world—one does not consciously reflect on, define, or analyze one's experiences. Valid ideas are those that help us to resolve our problems and doubts and return to a satisfied condition. So a scientific theory is held to be true if we can apply it to future cases. An ethical principle is true if it can be used to resolve the problems that confront people. When the theory or principle leads to problems and is not part of the solution, we begin to say that it is not true (Dewey, 1957, 1960). As Dewey (2002) puts it, "A moral law, like a law in physics, is not something to swear by and stick to at all hazards: it is a formula of the way to respond when specified conditions present themselves. Its soundness and pertinence are tested by what happens, when it is acted upon" (p. 431).

Dewey's argument for a reconstruction in the philosophy of knowledge is paralleled by his critique of traditional educational theory. Classic philosophies of education suggested that students should be taught basic facts and principles, which, having been mastered, could be used as a basis to approach future problems. On this traditional model, the goal of education is to get the student to acquire the core facts and theories that an educated person must know (Hutchins, 1953; Locke, 1997; Mill, 1997). The method of education is usually didactic; the student is lectured to about material that is to be memorized, with some reinforcement through repetition.

For Dewey, by contrast, the fact that reflection always orients us in experience means that the acquisition of knowledge should be continually related to concrete situations and the challenges they present. This suggests that traditional education and its goals must be abandoned in favor of active, progressive education. This active, practical form of learning has at least two benefits from his instrumentalist perspective.

First, students learn ideas, theories, and facts in the actual life contexts that give them their true meaning and validity. One does not really understand the concepts of science or humanities if one does not know how to apply them to concrete situations in all their complexity. Students who learn concepts through directly realizing their useful application know them better and more genuinely than those who have simply memorized abstract theories and facts. Learning in actual life contexts also tends to involve the full engagement of the student, as he or she is physically and emotionally involved in the subject of study. This engagement contrasts with traditional education in which study is abstracted from meaningful life experiences to prepare the student for the distant future. Dewey notes that traditional educators are always trying to think of how to make their material interesting to students. He comments that the need to make the material interesting is because of its separation from real-life contexts. By contrast, when students are involved in real-life contexts, there is no need to make material interesting (Dewey, 1913).

In addition to what Dewey calls "interaction" with one's situation, progressive, experiential education also involves what Dewey calls "continuity." Continuity gives students practice testing theories and solving problems so that they can respond intelligently to future situations that are characterized by changing circumstances and new problems. This capacity for reflective problem solving is the mark of an educated individual. The world is constantly changing and along with it the facts and theories. By schooling a student to both interact with a specific situation and recognize continuities in experience, progressive education integrates knowledge and practical application (Dewey, 1963; Giles & Eyler, 1994).

Dewey (1963) famously argued for an "education of, by and for experience" (p. 29). Most obviously, an education *by* experience is one in which students learn by having experiences. By an education *of* experience Dewey is suggesting that students' capacity to understand their world should be increased. For Dewey, experience is an active response to a situation and can therefore be more or less reflective and intelligent. Education seeks to make experience intelligent. Finally, education is *for* experience in that it should prepare students to deal with future situations. Presumably any education, even the most didactic, would involve some form of experience. However, Dewey (1963) emphasizes that "the belief that all genuine education comes about through experience does not mean that all experiences are genuinely or equally educative" (p. 25). Experiences must open the mind to future inquiry and orient the individual to intelligently respond to concrete situations. The task of the educator is to plan the experiences of the student for such resourceful intelligence.

It is already clear from what has been said that service-learning could be a form of progressive education based on Dewey's model. Insofar as service-learning involves grappling with real social problems, requiring students to attempt to come up with solutions to them, and applying ideas studied in the classroom, this type of education is thoroughly Deweyan. Of course, progressive education would not have to take the form of service-learning. Other types of hands-on, problem-solving tasks could be undertaken, with students solving their own self-interested problems or engaging in internships with businesses. However, other aspects of Dewey's educational philosophy that relate to his social and political theory lend further support specifically to service-learning as a pedagogical method.

Dewey held that knowledge and learning were fundamentally social activities. Dewey's thought was very much influenced by his study of Hegelian idealism as well as the earlier pragmatism of Charles Sanders Peirce (1972). From them he received the idea that knowledge can only exist in a community with a shared recognition of its validity. In Dewey's experimental pragmatism, this yielded the result that valid theories are those that solve problems for a community and not just for an individual.

For Dewey, the attempt to come up with solutions that work for a community inevitably suggests the structure of democracy as the best method for solving problems. He goes on to argue in favor of democratic decision making as the way to resolve social conflicts. Dewey recommends democracy not because of any inherent moral rights to political participation but rather because he sees it as the most sensible way for people who have conflicts of interest to collectively solve their problems. For Dewey, voting rights alone did not constitute democracy. He was an early theorist of what is now called participatory democracy (Pateman, 1976), which calls for active citizen participation in identifying social problems and proposing and implementing solutions. Only by encouraging such participation, Dewey argued, could a community retain the cooperation required for a productive and fulfilling society. Dewey, whose philosophical tendency was always to avoid dichotomies, argued that democracy is an alternative to the opposing destructive ideologies of individualism and collectivism. On one hand, he argued that individuality requires community support and community involvement, so a society of detached egoistic individuals would be neither fulfilling to individuals nor self-sustaining as a whole. On the other hand, Dewey was opposed to any form of collectivist theory that attempted to suppress individuality for the greater good. He argued that a functioning society required independent individuals to engage in their own reflection and activity separately from that of the state. Social problems could only be solved if private but socially engaged citizens took an active part in describing the nature of the problems and proposing solutions (Dewey, 1916, 1960).

The idea of the social nature of the individual and the necessity of democratic participation has implications for the process of education. It follows that education should be a social task in which the process of inquiry is a joint venture. Students should solve problems as groups rather than just as individuals, thereby once again learning the context of real situations and being prepared to enter the social world and face problems in which solutions require cooperation with others. This pedagogical model aims to develop citizens who would be simultaneously mature and independent in thought, on one hand, and oriented to cooperation and contribution to the civic good on the other. Dewey was explicit about the close links among democracy, individuality, community, and education: "A society which makes provision for participation in its good of all its members on equal terms and which secures flexible readjustment of its institutions through interaction of the different forms of associated life is in so far democratic. Such a society must have a type of education which gives individuals a personal interest in social relationships and control, and the habits of mind which secure social changes without introducing disorder" (1916, p. 99).

Dewey himself never outlined a system of community-service-based learning, much less used the term *service-learning*. However, the pedagogical goals and methods of service-learning find a clear basis in his educational theory. In the course of education in various subjects, students are presented with genuine social problems and are challenged to inquire into them and test solutions for them. This is done in cooperation with others—both other students and other members of the community—to find solutions that are mutually acceptable. Community service makes theories and concepts concrete, teaches the process of engaged social inquiry, and prepares the individual to actively participate in the democratic process.

Not only does Dewey's theory offer general theoretical support for service-learning, but it also has implications for the form that this education should take. If service-learning is to foster problem solving and democratic social engagement, it should involve more than students devoting time to useful or well-intended community service tasks, such as picking up garbage or delivering food to the needy. Rather, progressive educational thought suggests that students should be involved in the process of defining the problem to be solved, thinking through solutions, and working with others to achieve a commonly acceptable result. In short, it suggests that service-learning should take the form of education in community organizing and community building.

At the University of Chicago where Dewey spent the majority of his academic career, Dewey and colleagues founded what they called the Laboratory School (which later became known as the Dewey School), where progressive education was put into practice. There, students would learn mainly through conducting various group projects in which they would solve practical problems. The school was a laboratory in a dual sense— for University of Chicago educators experimenting with new hands-on, progressive curricula and for the students of the school who learned by scientifically approaching practical problems (Hines, 1972).

Dewey influenced a whole generation of progressive theorists and educators who rejected traditional educational methods and attempted to organize schools on this basis. Dewey's disciple William Kilpatrick developed what he called the "project method" in which education was always organized around projects. Kilpatrick provides the foreword for an early explicit proposal for service-learning, Paul Hanna's *Youth Serves the Community* (1936). In this text, the idea of progressive, project-based education is applied to various forms of social problems. Hanna outlines an array of potential projects in which young people can both serve their communities and develop their own skills. Chapters include recommendations for service regarding public safety, civic beauty, community health, industrial improvement, protection of resources and local history, and the fostering of the arts (Hanna, 1936). Such early works inspired by progressive educational theory are predecessors of current service-learning initiatives.

THEORETICAL OPPOSITION TO PROGRESSIVE EDUCATION AND SERVICE-LEARNING

From their incipience, progressive education and service-learning met with objections and challenges. Hands-on project learning was criticized as impure, insufficiently rigorous, ethically and politically biased, and detracting from objective study and the broader goals of a liberal education. Traditional liberal educators argued for the promotion of an education not tailored to practical success as directly as to general knowledge. Progressive education's emphasis on practical problem solving and contextual learning was at odds with giving the students a comprehensive background in generally valid theories and the most important facts. Concepts and ideas could be amassed without always having to immediately apply them, especially to a drawn-out, concrete project. The time-consuming and complex nature of practical projects might keep students from developing mastery of basic knowledge and intellectual disciplines (Hutchins, 1953).

Progressive, project, and service movements in education have been resisted by a few competing conceptions of what is of central curricular import. First, some became concerned with a failure of students to learn basic skills such as reading, writing, and arithmetic. Higher education also faces concern for these basics as well as a call to return to giving a broader intellectual background in the liberal arts, including knowledge of history, literature, economics, and politics. When the Soviet Union appeared to be surpassing the United States in science and technology after the launching of the first Sputnik space flight in 1957, calls were made for the United States to return to a more scientifically rigorous educational system. This included calls to abandon progressive, hands-on programs, whose methods appeared less rigorous and whose subject matter had little direct relationship to national defense (Patton & Mondale, 2001). This sense of a lack of rigor and commitment to science and applied science was repeated again in the 1980s after economic recession and the relative success of Japan, which began to outperform the United States in the automobile and other technology-intensive industries. In the 1983 *Nation at Risk* report condemning the state of American education, Secretary William Bennett and others pointed to new, unproven educational methods as a reason for the slipping test scores of U.S. children as compared to the rest of the world (National Commission on Excellence in Education, 1983). For critics calling for a return to basic, liberal, and scientifically rigorous education, progressive approaches to education were seen as part of the problem that needed fixing.

Another objection to progressive education, which applies particularly to service-learning, is that it eschews the neutrality befitting a liberal government and objective academicians in their education of citizens. Opponents of government indoctrination have held that education should not indoctrinate individuals into particular social ideals or forms of life. Rather educators should give the students knowledge about facts and about different kinds of values and allow students to decide how to put this knowledge to use, that is, which values to pursue. Following the influential epistemological theory of positivism, value neutrality also became an ideal of academic research. Values, holds positivism, cannot be reflected upon rationally but are arbitrary matters of subjective or cultural choice. Genuine knowledge, then, must involve empirically or logically testable theories characteristic of science and math. Students can study—in humanities and social science—what people have held to be valuable, but educators and students have no defensible basis for making judgments of value. A frequent criticism of project-based education is that it violates neutrality by promoting a certain form of citizenship, encouraging particular social ideals, and coercing students to engage in particular types of social activism (Fish, 2003; Flathman, 1996).

Adding to the sense that progressive education was impure were certain experiments in technical education, in which high schools and colleges developed curricula tailored to prepare students to perform particular jobs. In Cleveland, the cooperation of the school system with the automotive industry, with students building cars during school time, led to the charge that progressive education was narrowly training students to be productive workers rather than educating them to be free human beings and citizens capable of choosing between a range of life goals and activities (Patton & Mondale, 2001).

Dewey and other progressives have continually defended themselves against these objections. To charges that progressive education was one-sided in its emphasis on application and deficient in academic rigor, Dewey responded by arguing for an intelligent progressive approach that drew on traditional didactic methods in combination with project learning. He repeatedly argued that it would be a mistake to assume that students should be entirely left alone to grapple with new experiences. "The belief that all genuine education comes about through experience does not mean that all experiences are genuinely or equally educative" (Dewey, 1963). The progressive movement's emphasis on hands-on learning may have influenced the subsequent free schools movement. Advocates of the latter, such as leading theorist and practitioner A. S. Neill (1944), held that student experiences should not be constrained by structured lesson plans. Yet it should be emphasized that Dewey was completely opposed to such an unstructured curriculum and pedagogy. The current conservative educational tendency to reject Deweyan progressivism in the same breath as postmodern and anarchical calls for deschooling children is particularly odd (Ryan, 1998). For Dewey, instruction should give background information, concepts, and theories of use in entering projects, and instruction should construct and advise projects in a way to facilitate their educational value. In short, Deweyan progressivism seeks to alter and expand on traditional educational methods but not reject them outright (Dewey, 1963).

While some programs influenced by progressive education's emphasis on experiential, hands-on learning were guilty of narrow training, Dewey and progressive education in general certainly could not be accused of narrowness. His emphasis was repeatedly upon educating the individual to be prepared to respond intelligently to new situations, not to train the individual for a particular task or condition a set of behaviors. As much as traditional liberal educators, Dewey stressed the need for education to prepare students broadly in their development as individuals and citizens (Dewey, 1916, 1963; Ryan, 1998).

Regarding the charge of ethical and political bias, Dewey could respond that his platform was specifically opposed to the promotion of particular values in education. His own pragmatic approach to ethics stemmed from the belief that there was no set of general, timelessly valid moral principles that could be assumed to apply to every social issue (Dewey, 1960). He thought new problematic situations, such as those confronted in service-learning programs, needed new solutions. For example, contrary to suspicions that progressive and service education must be socialist and antimarket and anticapitalist, Dewey did not want education to try to foster a socialist revolution or even, necessarily, a greater extension of social services. He did not presuppose that the solution to all problems lay exclusively in government, market, or charitable solutions. Instead, he welcomed experimentation with combinations of the three as students sought to solve problems in their schools and communities (Dewey, 1916, 1963). Thus, Deweyan service-learning could be said to be neutral in avoiding commitment to any particular moral or political principle or economic arrangement.

However in other, more general, senses, Dewey would have to accept the charge of nonneutrality. First, while Dewey does not believe there are other unquestionable ethical principles that should be pushed, he does think that education should give practice in solving ethical problems, in which there are better and worse methods and solutions. Thus, Deweyan education would promote the idea of there being nonrelative, scientifically based answers to ethical and political questions. Second, Dewey's model seeks to use education to promote individual lives and social communities characterized by reflection, social engagement, and democratic participation. These are themselves particular values, about which some might have reservations. In practice, individual reflection and democratic cooperation will favor some worldviews over others. For Dewey, however, these are unavoidable values, to which any society will naturally be led as it attempts to respond to the practical problems that confront it. Third, Dewey's plan to foster active democratic response to social problems follows from a belief that there are systematic social problems that neither the free market nor unprodded government bureaucracies are prepared to solve.

If the progressive program for dealing with values can be charged with not being neutral, progressives will point out that supposedly value-neutral educational proposals themselves assume particular value orientations. For example, the call for education to focus on basic skills and rigorous background in technologically applicable knowledge, as opposed to ethics or politics, is designed to further particular social goals, namely, individualism and economic competition and growth. Recommendations of value neutrality are themselves value laden. Dewey presupposes that his goal of a democratic society of worker-citizens is more viable than competing conceptions, including either obedience to tradition or authority, or the unfettered pursuit of private profit. So Dewey would argue that he is not recommending the indoctrination of students into particular values in an authoritarian, biased, and questionable manner, but rather is spreading one general overarching value of democratic problem solving and the accompanying skill in being able to solve particular problems in which values play a role.

In any event, after its initial vitality during Dewey's rise, the progressive democratic approach that Dewey outlined was in decline at the end of his life. The concerns for rigor and breadth in education as well as for economic and military competitiveness were used to defend a return to traditional methods. Progressivism came to be widely regarded as impure, biased, or lacking in academic rigor.

This shift in educational theory may have been influenced by the rise of logical positivism as an overarching epistemological theory. Logical positivism sought to preserve an account of the possibility of objective empirical knowledge through a formal analysis of the reference of language use (Ayer, 1936; Carnap, 1967). Positivists portrayed pragmatist as well as phenomenological approaches to knowledge as lacking an appropriate analysis of the nature of objective truth and consistent meaning. The radically democratic social philosophy suggested by Dewey was also eclipsed in the course of the twentieth century. Dewey's hope for a community of activists began to appear unrealistic to many with the growth of political complexity, social fragmentation, and political alienation. Political philosophy began to emphasize the nature of individual rights and justice in balancing competing interests between citizens (Schumpeter, 1947). Thus, several intellectual and practical movements resulted in the declining influence of progressivism. In the middle to later part of the twentieth century, from around 1940 to 1985, the theories of Dewey were out of vogue. At the same time, experiments in project-oriented service-learning remained exceptional (Kraft, 1996).

THE RESURFACING OF EDUCATIONAL PROGRESSIVISM AND SERVICE-LEARNING: ARGUMENTS BORN OF LATE-TWENTIETH-CENTURY ALIENATION

A quick survey of recent literature in epistemology, social philosophy, and educational theory shows that all of this has changed again, as of the end of the twentieth century. Progressivism, Dewey, and service-learning have all received renewed interest of late. Several recent trends in the philosophies of education, knowledge, society, and politics theoretically undergird this renewal of interest in and support for project learning and, especially, service-learning.

First, logical positivism and other objectivist epistemologies are once again in decline. The attempt to derive formal and objectively verifiable conceptions of truth, knowledge, justification, and meaning failed, re-placed by a renewed interest in the role of the active interpretation of thinking subjects, of concern for practical goals, and of social context in knowledge. This has resulted in reinvigoration of pragmatic, phenome-nological, and hermeneutic approaches to the nature of knowledge. Many of the most influential epistemological theorists of recent years—for ex-ample, Quine (1953), Rorty (1979), and Habermas (1972)—are critical of traditional empiricism and define themselves as pragmatists. In this re-discovery of the import of human interests and social context to the for-mulation of knowledge, Dewey has come to be among the most widely cited epistemological thinkers.

If these trends characterize the philosophy of knowledge in general, they are especially prevalent in the philosophies of education (Liu, 2000). Here, phenomenological and pragmatic conceptions of the roles of the individual and society are thought indispensable to understanding hu-man knowledge and development. Dewey's instrumentalist conception of inquiry has been researched and theoretically updated by educational psychologists such as David Kolb (1984).

Perhaps even more influential on pedagogical theory than recent trends in epistemology have been movements in social and political philosophy in which the theory of knowledge and education is related to conceptions of citizenship (Barber, 1992; Boyte, 1989; Lisman, 1998). Political philoso-phy at the end of the twentieth century became concerned with the status of democracy and citizenship. Many thought that the complexity of mod-ern societies and economies, the political influence of big money and mass media, and citizen reliance on specialized, expert knowledge were making social engagement and political participation obsolete. Several interre-lated critiques of social and political culture arose, with corresponding recommendations for a rejuvenation of participatory democracy. Almost all of these considerations lend support to the newly emerging interest in service-learning.

First many argued that the eighties brought about a growing egoism and career-centeredness and a corresponding alienation from political and social life. While the country grew economically, traditional concern for others and accountability diminished (Bellah, Madsen, Sullivan, Swidler, & Tipton, 1985). Political philosophers became concerned that a society could not be held together without an underpinning of social solidarity and commitment to the common good as well as individual advancement. While individual pursuits of success may lead, through the well-touted invisible hand of efficient production and distribution, to the fostering of the community, few would assert that markets are able to meet all social needs and avoid deleterious side effects on communities. In fact, as the aftereffects of recent corporate scandals demonstrate, excessive individualism may lead to a corruption in business that ultimately undermines economic stability. A functioning market society requires an underpinning of ethics on the part of individuals both to keep business practices themselves free of corruption without continual government enforcement and to voluntarily commit time and resources to social problems not addressed by the market (Velasquez, 1998). This has led to a concern among political theorists about how a sense of community and ethical relationships to others can be renewed.

In this social and political climate, service-learning is seen as one way in which students might become motivated to be concerned with social problems, the plight of others, and politics in general. Arguably traditional classroom education perpetuates egoistic individualism, insofar as students study on their own in an attempt to get the best grades, with a goal of quickly moving through their programs and advancing to a lucrative career. Other students are encountered merely as competition for good grades and positions. At best, students see their professors and other students as possible sources of help in their own advancement. Service-learning is a way of introducing projects whose successful completion involves working and communicating with others, assessing their needs, and providing assistance. It may renew a commitment to the common good as well as to individual accomplishment. Service-learning thus gains support from the concern for a renewal of ethical concern and communal solidarity and responsibility. A century ago William James argued that modern societies have tended to solve the problem of their communities' need for solidarity and a sense of shared purpose through military mobilization. James argued that if societies were to attain the fruits of social mobilization without war's concomitant death and destruction, what was needed was a "moral equivalent of war," that is, other types of social projects that could bind people to one another and give a sense of community. James suggested the encouragement of community service projects, especially for youth. Current advocates of service-learning are renewing James's call for nonviolent forms of community building (James, 1910).

In addition to a renewed commitment to individual ethics and social concern, service-learning is supported by political theorists concerned with the status of democracy. As was noted in the discussion of the causes of the abatement of service-learning, the ability, inclination, and felt responsibility of citizens to participate in politics has declined. Studies of Americans' attitudes about politics repeatedly find apathy or cynicism. This is reflected statistically in the low numbers who vote or participate in political campaigns (Barber, 1984; Boyte, 1989). The word *political* itself has come to have a negative connotation so that to call a speech, piece of writing, or action political is to accuse it of empty rhetorical strategy in a struggle for self-interest and unjustified power.

American alienation from political life may result in part from a basic satisfaction and comfort with the freedoms and productivity of American economic life, or it may result from a sense that political and economic affairs are too complex for ordinary citizens to make a substantial contribution. Such concerns tend to encourage citizens to leave politics to the bureaucratic class, trusting in the latter's managerial expertise. While trust in experts is one side of citizen apathy, despair about exercising positive political influence is another. The cynical view that politics is ultimately determined by money and power lobbies rather than rational argument or concern for the common good has become so widely held as to be almost common sense.

While there are some differences in analysis about the cause and severity of the problem, social philosophers of various political stripes have argued that there is a crisis of democracy, with little genuine input from citizens. Political decisions are made by an expert elite who are supposed to steer society and the economy in a positive direction. While citizens, through elections, hold occasional referendums on the particular elites who have been in power, there is little political debate or participation in the formulation of social ideals and public policy.

The problem of citizen willingness to participate in politics and civic debate is related to concern for the loss of what has been called social capital. Robert Putnam (2000), in his instant classic *Bowling Alone*, and other commentators, have argued that Americans have fewer social connections with opportunity and ability to engage in social and political debate today than earlier in American history. Whereas citizens used to participate in clubs, associations, churches, and other public spaces that served as places of debate, consciousness raising, and collective action, today they stay at home or engage in consumer activities, such as bowling, on their own. When people do associate with others, there is less active political discussion and debate. Putnam argued that this constitutes a crisis of social capital, wherein, although well-off materially, Americans are poor in terms of social connection (Putnam, 2000; see also Barber, 1984; Bellah et al., 1985).

Many critics have questioned whether such a disengaged society can be called genuinely democratic (Barber, 1984; Pateman, 1976). It is questionable whether governments are willing and able to adequately meet the needs and interests of the people without their active participation in articulating their concerns and discussing solutions. Political theorists have argued that what is needed is rejuvenation of civil society and citizenship, concepts which played little role in political theory in the post–World War II focus on individual rights.

Some argue that the terrorist acts of September 2001 have created a renewed interest in politics, social solidarity, and concern for the common good (Colby, Ehrlich, Beaumont, & Stephens, 2003). However, the consequences of the war on terrorism on American political culture might be mixed and not yet fully clear. While there is social concern, the prevalence of concern for national security leads once again to reliance upon bureaucratic decision makers who possess government authority and classified information. The United States has also responded to terrorism with a demand for social unity, which may make the voicing of independent political views, and hence political debate, more difficult (Arato, 2002). In any case, if participatory democracy is to be revived, it will require the channeling of social and political impulses into the reflective and civic-minded directions suggested by Dewey.

In the course of reflecting on the conditions under which a complex and independent society can encourage social and political engagement, it is not surprising that attention has turned to education (Barber, 1992; Colby et al., 2003). In light of contemporary political theory's assessment of the deficit of democratic motivation and ability, service-learning is seen as a way of cultivating a habit of civic engagement and activism. Furthermore, service-learning is a way of providing community connections and fostering political skills that today's youth tend to lack. Students going through school would be prepared not only to enter the workforce with job training but also to have connections to the community and knowledge of how to go about building such connections.

In addition to building knowledge and connections on the part of students, some have emphasized the need for knowledge of the politics of interpersonal relationships and community problems. Here service-learning gains support from the movement called critical pedagogy. In critical pedagogy, the focus of education should be on learning about the functioning of power, and the teaching method itself should attempt to unmask and disperse power. Critical pedagogy critiques the instructor as a dispenser of knowledge and attempts to emphasize the agency of the learners (Freire, 1970; Giroux, 1988). This is generally achieved through presenting the instructor as just a partner in the pursuit of knowledge.

Service-learning can involve such a "decentering" of the instructor, as education occurs outside the classroom and the lectures of the instructor. The experiences of the student outside of class—in the service environment—tend to be recognized as having a validity of their own, testing, supplementing, or even undermining the theoretical and factual knowledge discussed in class. Instructor, students, and community all become collaborators in the course of the project.

Service-learning also gives students instruction in political dialogue and the negotiation of complex power relationships (Esquith, 2000). In addition to learning about the problems of a community and developing a disposition to help, the student learns the ethical problems and political challenges inherent in paternalistically undertaking community service. Whether helping with food, shelter, medicine, or legal aid, the student comes up against hierarchies in the community and barriers to his or her own successful ability to influence without either coercing others or being overpowered himself or herself. Political theorist Steve Esquith (2000) argues that in completing a project in such a situation, a student gains practice in understanding such power relationships and negotiating them with poise and sensitivity.

For some educational and political theorists emphasizing critical pedagogy, the goal of community service would be de-emphasized in service-learning. The student would not be viewed as a missionary going out to help the masses so much as an individual being thrown into complex social situations to expand his or her own worldview. Exemplifying this approach is Ivan Illich, who, in a paper called "To Hell With Good Intentions" (1990), argues that students need to come to understand that they have no simple solutions to offer the disadvantaged. Illich argues that middle- and upper-class students tend to think that a little bit of charity and dissemination of their own middle-class values will suffice to lift the impoverished and exploited out of their conditions. For Illich, by contrast, the principle value of experiential learning is precisely to deconstruct this arrogant and misguided missionary self-understanding of the student. The service-learning student, like many Peace Corps volunteers, should come to bear witness to the extent of cultural differences and the complexity of world problems. While most progressive educators would want to emphasize possible bases for positive influence to a greater extent than Illich, the goals of understanding and negotiating differences and bearing witness are additional concerns that a democratic and just society might foster through service-learning.

We have seen that social theory describes several social crises and challenges for contemporary citizens that can be argued to underpin the recent interest in service-learning. Service-learning may foster ethical responsibility, community solidarity, democratic engagement, and poise and savvy in dialoguing across differences in situations laden by social power.

A final set of concerns leading to a renewed interest in progressive education and service-learning arises from the current state of academia itself. Namely, there is concern among professors and universities that they have become overly separate from surrounding communities and that education is not seen as having immediate implications for students' lives or society. Perhaps there has always been some separation between the intellectual elite who operate universities and local communities. One might expect the separation between university and life to diminish as more individuals receive a college education and as universities are under more pressure to justify the state funding that they receive and the tuitions that they charge. However, many argue that academia is more remote from daily life than ever. Fields of academic knowledge have become increasingly specialized, such that the research of an individual academic is further removed from problems in their complete social context. Secondly, the overarching concern for publication as the criteria for academic advancement gives incentive for research into cutting-edge theoretical work as opposed to practical application. For universities concerned to promote world-quality scholarship and obtain grants from outside the community, there may be little incentive to engage in community service projects. This can result in a mutual disinterest or enmity between university and community. Universities may miss out on opportunities to contribute to and connect with their social surroundings in ways positive for campus and the community. In this climate, there is concern to make a university not just a collection of expert theorists, but rather an institution through which expert knowledge is used to assist and organize the public in its attempt to reproduce and improve society. Universities and faculty, concerned to reconnect with surrounding communities, are finding service-learning to be an opportunity consistent with their own educational missions (Lisman, 1998).

In the classroom, one also finds a concern for, and potentially a crisis of, social relevance. Particularly in the relatively abstract and theoretical sciences and humanities, faculty, concerned to engage students or to respond to objections of irrelevance, are interested in demonstrating the concrete applicability of their material. Professors of philosophy, sociology, history, political science, and anthropology tend to use textbook examples to illustrate theories. Students, increasingly from various economic strata of society and concerned for practical gain in their education, wonder whether there is any application for their liberal studies in their own lives. One traditional answer has been that some students will go on to government or other leadership positions in which it will have been good for them to have an understanding of society and explanatory theories and ethical principles (Nussbaum, 1994). However, this is a remote application and is not relevant to many students in the university, particularly those who will not serve as political or social leaders.

As philosophy professor John Wallace puts it in his discussion of pedagogy and the relationship of theory to practice, he came to feel that he owed his students an immediate demonstration of the applicability of the concepts and arguments quibbled over in philosophy class (Wallace, 2000). Having students undertake projects in which they draw on, apply, and ultimately, criticize conceptions of ethics discussed in class allowed him to do this. For any course that theoretically discusses society or social events, service-learning projects lend the possibility of providing concreteness. The natural sciences, no less than the social sciences, may be in need of and amenable to the integration of community service projects that demonstrate their practical application (Colby et al., 2003).

CONCLUSION

In conclusion, several interrelated trends in society and theory have influenced a renewed interest in progressive education and service-learning. It is not surprising that this has been accompanied by a revival of interest in the philosophy of Dewey, whose writings on the active nature of understanding and the benefits of and conditions for participatory democracy provide an early theoretical foundation for a pedagogy in which students cooperatively engage actual social problems.

REFERENCES

Arato, A. (2002). Minima politica after September 11. *Constellations, 9*(1), 46–52.

Aristotle (1997a). Nicomachean ethics (D. Ross, Trans.). In S. M. Cahn (Ed.), *Classic and contemporary readings in the philosophy of education* (pp. 111–131). New York: McGraw-Hill.

Aristotle (1997b). Politics (D. Ross, Trans.). In S. M. Cahn (Ed.), *Classic and contemporary readings in the philosophy of education* (pp. 131–143). New York: McGraw-Hill.

Ayer, A. J. (1936). *Language, truth and logic.* New York: Dover.

Barber, B. R. (1984). *Strong democracy: Participatory politics for a new age.* Berkeley: University of California Press.

Barber, B. R. (1992). *An aristocracy of everyone: The politics of education and the future of America.* New York: Ballantine Books.

Bellah, R. N., Madsen, R., Sullivan, W., Swidler, A., & Tipton, S. M. (1985). *Habits of the heart: Individualism and commitment in American life.* Berkeley: University of California Press.

Boyte, H. C. (1989). *Commonwealth: A return to citizen politics.* New York: The Free Press.

Carnap, R. (1967). *The logical structure of the world* (R. A. George, Trans.). Berkeley: University of California Press.

Colby, A., Ehrlich, T., Beaumont, E., & Stephens, J. (2003). *Educating citizens: Preparing America's undergraduates for lives of moral and civic responsibility.* San Francisco: Jossey-Bass.

Dewey, J. (1913). *Interest and effort in education*. New York: Augustus M. Kelley.

Dewey, J. (1916). *Democracy and education*. New York: The Free Press.

Dewey, J. (1957). *Reconstruction in philosophy*. Boston: Beacon Press.

Dewey, J. (1960). *The quest for certainty*. New York: Capricorn Books.

Dewey, J. (1963). *Experience and education*. New York: Collier Books.

Dewey, J. (2002). The quest for certainty. In S. M. Cahn & P. Markie (Eds.), *Ethics: History, theory and contemporary issues* (2nd ed., pp. 420–434). New York: Oxford University Press.

Esquith, S. L. (2000). Service-learning, citizenship and the philosophy of law. In D. Lisman & I. Harvey (Eds.), *Beyond the tower: Concepts and models for service-learning in philosophy* (pp. 113–121). Washington, DC: American Association for Higher Education.

Fish, S. (2003, May 16). Aim low. *Chronicle of Higher Education*, p. C5.

Flathman, R. (1996). Liberal versus civic, republican, democratic, and other vocational educations. *Political Theory, 24*(1), 4–32.

Freire, P. (1970). *Pedagogy of the oppressed*. New York: Herder & Herder.

Giles, D. E., & Eyler, J. (1994). The theoretical roots of service-learning in John Dewey: Toward a theory of service-learning. *Michigan Journal of Community Service-Learning, 1*(1), 77–85.

Giroux, H. A. (1988). *Schooling the struggle for public life*. Minneapolis: University of Minnesota Press.

Habermas, J. (1972). *Knowledge and human interests* (J. J. Shapiro, Trans.). Boston: Beacon Press.

Hanna P. R. (1936). *Youth serves the community*. New York: D. Appleton-Century.

Hines, V. (1972). Progressivism in practice. In Association for Supervision and Curriculum Development (Ed.), *A new look at progressive education* (pp. 118–164). Washington, DC: Association for Supervision and Curriculum Development.

Hutchins, R. M. (1953). *The conflict in education in a democratic society*. New York: Harper & Row.

Illich, I. (1990). To hell with good intentions. In J. C. Kendall & Associates (Eds.), *Combining service and learning: A resource book for community and public service*. (Vol. 1, pp. 314–320). Raleigh, NC: National Society for Internships and Experiential Education.

James, W. (1910, August). The moral equivalent of war. *McClure's Magazine*, pp. 463–468.

Jefferson, T. (1964). *Notes on the state of Virginia*. New York: Harper & Row.

Kant, I. (1997). Thoughts on education (A. Churton, Trans.). In S. M. Cahn (Ed.), *Classic and contemporary readings in the philosophy of education* (pp. 198–222). New York: McGraw-Hill.

Kolb, D. A. (1984). *Experiential learning: Experience as the source of learning and development*. Englewood Cliffs, NJ: Prentice Hall.

Kraft, R. J. (1996). Service-learning: An introduction to its theory, practice and effects. *Education and Urban Society, 28*(2), 131–159.

Lisman, D. (1998). *Toward a civil society: Civic literacy and service-learning*. Westport, CT: Bergin & Garvey.

Liu, G. (2000). Knowledge, foundations, and discourse: Philosophical support for service-learning. In D. Lisman & I. Harvey (Eds.), *Beyond the tower: Concepts and models for service-learning in philosophy* (pp. 11–33). Washington, DC: American Association for Higher Education.

Locke, J. (1997). Some thoughts concerning education. In S. M. Cahn (Ed.), *Classic and contemporary readings in the philosophy of education* (pp. 145–161). New York: McGraw-Hill.

Mill, J. S. (1997). Inaugural address at Saint Andrews. In S. M. Cahn (Ed.), *Classic and contemporary readings in the philosophy of education* (pp. 224–260). New York: McGraw-Hill.

National Commission on Excellence in Education. (1983). *A nation at risk: The imperative for educational reform. A report to the nation and the Secretary of Education.* Washington, DC: United States Department of Education.

Neill, A. S. (1960). *Summerhill: A radical approach to child rearing.* New York: Hart Publishing Co.

Nussbaum, M. (1994). *The therapy of desire: Theory and practice in Hellenistic ethics.* Princeton, NJ: Princeton University Press.

Pateman, C. (1976). *Participation and democratic theory.* Cambridge, UK: Cambridge University Press.

Patton, S. & Mondale, S. (Producers). (2001). *School: The story of American public education* [Film]. Princeton, NJ: Films for the Humanities & Sciences.

Peirce, C. S. (1972). *Charles S. Peirce: The essential writings* (E. C. Moore, Ed.). New York: Harper & Row.

Plato (1961). The republic (P. Shorey, Trans.). In E. Hamilton & H. Cairns (Eds.), *The collected dialogues of Plato* (pp. 576–844). Princeton, NJ: Princeton University Press.

Putnam, R. D. (2000). *Bowling alone: The collapse and revival of American community.* New York: Simon & Schuster.

Quine, W. V. O. (1953). *From a logical point of view.* Cambridge, MA: Harvard University Press.

Rorty, R. (1979). *Philosophy and the mirror of nature.* Princeton, NJ: Princeton University Press.

Rousseau, J. (1979). *Emile* (A. Bloom, Trans.). New York: Basic Books

Ryan, A. (1998). *Liberal anxieties and liberal education.* New York: Hill & Wang.

Schumpeter, J. A. (1947). *Capitalism, socialism, and democracy* (2nd ed.). New York: Harper & Row.

Velasquez, M. G. (1998). *Business ethics: Concepts and cases* (4th ed.). Upper Saddle River, NJ: Prentice Hall.

Wallace, J. (2000). The use of a philosopher: Socrates and Myles Horton. In D. Lisman & I. Harvey (Eds.), *Beyond the tower: Concepts and models for service-learning in philosophy* (pp. 69–90). Washington, DC: American Association for Higher Education.

CHAPTER 2

The Historical Origins of Service-Learning in the Nineteenth and Twentieth Centuries: The Transplanted and Indigenous Traditions

Gregory R. Zieren and Peter H. Stoddard

Modern definitions of service-learning and community learning can trace their roots deep into the history of American democracy and higher education. Government that relies upon the consent of the governed must reckon with the certainty that education plays the key role in socializing the people into proper functions as citizens and shaping public opinion in incalculable ways. The relationship between the citizen and government, between individuals and their constituent communities, must always be a work in progress without a definitive beginning or end, and the role education plays in the relationship must be evaluated and strengthened anew by each generation. The founders of Harvard and Yale (Hofstadter, 1955) understood this in the mid-seventeenth century, as did the creators of the University of Georgia (Rudolph, 1962) and Thomas Jefferson's University of Virginia (Cunningham, 1987) in the late eighteenth century. What these men understood as service to the community and practical learning for the times may seem limited by the resources devoted to the task, the remoteness from European centers of learning, or the modest scope the professions played in Colonial and Federalist times. But the prevalence of literacy (Lockridge, 1974), the commitment to public education in the Northwest Ordinances (Ostrander, 1999), and the need for an informed electorate in a society devoted to government by the people, of the people, and for the people were evident by the end of the eighteenth century.

What set American colleges and universities apart in their earliest years from European models was the extremely limited role the state played in education. European universities still taught the original disciplines of law, medicine, theology, and philosophy and certified students as qualified to function in law courts, state bureaucracies, and established churches (Hofstadter, 1955). American governments at all levels needed only the barest minimum of personnel for state purposes and never relied on early institutions for certification. These circumstances reduced state support to little or nothing for most colleges but offered important advantages for the future of higher education. American colleges and universities were freer to adapt curriculum to changing societal needs, freer to experiment with new forms of learning, and freer to make learning serve the community. Ironically, the freedom to experiment often entailed importing educational innovations from Great Britain, Germany, France, and even Russia to enrich the scope of learning for American students (Cremin, 1961).

Despite a promising start—new state universities and the founding of hundreds of colleges with denominational affiliations—American higher education faced what Rudolph (1962) has called a crisis in the years just before the Civil War (p. 240). Questions of quality, standards, and excellence had yet to be answered systematically among the bewildering array of institutions that called themselves colleges or universities. They reflected a largely agrarian and rural society, serving to provide a supply of doctors, lawyers, and preachers to staff the professions and educate the sons of gentlemen but accomplished little else. Contemporaries complained that even the education of professionals was second-rate and often incomplete (Hofstadter, 1955).

These colleges were intellectual backwaters from the main currents of advanced nineteenth-century thought and served only a tiny fraction of the college-aged cohort. Indeed, on the eve of the Civil War the percentage of the population in New England that was college educated was declining. In 1859 in Ohio the average enrollment of 22 colleges there was just 85 students, and not until 1860 did Harvard graduate its very first class of 100 students (Rudolph, 1962). New York City's population was approaching half a million by the late 1840s, but it supported just two colleges with a total enrollment of 247 (Rudolph, 1962).

The pedagogy of most colleges relied on quizzes, recitations, and committing to memory textbooks full of Greek, Latin, mathematics, and theology (Metzger, 1955). The high point of the college year was the annual public-speaking contest and recitations on patriotic or religious themes. Governing boards were made up of local clergy and business donors who made sure professors and students adhered to orthodox thinking, and the seniors' capstone course was the college president's own class in moral philosophy (Metzger, 1955). As Rodgers (1998) noted, the consequence of such devotion to a calcified curriculum "was a structured commitment to the simplified and out of date" (p. 81).

PRACTICAL AND TECHNICAL EDUCATION
BEFORE 1860

A few bright exceptions to the tyranny of classical learning and rote memorization did stand out as alternatives. The United States Military Academy at West Point provided practical training in advanced mathematics, chemistry, technical drawing, and civil engineering (Pahl, 1987). The value of this curriculum was apparent not only to the officer corps of the U.S. Army. West Point-trained engineers proved their worth as builders of the nation's largest civil engineering projects, the early railroads (Eddy, 1957). Nearby Rensselaer (Polytechnic) Institute in Troy, New York, devoted its curriculum to engineering, surveying, collecting botanical specimens, touring workshops, and gardening (Rudolph, 1962). A visit to a bleaching factory, tannery, or mill preceded appropriate laboratory experiments. Van Rensselaer described his purpose in creating his benefaction as training teachers who could instruct "the sons and daughters of farmers and mechanics . . . in the application of experimental chemistry, philosophy and natural history to agriculture, domestic economy, the arts and manufactures" (Rudolph, 1962, p. 231). Both institutions looked to the French Ecole Polytechnique for curriculum and example (Ferguson, 1992).

A third important start in the direction of practical and applied learning was the founding of Michigan Agricultural College in 1857 in East Lansing, Michigan, the first state agricultural college in the nation (Eddy, 1957). The new state legislature called for "the promotion of intellectual, scientific and agricultural improvement . . . [in] the establishment of an agricultural school." Its first president, Joseph R. Williams, dedicated the institution to the moral, physical, and intellectual improvement of the farmer because he is also a citizen of a democracy who should execute "the duties of even high responsible stations with self-reliance and intelligence" (Eddy, 1957, pp. 16–17). Williams's ambitious agenda included training in chemistry, physiology, entomology, mechanics, electricity, and the veterinary arts. The new college also mandated manual labor for students for three to four hours every day, a requirement kept in place until the 1890s. Iowa, Pennsylvania, Maryland, and New York all took steps to start agricultural colleges in the years immediately preceding the Civil War (Eddy, 1957).

THE MORRILL LAND GRANT COLLEGE
MOVEMENT

These practical examples of applied learning and a new curriculum fit for the educational requirements of the age inspired Congressman, later Senator, Justin Morrill from Vermont to sponsor legislation that some called "the common man's educational Bill of Rights" (Eddy, 1957, pp. 23–45). The Morrill Act followed the precedent of the Northwest Ordinance and devoted the proceeds from the sale of millions of acres of public land for public education, but this time, public higher education for the sons of farmers and mechanics. Morrill defended the legislation by pointing out that European nations were investigating farming methods in institutions of higher learning. American farmers, too, needed scientific field and laboratory experiments if farm productivity were to continue to improve (Eddy, 1957).

The Morrill Land Grant College Bill must be seen in the context of the new Republican Party's appeal to ordinary Americans as the party of "Free Men, Free Soil, Free Labor" (Foner, 1970). Like its companion pieces of legislation, the Homestead Act, the Transcontinental Railroad Act, and the creation of a new Department of Agriculture, the Morrill Act was social policy for reaffirming the Jeffersonian virtues of the yeoman farm, the necessity of fostering an informed citizenry in a democracy, and the need for practical education to benefit everyone. The Morrill Act was the first national attempt to combine the liberal arts with practical and vocational learning, an experiment funded with a permanent endowment from set-aside land sales (Eddy, 1957; Rudolph, 1962).

Like the founders of Michigan Agricultural College, the creators of the earliest land grant colleges insisted that, in Iowa State College professor Isaac Roberts's words, "All college students were then required to work two and one-half hours daily" (Eddy, 1957, p. 63). The interest in practical learning was also evident in the emphasis on "the mechanic's art" in the early curriculum of the land grant colleges. This emphasis found form in civil and mechanical engineering courses. Drawing and surveying courses were common, and as scientific coursework became vital to the engineering curriculum, chemistry, mathematics, and physics found their way into the course lists (Eddy, 1957).

The practical education of women was part and parcel of the land grant college ideal. The course of study introduced in the 1870s as domestic economy eventually became known as home economics (Eddy, 1957, pp. 61–62). Typical of the broad gauge of education was the motto the new Illinois Industrial University (later University of Illinois) adopted, "Learning and Labor" (Rudolph, 1962, p. 257).

The broadly democratic character and service orientation of the land grant colleges was evident when they expanded their scope to include the underserved educational needs of African American citizens in 1890 (Eddy, 1957). Morrill's supplemental appropriation to the original bill forbade the land grant colleges to discriminate against students based on race. Practically speaking, in southern states where Jim Crow laws predominated, the legislation led to the founding of agricultural and technical colleges such as Tennessee Agricultural and Industrial State College in Nashville, now Tennessee State University (Eddy, 1957, p. 291).

THE PHILADELPHIA CENTENNIAL AND MANUAL TRAINING

The next impulse for higher education that stressed practical and applied learning came from the international showcase of America's centennial celebration in 1876. Education for democracy and for an emerging industrial order was one of the themes promoters had stressed in sending out invitations to American states and foreign governments (Post, 1976). Sweden sent a complete rural schoolhouse, as did Indiana and other states. Pennsylvania devoted an entire building to displays documenting the commonwealth's educational endeavors from the common school to higher education. The Women's Centennial Executive Committee set up next to the Women's Pavilion one of the nation's first kindergartens, a German innovation, and "selected a class of sixteen tiny pupils from the inmates of the Northern Home for Friendless Children" (Ingram, 1876, p. 714).

Fairgoers interested in innovations were especially impressed by the German and Russian displays of educational tools. Prof. Franz Reuleaux became Germany's most renowned engineering professor in 1875 when he published a text for mechanical engineers. He also designed a set of nearly 300 models of gears, crank mechanisms, and power transmission devices that were intended to accompany the text. Reuleaux's models, sturdily constructed of iron and brass, were sold to engineering schools in Europe and the United States (Ferguson, 1992).

The larger Russian display of tools from the new Moscow and St. Petersburg Technical Institutes attracted even more attention. Instruction in physics, mathematics, and engineering in these institutes was combined with on-the-job training in construction shops built to facilitate teaching (Cremin, 1961). Though the workshops sold their products, the training of apprentices was the main purpose. The display consisted largely of tools used for instruction and models of finished work that students were to imitate to perfect their own skills. Carpenters, joiners, blacksmiths, machinists, and engineers all found the tools of their trades on display (Ingram, 1876).

The Russian and German educational displays inspired two influential American visitors and, as Lawrence Cremin put it, "American education was never the same thereafter" (pp. 25–26). One of the two was President John D. Runkle of the new Massachusetts Institute of Technology. He found in the Russian exhibition the key to creating practical shops for engineering students. He also created a new School of Mechanics Arts to offer manual training, as it was called, "for those who wish to enter industrial pursuits rather than become scientific engineers" (Cremin, 1961, p. 25).

The manual training concept swept American higher education in the 1880s with its vision of education for the great mass of students in fields both practical and useful. Runkle promoted the idea as a new balance of the mental and the manual, thereby preparing people pragmatically for life in a society both democratic and industrial in nature (Cremin, 1961).

Calvin Woodward of Washington University in St. Louis was the second influential visitor to the Russian exhibit in 1876, and he became an even more enthusiastic promoter of the manual training ideal. Woodward opened the first school devoted to it in 1880 in St. Louis. By 1890 manual training schools had opened in 36 cities representing 15 states and the District of Columbia. The schools were not merely vocational in nature. The three-year curriculum was divided between mental and manual labor, with mathematics, drawing, science, language, history, and literature taught alongside carpentry, wood turning, pattern making, soldering, and machine work (Cremin, 1961).

Despite Woodward's insistence that balance prevail between the manual and the mental, the needs of an industrial society for trained mechanics, woodworkers, and the like pushed most schools increasingly in the direction of the vocational. Some manual training schools maintained the balance and evolved into institutions of higher learning with strong engineering and technical curriculum, like the University of Toledo. Most, however, transformed themselves into secondary schools where vocational and technical training prevailed (Cremin, 1961).

THE CHICAGO WORLD'S FAIR OF 1893 AND THE GERMAN INFLUENCE

Practical learning got a boost from the second great American world's fair, the Chicago Columbian Exposition of 1893. This time the impetus came not from foreign exhibits but from foreign competition. Germany was the big prizewinner in machine tools, mechanical devices, and chemical compounds in competition with the U.S., Great Britain, and other industrial nations (Lewis, 1997). The Germans were not just capable exhibitors of industrial products but were also busy exporters conquering overseas markets through the excellence of their methods of production. This posed a challenge for American business because German technical education was a key component of their success and ranked as perhaps the best in the world (Chandler, 1990).

German technical instruction at both the secondary level and in technical universities had emerged in the late nineteenth century in tandem with the rise of Germany as a major industrial nation and major exporter. Just as American higher education served as a model for other nations in the late twentieth century, German technical education began serving as a model by the late nineteenth century (Wegner, 1995). One crucial element of the German model was the combination of classroom instruction and on-the-job training. Most college graduates worked as state employees, at least for a time, and served a practical internship related to the student's field of study. Lawyers, doctors, teachers, engineers, and other graduates worked for a year or two as interns before completing the second, and final, state examinations (Linton, 1995).

The example was such a powerful impetus that the National Association of Manufacturers in 1896 set up a Standing Committee on Education to promote German-style technical training with practical internships (Wegner, 1995). The problem of lack of experience was not limited to the education of mechanics or engineers in this country. Three-quarters of new public school teachers in 1886 began the school year with no prior teacher training. They were, in the words of one national education report, an "army of novices" (Wegner, 1995, p. 61) preparing to educate America's youth. The clinical training of American doctors was also deficient in comparison with the German system. In Germany senior medical professors supervised internships and hospitals were equipped with laboratories suitable for diagnostic work and even research purposes (Bonner, 1995). In contrast, American training in hospitals relied on local physicians to supervise and only a few of the best university hospitals provided laboratories for any purpose.

Doctors, lawyers, teachers, social workers, engineers, and a variety of educated professions began to form professional organizations in the 1880s and 1890s to lobby state legislatures to provide standards of education and training for the certification of new members. Educational and competence requirements implied not only restricting entry into the professional classes but guaranteeing a standard of professional achievement as well. As Robert Wiebe (1967) demonstrated, the new professional organizations usually included a period of internship in their demands on colleges and universities for education suitable to sustain the standards of what could now be legitimately called professions.

PROGRESSIVE ERA INITIATIVES IN SERVICE-LEARNING

The Progressive Era marked the coming of age of the American university as an institution committed to service and distinct from the models of Great Britain or Germany. Until the late nineteenth century American colleges continued to play the role of conservators of knowledge and transmitters of mostly foreign culture. Latin, Greek, mathematics, anatomy, and rhetoric were the legacies of a European civilization transplanted into the New World. Like acolytes tending an altar, American colleges kept alive that learning and civilization on the fringes of a wild, new continent. The land grant colleges after the Civil War broadened the scope of learning to incorporate new and practical subjects, but the task was still conservative in nature.

In the years around 1900 new concepts of what tasks a university should perform and the role it should play in a democratic society began to shape American universities. Like the German universities, research in the United States came to mean adding to the sum of knowledge available to humanity. But the process of discovery also entailed spreading the benefits of knowledge to new segments in society and to society at large. In the words of the Reverend Lyman Abbott, the purpose of scholarship in the American university "has been regarded as an equipment for service" (Rudolph, 1962, p. 312). In 1899 James Burrill Angell, president of the University of Michigan, noted the contrast between the ideal of public service that inspired the great universities and made them servants of American democracy and the college earlier in the century that most citizens regarded as "a home of useless and harmless recluses" (Rudolph, 1962, p. 321).

The service function of American universities first flowered in that uniquely optimistic age known as the Progressive Era, a time when many believed that informed and enlightened voters were the essential catalyst in remaking American democracy to suit the modern age (Cooper, 1990). Who better to inform the citizenry than the newly minted army of fresh college graduates? Colleges and universities became more prominent in community life as enrollment grew and a greater percentage of young adults took part in higher education. Between 1890 and 1910 enrollment doubled to over 355,000 students (Eddy, 1957). Furthermore, as the numbers grew and the range of curriculum offerings became more diverse, graduates found places in all sectors of society. Colleges trained and certified teachers, social workers, and librarians, and college graduates went on to earn graduate degrees in law, medicine, engineering, and business.

The model for university graduate engagement in reform and democracy was Wisconsin and its university in Madison. President Charles Van Hise called it "the Wisconsin Idea," a broadly conceived project to foster reform and civic improvement based on the specialized knowledge embodied by the university and its graduates (Rudolph, 1962). Agricultural economists aided farmers to find the most profitable mix of crops and activities, public policy analysts examined the rate structure of railroads and street railways to set rates in the public interest, and labor experts on the Industrial Commission studied wages and working conditions to improve the status of the working class (Thelen, 1976). The Wisconsin Idea rested on the conviction that students and university-trained experts could apply themselves to the problems of modern society and make democracy work more effectively.

Part of the democratic appeal of the Wisconsin Idea came from its popular extension program. Wisconsin and other Middle Western states gave birth to the idea in the 1880s when the programs were called "Farmers' Institutes" (Eddy, 1957). The faculty of land grant colleges offered lectures and short courses to farmers and townspeople in counties all over the state. The curriculum initially reflected the agricultural nature of late-nineteenth-century rural America with course offerings in soils and crops, fertilizer, and animal nutrition. But by 1900 the offerings included topics of interest to women, such as home economics, as well as citizenship for immigrants and civic education for all (Cogan, 1999; Mattson, 1998). In 1914, for example, extension programs reached an estimated 3 million; the passage of the Smith-Lever Act (Eddy, 1957) that year to provide federal funds for extension work reflected the popularity of the movement and the broad connection between higher education and the average American citizen. The Smith-Hughes Act of 1917 (Uffelman, 2003) provided federal funding for vocational education, another example of promoting education in practical subjects to benefit the masses.

Two other initiatives from the Progressive Era deserve mention as predecessors of service-learning. In 1901 the University of Cincinnati introduced cooperative education patterned on the German dual system of classroom instruction alongside work in the field in the student's occupation (Stanton, Giles, & Cruz, 1999). Also in 1901 the first community college, then called junior college, opened its doors in Joliet, Illinois (American Association of Community Colleges, 2001). Both were experiments designed to connect more closely the worlds of work and education, and education with the community.

Finally, no treatment of Progressive Era beginnings in service-learning would be complete without at least a mention of John Dewey's contribution. In 1902 Dewey insisted that higher education must meet public needs and that the culture must adapt to "the conditions of modern life, of daily life, of political and industrial life, if you will" (Veysey, 1965, p. 115). He reiterated that belief in his 1916 classic statement of educational philosophy, *Democracy and Education*, in terms that have inspired advocates of service-learning down to the twenty-first century (Rudolph, 1962).

SOCIAL WORK'S CONTRIBUTION TO SERVICE-LEARNING

The keepers of the flame of service-learning since the Progressive era can be seen variously as believers in democracy (Brookfield, 1987; Lindeman, 1991; Stewart, 1987), missionaries for social change (Alinsky, 1971; Rivera & Erlich, 1992), proponents for civic education and competence in adults (Adams, 1975; Egerton, 1983), and government reformers and proponents of the humanistic bureaucracy (Hopkins, 1999).

One profession in particular, social work, has served as both the focus of service-learning experiments and as the self-appointed beacon for service-learning in society (Konopka, 1958; Specht & Courtney, 1997). Through its rise to professionalism and its position as advocate in society, social work and social workers have made dramatic contributions to the modern day conception and practice of service-learning (Hamilton, 1954; Hopkins, 1999). As a result, social work today, in its practice and in its curriculum, provides a strong traditional base and functional model for service-learning in the university (Council on Social Work Education, 1992(a), 1992(b), 1994; Jansson, 1999).

Key events in American history—the Depression, the Civil Rights movement, and the War on Poverty—have helped social work (and through social work, society itself) maintain a clear conceptualization of service-learning and an understanding of its importance to society. Early social work proponents of service-learning helped lay the foundation for service-learning in society and to develop its rationale (Boehm, 1959). A review of the combined historical development of service-learning and social work will help to explain this phenomenon.

EARLY DEMOCRATS AND THE DISCIPLES OF JOHN DEWEY

The concept of democracy as based upon fully knowledgeable partici-pation of adults in society and the equal access of all adults to education became an important goal of early social workers and social activists. This thrust for social democracy came from an unexpected source.

Adult education and the responsibility of those learning a profession to participate in service-learning was the message proposed by early social work educator and reformer Eduard Lindeman who rose to prominence in the 1920s and 1930s after the progressive movement. His definition of the *democratic man* called for an effort by society to insure that all adults had the necessary civic skills to create the best possible society (Brookfield, 1987).

Lindeman, adopting Dewey's philosophy and methodology, proposed service-learning and involvement in adult education as one of the key bases for the social work profession. It was through his work at Columbia University, the New School for Social Research, and many other social work and social sciences programs that the democratic movement took shape and direction (Lindeman, 1926). Lindeman's influence was particu-larly strong among social work educators in the 1920s and 1930s. For over a 30-year period he helped define not only social work education, but also a place for social work in society through service-learning (Lindeman, 1991).

A key argument that Lindeman made was that the individual's civic participation was critically important for a democratic society (Geisner, 1956). Increased education would lead to increased civic participation. Lindeman's work then focused on a methodology to obtain greater civic participation. He argued that professionals, especially social workers, have as their primary responsibility the participation in and the development of service-learning as a tool to increase the overall educational level of all adults in society. In *The Meaning of Adult Education* (Lindeman, 1926), he proposes a strong involvement of social work education and of social work professionals in the civic training and education of those in society who have not received educational opportunities to help them participate fully in the discussions necessary to sustain a democratic form of government.

Lindeman outlined an argument that has since become a major focus of social work (Congress, 1999), that lower-income and disenfranchised individuals who were more likely to have less education were also less likely to participate in the workings of a democracy. For that reason they would suffer a lack of advancement and material gain in society as well as a loss of economic self-determination. It was social work's responsibility to create a fully participatory democratic society, and to that end it became imperative that social workers participate in service-learning.

An important response of social work education to Lindeman's argument was the refinement of its internship model of learning, referred to in social work as the field practicum. More than an internship, the social work field practicum is a guided learning experience with service to the community as its primary task (Compton & Galaway, 1999; Germain & Gitterman, 1980).

The traditional participation of service-learning in civic education is described by Hepburn (1999). This was an emphasis of the social work model of service-learning from its very beginnings (Meyer, 1970). Social work was able to define itself through service-learning as an important part of society (Popple, 1995). This was an attempt to increase the distribution of power in the society and at the same time increase the roles of everyday people in determining their lives (Ricci, 1971). A strong civic ideology was to develop within the social work profession to buttress service-learning in social work education. This has provided society with an ongoing model, which has developed over time, for service-learning (Hamilton, 1954).

ADULT EDUCATION: THE PATH TO CIVIC ACTION

A portion of the foundation for service-learning in social work came from an early source of civic activism that also had its roots in adult education. Loosely based upon the Folk Schools or people's schools of Europe

in the early twentieth century, the work of Myles Horton and the participants at his Highlander School paved the way for teaching civic activism
with the goal of improving the conditions for all citizens in society (Egerton, 1983; Glen, 1988). The founder of Highlander, Myles Horton, spent
several years in Denmark and other European countries learning of the
early effort of adult education pioneers in those countries. He saw students and teachers at universities involved in an effort to both educate
and motivate more people to increase their civic involvement.

It was Horton's interest in adapting such a model to work with the
social inequalities of poverty and race in the American South that created
an additional influence on the service-learning model. Horton's Highlander School was the epitome of service-learning in action. Knowledgeable professionals as well as nonprofessionals who lacked civic skills were
brought together in a school setting where they learned ways to take the
concepts of civic involvement to the public at large. People from throughout the South were encouraged to attend the school to discuss civic issues
and to learn of democracy and principles of service to others. The school
especially focused on its participants' returning to their communities to
train others, a concept at the heart of service-learning.

The service-learning concept was to have a tremendous impact. Egerton
(1983) argues that it was one of the key elements in black Americans'
acquiring the skills needed for the difficult tasks ahead in the civil rights
movements of the 1950s and 1960s. In his review of the impact of Highlander, Adams (1975) speaks of the powerful model developed at the
school that pervaded the entire civil rights movement. The impact also
spread to the profession of social work, which was growing increasingly
eager to find more new and relevant roles in society (Brieland, 1995). At
the core of the Highlander experience was the individual's commitment
to society, democracy, civic action, and social change. Each of these was
adopted into social work education and found its place in the service-
learning approach (Cotton, 1989).

Both of Highlander's themes of civic education and of civic service resonated with social work and its service-learning model already in place.
Brager and Holloway (1978) illustrate how Highlander's philosophy of
civic activism took root in the social work service-learning tradition. Since
its first years as a profession, social work was concerned about education
that was more than just education of the individual, but rather education
of the individual through service to society. The early social workers all
developed strong civic activism in areas from child labor to immigrant
rights.

Social work pioneers Mary Richmond and Jane Addams both spent a
large portion of their time in civic affairs. Addams, who modeled her Hull
House around the concept of civic-based service-learning stands as a continuing model for the profession (Lubove, 1965; Specht and Courtney,

1997). In later years, that model would come to dominate an entire field of practice within social work.

FEDERALISM AND SERVICE-LEARNING

A key point in the development of service-learning came at the hands of a small but highly influential group of social workers who were an integral part of the 1930s New Deal. Inspired by social workers Harry Hopkins and Aubrey Williams, Eleanor Roosevelt convinced her husband and other members of the Roosevelt administration of the need for a massive employment program for youth. As a result, Roosevelt launched the most extensive service-learning project up to that date through the National Youth Administration, created by presidential executive order in June, 1935. It not only created a role for the federal government in education, but it also revived the concept of education for democracy as an outgrowth of Dewey's ideals (Tyack, Lowe, & Hansford, 1984).

The National Youth Administration (NYA) provided jobs and educational opportunities for more than 700,000 youth from 16 to 25 years of age in both vocational and academic settings. In the vocational section, the Works Projects Program, NYA program participants worked in full-time jobs in industrial and community settings. For the youth in that half of the NYA program the goal was skills attainment, but skills attainment with a focus on the industrial needs of the community. Students were expected to pay back to the communities the benefits of their education upon completion of their training (Reiman, 1992). In the academically oriented Student Aid Program, students participated in what we now know as work-study programs on academic campuses, but work-study that was geared to working in the community and focusing on community problems. Reiman (1992) quotes NYA documents that point out that the program's purpose was to teach by example "the practice, responsibilities and rewards of citizenship" (pp. 1–15).

The NYA program exposed a new generation to the social work concepts of service to others and community betterment gained from the idealism of the turn-of-the-century social workers who formed settlement houses as hubs for community service by college students. This was not by accident. Williams, and her boss, Harry Hopkins, had both participated in settlement house work, Hopkins with the famous Jane Addams and her Hull House in Chicago around 1910 (when he was a student at Grinnell College in Iowa) and Williams at a settlement house on the east coast when she was a university student (Hopkins, 1999; McJimsey, 1987).

The federal influence on the concept of service-learning was that it should primarily be a process of contribution to the least of society by those who stood to become the top of society. They would pay back the people who had taught them (those in the communities with which they worked) by working in service to them. It was the epitome of Dewey's philosophies of practical education—and it came straight from Harry Hopkins (Black, 1996; Hopkins, 1999; Sherwood, 1948). The settlement house experience had strongly influenced Hopkins and it led to his democratic ideals for social service for the rest of his life. These were ideals that always held the poor and low-income as people with dignity who should be respected, "for there but for the grace of God go I," Hopkins would tell staff (McJimsey, 1987).

The program spread, its ideas spilling into other federal agencies, most notably the Department of the Interior where Harold Ickes established the Civilian Conservation Corps (CCC) at the urging of Roosevelt (Watkins, 1990). The CCC too was built around ideals of service to the community and learning from the community. Closely modeled on the NYA programs as a result of the involvement of Eleanor Roosevelt in its planning, the CCC was another attempt to take youth out of one environment and to place them into another where they would both learn and serve at the same time (Black, 1996; Watkins, 1990).

The most important aspect of the federal programs is that they were large, larger than any other service-learning programs the nation has seen. Because of their size they involved a whole generation of youth in education as a commitment to service to others. If one combines the numbers of participants in the NYA and CCC programs, over 1.4 million youth participated in service-learning in the years between 1935 and 1939 (Black, 1996; Watkins, 1990), giving American society, in terms of number of students in service-learning, a program with more impact, both direct and long-term, than all of higher education at the time.

The federal program, perhaps, also put a definitive social work stamp on the concept of service-learning—first, by getting its inspiration from early social workers such as Jane Addams and second, by being implemented by a second generation of social workers who would later go on to have a marked influence on the profession. (Harry Hopkins helped found the American Association of Social Workers and later went on to be its president as well as playing an important role in the founding of the current National Association of Social Workers.) But it may also have defined service-learning as a truly service-oriented activity from which the ultimate benefits accrued to society more than to the learner or the community that would teach that learner.

THE COMMUNITY AS A SERVICE-LEARNING FOCUS

Beginning with the Depression, and extending through the Civil Rights movement, social work became increasingly interested in public advocacy and training others to advocate for themselves. This is what was meant in the profession by *community organizing* (Cox et al., 1997).

Initially, social work found itself on the sidelines of the community activist movement in the Depression. Free thinkers such as Alinsky (1971) appeared to break professional boundaries in their active involvement in social change efforts. The more social work was confronted with the need for social change through its involvement in service-learning and outreach with the communities it served, the more social change through broad-based advocacy and community organizing became a part of social work. In time, the profession would come to see such community organizing as providing a rich heritage for the profession (Garvin & Cox, 1979).

After its adoption by social work in the Depression, community activism was reinforced as an area of the profession in the Civil Rights movement (Ross, 1955; Whithorn, 1984). Social work became increasingly interested in involving both students and the community they served in the same educational process. Over time this led to a more complex model of service-learning for the profession that stressed the autonomy of the community in the change-as-learning effort. Fellin (1995) explains how the framework for uniting social work service-learning with community principles evolved.

First came a definition of the purpose of both social work and service-learning as one of advocacy for communities (Sosin & Caulum, 1983). That in turn was followed by broader and more inclusive definitions of social activism as being a major component of democracy (Boyte, 1980). The limits of the purpose and methods of community organizing and advocacy were broadened (Cox, 1987). Emerging populations were investigated and their problems incorporated into the social work curriculum; first lower income, then minorities, and then women were each brought into the organizing and advocacy area (Hyde, 1986, 1990; Rivera & Erlich, 1992).

Organizing as a specific methodology within social work was developed. Key social work authors such as Kramer and Specht (1983) developed models for what was called community practice. No longer was Alinsky intimidating to the social work profession; he was incorporated into it.

Service-learning, through the social work curriculum, began to be designed specifically for community organizing. Meenaghan, Washington, and Ryan (1982) described the process as one of broadening the goals for the profession. Bartlett (1970) shows how the profession incorporated such new areas into its ideals, which led in turn to the guiding principles of service-learning. A key step was social work's recognition of community organizing and civic action as being part of its value base (Dluhy, 1981; Gibelman, 1995; Reamer, 1990, 1995; Verscheldren, 1983).

The key task then became for social work to define exactly how students participated in community change as a service-learning process. Vayda and Bogo (1992) explain that the tasks of focusing on disempowered or disenfranchised groups became the uniting theme. Eventually this led to a generic form of service-learning that focused all methods of the profession (Cox, Erlich, Tropman, & Rothman, 1987; Johnson, 1998; Kirst-Ashman & Hull, 1999; Pincus & Minihan, 1973). The term *generalist* was coined and social work began to focus on the investigation of the social problem within the civic environment as the most important task (Johnson, 1998; Kirst-Ashman & Hull, 2001; Saleebey, 1999; Shaefor, Horejsi, & Horejsi, 2000).

These authors chronicle the development of the idea that social work and community service are intertwined. It was through this process that service-learning was broadened and strengthened within the social work curriculum. Social work's preeminent theorist has shown how the concept of community service was eventually inseparable from the profession (Schorr, 1985). For students in social work the model was now complete (Barr, 1991; Burghardt, 1982; Corey & Corey, 1998).

SOCIAL WORK'S HISTORICAL CONTRIBUTION

Service-learning, as a direct linkage between the learner and the community in a service-oriented project, has been incorporated more heavily into the profession since the 1960s. Social work now provides a model for other disciplines interested in becoming more involved in service-learning. It also provides a mechanism by which the service-learning experience can be constructed. Founded on the democratic commitment to educating citizens for democratic change and the enfranchisement of minorities through social action, service-learning has taken on the task of inclusion in American society, a concept now described as empowerment (Gutierrez, 1990; Gutierrez, Parsons, & Cox, 1998; Hamilton, 1994; Haynes & Mickelson, 2000).

REFERENCES

Adams, F. T. (1975). *Unearthing seeds of fire: The idea of Highlander.* Winston-Salem, NC: Blair.

Alinsky, S. (1971). *Rules for radicals.* New York: Vintage Books.

American Association of Community Colleges. (2001). *America's community colleges: A century of innovation.* Washington, DC: Community College Press.

Barr, A. (1991). Placements in neighborhood community work: Evaluation of student performance. *Community Development Journal, 16,* 11–20.

Bartlett, H. (1970). *The common base of social work practice.* Silver Spring, MD: NASW Press.

Black, A. (1996). *Casting her own shadow: Eleanor Roosevelt and the shaping of postwar liberalism.* New York: Columbia University Press.

Boehm, W. (1959). *Objectives of the social work curriculum of the future*. New York: Council on Social Work Education.

Bonner, T. N. (1995). German influences on American clinical medicine, 1870–1910. In H. Geitz, J. Heideking & J. Herbst (Eds.), *German influences on education in the United States to 1917* (pp. 275–293). New York: Cambridge University Press.

Boyte, H. (1980). *The backyard revolution: Understanding the new citizen movement*. Philadelphia: Temple University Press.

Brager, G., & Holloway, S. (1978). *Changing human service organizations*. New York: Free Press.

Brieland, D. (1995). Social work practice: History and evolution. In *The Encyclopedia of Social Work* (19th ed., pp. 2247–2258). Silver Spring, MD: NASW Press.

Brookfield, S. (1987). *Learning democracy: Eduard Lindeman on adult education and social change*. Beckham, Kent, UK: Croom Helm.

Burghardt, S. (1982). *The other side of organizing*. Cambridge, MA: Schenkman.

Chandler, A. D. (1990). *Scale and scope: The dynamics of industrial capitalism*. Cambridge, MA: Harvard University Press.

Cogan, J. J. (1999). Civic education in the United States: A brief history. *International Journal of Social Education, 14*, 52–64.

Compton, B. R., & Galaway, B. (1999). *Social work processes* (6th ed.). Pacific Grove, CA: Brooks/Cole.

Congress, E. P. (1999). *Social work values and ethics*. Chicago: Nelson-Hall.

Cooper, J. M. (1990). *Pivotal decades: The United States, 1900–1920*. New York: W. W. Norton & Co.

Corey, M. S., & Corey, G. (1998). *Becoming a helper* (3rd ed.) Pacific Grove, CA: Brooks/Cole.

Cotton, D. (1989). Reflections on an experience in social change. *The Legacy, 1*, 4–6.

Council on Social Work Education. (1992a). *Curriculum policy statement for the baccalaureate degree programs in social work education*. Alexandria, VA: author.

Council on Social Work Education. (1992b). *Curriculum policy statement for the master's degree programs in social work education*. Alexandria, VA: author.

Council on Social Work Education. (1994). *Handbook of accreditation standards and procedures*. Alexandria, VA: author.

Cox, F. M. (1977). Exercising influence. In F. M. Cox, J. L. Erlich, J. Rothman, & J. Tropman (Eds.), *Tactics and techniques of community practice* (pp. 195–198). Itasca, IL: Peacock Publishers.

Cox, F. M. (1987) Communities: Alternative conceptions of community: Implications for community organization practice. In F. M. Cox, J. L. Erlich, J. Rothman, & J. E. Tropman (Eds.), *Strategies of community organization macro practice* (pp. 232–242). Itasca, IL: F. E. Peacock.

Cox, F., Erlich, J. L., Tropman, J., & Rothman, J. (1987). Models of community organization and macro-practice. In F. M. Cox, J. L. Erlich, J. Tropman, & J. Rothman (Eds.), *Strategies of community organization macro-practice* (pp. 3–26). Itasca, IL: F. E. Peacock.

Cremin, L. A. (1961). *The transformation of the school: Progressivism in American education, 1876–1957*. New York: Vintage Books.

Cunningham, N. E. (1987). *In pursuit of reason: The life of Thomas Jefferson.* Baton Rouge: Louisiana State University Press.

Dluhy, M. J. (1981). *Changing the system: Political advocacy for disadvantaged groups.* Beverly Hills, CA: Sage Press.

Eddy, E. D. (1957). *Colleges for our land and time: The land-grant idea in American education.* New York: Harper & Brothers.

Egerton, J. (1983). *Speak now against the day: The generation before the civil rights movement in the South* (pp. 158–162). New York: Alfred A. Knopf.

Fellin, P. (1995). *The community and the social worker* (2nd ed.). Itasca, IL: F. E. Peacock.

Ferguson, E. S. (1992). *Engineering and the mind's eye.* Cambridge, MA: MIT Press.

Foner, E. (1970). *Free soil, free men, free labor: The ideology of the Republican Party before the Civil War.* New York: Oxford University Press.

Garvin, C. D., & Cox, F. M. (1979). A history of community organizing since the Civil War with special reference to oppressed communities. In F. M. Cox, J. L. Erlich, J. Rothman, & J. Tropman, *Strategies of community organizing: A book of readings* (pp. 45–75). Itasca, IL: F. E. Peacock.

Geisner, R. (1956). *The democratic man: Selected writings of Eduard C. Lindeman.* Boston: Beacon Press.

Germain, C., & Gitterman, A. (1980). *The life model of social work practice.* New York: Columbia University Press.

Gibelman, M. (1995). *What social workers do.* Silver Spring, MD: NASW Press.

Glen, J. M. (1988). *Highlander: No ordinary school, 1932–1962.* Lexington: University Press of Kentucky.

Gutierrez, L. (1990). Working with women of color: An empowerment perspective. *Social Work, 35,* 149–154.

Gutierrez, L., Parsons, R. L., & Cox, E. O. (Eds.). (1998). *Empowerment in social work practice: A sourcebook.* Pacific Grove, CA: Brooks/Cole.

Hamilton, G. (1954). Self-awareness in professional education. *Social Casework, 35,* 371–379.

Haynes, K. S., & Mickelson, J. S. (2000). *Affecting change.* New York: Longman.

Hepburn, M. (1999). Service-learning in civic education: A concept with long, sturdy roots. In T. Stanton, D. Giles & N. Cruz (Eds.), *Service-learning: A movement's pioneers reflect on its origins, practice, and future.* San Francisco: Jossey-Bass.

Hofstadter, R. (1955). *Academic freedom in the age of the college.* New York: Columbia University Press.

Hopkins, J. (1999). *Harry Hopkins: Sudden hero, brash reformer.* New York: St. Martin's Press.

Hyde, C. (1986). Experience of women activists: Implications for community organizing theory and practice. *Journal of Sociology and Social Welfare, 13,* 542–562.

Hyde, C. (1990). A feminist model for macro practice: Promises and problems. *Administration in Social Work, 13,* 145–181.

Ingram, J. S. (1876). *The centennial exposition.* Philadelphia: Hubbard Bros.

Jansson, B. (1999). *Becoming an effective policy advocate.* Pacific Grove, CA: Brooks/Cole.

Johnson, L. C. (1998). *Social work practice: A generalist approach* (6th ed.). Boston: Allyn and Bacon.

Kirst-Ashman, K. K., & Hull, G. F. (1999). *Understanding generalist practice.* Chicago: Nelson-Hall.

Kirst-Ashman, K. K., & Hull, G. F. (2001). *Generalist practice with organizations and communities* (2nd ed.). Pacific Grove, CA: Brooks/Cole.

Konopka, G. (1958). *Eduard Lindeman and social work philosophy.* Minneapolis: University of Minnesota Press.

Kramer, R., & Specht, H. (1983). *Readings in community organization practice* (3rd ed.). Englewood Cliffs, NJ: Prentice-Hall.

Lewis, A. (1997). *An early encounter with tomorrow: Europeans, Chicago's Loop and the World's Columbian Exposition.* Urbana: University of Illinois Press.

Lindeman, E. (1926). *The meaning of adult education.* New York: New Republic Press.

Lindeman, L. (1991). *Friendly rebel: A personal and social history of Eduard C. Lindeman.* Adamant, VT: Adamant Press.

Linton, D. S. (1995). American responses to German continuation schools during the Progressive Era. In H. Geitz, J. Heideking & J. Herbst (Eds.), *German influences on education in the United States to 1917* (pp. 67–84). New York: Cambridge University Press.

Lockridge, K. (1974). *Literacy in Colonial New England.* New York: Norton.

Lubove, R. (1965). *The professional altruist: The emergence of social work as a career, 1880-1930.* Cambridge, MA: Harvard University Press.

Mattson, K. (1998). Can service-learning transform the modern university? A lesson from history. *Michigan Journal of Community Service-Learning, 5,* 108–113.

McJimsey, G. (1987). *Harry Hopkins: Ally of the poor, defender of democracy.* Cambridge, MA: Harvard University Press.

Meenaghan, T. M., Washington, R. O., & Ryan, R. M. (1982). *Macro practice in the human services.* New York: Free Press.

Metzger, W. P. (1955). *Academic freedom in the age of the university.* New York: Columbia University Press.

Meyer, C. (1970). *Social work practice: A response to the urban crisis.* New York: Free Press.

Ostrander, G. M. (1999). *Republic of letters: The American intellectual community, 1775–1865.* Madison, WI: Madison House.

Pahl, D. (1987). *West Point: The United States Military Academy.* New York: Exeter Books.

Pincus, A., & Minahan, A. (1973). *Social work practice: Model and method.* Itasca, IL: F. E. Peacock.

Popple, P. R. (1995). The social work profession: History. In *The Encyclopedia of Social Work* (19th ed., Vol. 3, pp. 2282–2292). Silver Spring, MD: NASW Press.

Post, R. C. (1976). *1876: A centennial exhibit.* Washington, DC: The Smithsonian Institution.

Reamer, F. G. (1990). *Ethical dilemmas in social service* (2nd ed.). New York: Columbia University Press.

Reamer, F. G. (1995). *Social work values and ethics.* New York: Columbia University Press.

Reiman, R. A. (1992). *The New Deal and American youth: Ideas and ideals in a depression decade* (pp. 1–15). Athens: University of Georgia Press.

Ricci, D. (1971). *Community power and democratic theory.* New York: Random House.

Rivera, F. G., & Erlich, J. L. (1992). *Community organizing in a diverse society.* Boston: Allyn and Bacon.

Rodgers, D. T. (1998). *Atlantic crossings: Social politics in a progressive era.* Cambridge, MA: Harvard University Press.

Ross, M. G. (1955). *Community organization: Theory and principles.* New York: Harper Bros.

Rudolph, F. (1962). *The American college and university: A history.* New York: Vintage Books.

Saleebey, D. (1999). The strengths perspective: Principles and practices. In B. Compton & B. Galaway (Eds.), *Social work processes* (6th ed., pp. 14–27). Pacific Grove, CA: Brooks/Cole.

Schorr, A. (1985, June). Professional practice as policy. *Social Service Review, 51,* 178–196.

Shaefor, B. W., Horejsi, C. R., & Horejsi, G. A. (2000). *Techniques and guidelines for social work practice* (5th ed.). Boston: Allyn and Bacon.

Sherwood, R. (1948). *Roosevelt and Hopkins: An intimate history.* New York: Random House.

Sosin, M., & Caulum, S. (1983). Advocacy: A conceptualization for social work practice. *Social Work, 28,* 12–17.

Specht, H., & Courtney, N. (1997). *Unfaithful angels: How social work has abandoned its mission.* New York: Free Press.

Stanton, T. K., Giles, D. E., & Cruz, N. I. (1999). *Service-Learning: A movement's pioneers reflect on its origins, practice, and future.* San Francisco: Jossey-Bass.

Stewart, D. (1987). *Adult learning in America: Eduard Lindeman and his agenda for lifelong education.* Malibar, FL: Robert E. Kreiger.

Thelen, D. P. (1976). *Robert LaFollette and the insurgent spirit.* Boston: Little Brown.

Tyack D., Lowe, R., & Hansford, E. (1984). *Public schools in hard times: The Great Depression and recent years.* Cambridge, MA: Harvard University Press.

Uffelman, M. D. (2004). Smith-Hughes Vocational Education Act of 1917. In J. Buenker (Ed.), *Encyclopedia of the Gilded Age and Progressive Era.* Racine, WI: M. E. Sharpe.

Vayda, E., & Bogo, M. (1992). A teaching model to unite classroom and field. *Journal of Social Work Education, 27* (3), 271–278.

Verscheldren, C. (1983). Social work values and practicum: Opportunities to work as a professional responsibility. *Social Work, 28,* 765–769.

Veysey, L. R. (1965). *The emergence of the American university.* Chicago: University of Chicago Press.

Watkins, T. H. (1990). *Righteous pilgrim: The life and times of Harold L. Ickes.* New York: Henry Holt and Co.

Wegner, G. P. (1995). Prussian *Volksschule* through American eyes: Two perspectives on curriculum and teaching from the 1890s. In H. Geitz, J. Heideking, & J. Herbst (Eds.), *German influences on education in the United States to 1917* (pp. 1–15). New York: Cambridge University Press.

Wiebe, R. H. (1967). *The search for order, 1877–1920.* New York: Hill and Wang.

Whithorn, A. (1984). *Serving the people: Social services and social change.* New York: Columbia University Press.

PART II

Theoretical Models

CHAPTER 3

A Justification of the Philanthropic Model

C. F. Abel

The challenge of this volume is to clarify the ethically proper form of service-learning. The question is neither whether service-learning is an effective pedagogical device nor whether it is ethical per se. Regarding the efficacy of service-learning the jury is still out, although there is some evidence that certain forms of community involvement may stimulate certain forms of learning regardless of class, gender, or ethnicity (Leighley, 1991; Tan, 1980). There is, for example, some documentation that involvement in community service stimulates students to think about political issues, to establish political identities, and to develop long-term habits of civic participation (Brody, 1994; Youniss & Yates, 1997). Unfortunately, though much of the literature argues that service-learning impacts significantly such affective dimensions as self-confidence, social responsibility, civic-mindedness, self-esteem, personal efficacy, and willingness to accept cultural differences (Astin & Sax, 1998; Boss, 1994; Markus, Howard, & King, 1993), none of it distinguishes effectively between its effects on the affective and cognitive domains. Thus, although "faculty and administrators are intensely interested in this issue . . . there is not yet convincing evidence of the importance of service-learning to subject matter learning" (Giles & Eyler, 1998, p. 109). Nevertheless, the apparent successes in the affective domain are sufficient to suggest that service-learning is at least worth considering as an option in certain contexts. Regarding the propriety of loosing callow students upon communities to experiment with recently acquired information and untested skills, it is assumed that so long as both agree to both the arrangement and the practices employed, each gets what is deserved.

The question goes instead to what should be agreed upon as the proper nature and focus of the service-learning experience and consequently what constitutes its proper practice. For some, the proper focus is external and interpersonal. The central mission of service-learning is to produce active, engaged citizen advocates. This mission is accomplished best through direct, active, and even ideologically (or anti-ideologically) focused political action at the community level. Accordingly, this civic education approach encourages educational partnerships between universities and communities, with communities actively involved in the role service will play in the education of students (Battistoni, 1997). Classrooms are considered proper venues for nurturing activist and confrontational forms of good citizenship. Thus, critical classroom discussion is combined with forms of service-learning designed to socialize students into the values, habits, and dispositions that promote partisan ideals and to alter dispositions, attitudes, and behaviors in ways conducive to issue advocacy. It is assumed that service-learning practiced in this way enhances a student's educational experience, sustains democratic culture, strengthens democratic institutions, and advances social justice (Barber & Battistoni, 1993; Boyte, 1993; Boyte & Skelton, 1997; Chesney & Feinstein, 1993).

Others are convinced that the proper focus is internal. The central classroom mission is to develop the student's capacity for judicious self-direction. Once developed, this capacity allows students to mold the relations they have with others as they see fit, perhaps refusing to interact politically at all. Among many of this philanthropic persuasion, service-learning is unnecessary though perhaps helpful in some respects. Exposing students to a number of social, political, and economic contexts might serve as object lessons, might deepen or broaden certain understandings, and might add a pragmatic dimension to their thought. On the other hand, students without sufficiently developed capacities for self-direction might be captured, as it were, by charismatic political leaders, romantic ideologies, or biased perceptions they cannot evaluate thoroughly or well. For those of this persuasion, the mission of producing political activists is the antithesis of education; and their concern is intensified by the fact that service-learning is now typically distinguished from both community service and civic education by the collaborative effort to "seek justice" by addressing "community problems" (Ehrlich, 1999, p. 246).

At the root of the debate over how we should practice service-learning, then, lies the question of how service-learning is justified. This chapter seeks to justify what is styled above as the philanthropic approach (Battistoni, 1997). It is distinguished from the civic approach by its neutrality regarding social issues and its placement of the student in the role of assistant observer as opposed to partisan collaborator. The chapter proceeds by considering first what constitutes a proper sort of justification for any pedagogy and then molding its argument to that form.

JUSTIFYING PEDAGOGIES

What does it mean to justify a particular form of educational practice (a pedagogy) and what types of justification may we use? For our purposes, the formal pedagogy will be addressed, not the detailed problems of realizing the pedagogy in practice. Asking how closely the image conforms to reality is certainly important to judging the extent of real service-learning that is going on. But that is not the same as justifying it in the first place.

One method of justifying a pedagogy that certainly seems erroneous is that of validation by origin. Thus, service-learning is sometimes justified by tracing its history to important thinkers wrestling with great educational issues. John Dewey and his quest for a "relevant" education is often mentioned in this regard, as are Boyd Bode and his concern with the "irresponsible individualism" he perceived at the root of traditional schooling and George Counts and his concern with the failure of schools to provide meaningful goals (Bode, 1938; Counts, 1952, Dewey, 1916). Each of these sought a remedy in social action by educators, but these origins alone neither justify nor invalidate any current pedagogy. Neither an appeal to such authorities nor an argument that it once was a good idea addresses our concern with the justification of service-learning today.

Justifying service-learning by reference to its intrinsic purposes seems equally erroneous. It does not seem to make sense to say that any pedagogy has an intrinsic or essential purpose. The purpose seems necessarily determined by whatever collective educational purposes we give it; and while different pedagogies may be suited better to different purposes, the idea that certain pedagogies are inherently better than others and should be employed for that reason alone seems nonsensical. Similarly, it doesn't seem to make much sense to suggest that service-learning be justified by what an education ought to accomplish. There seems to be no intrinsic purpose or value to an education beyond our individual and collective desires and perceptions of what we need.

However, justifying a pedagogy within a more modest discourse on educational purposes and the social function of education does seem appropriate. We might, for instance, specify the goals that education should pursue and then justify service-learning on the instrumental ground that it can best attain these goals. Within such discourses we are not deducing the justification of service-learning from any purportedly intrinsic goals but evaluating it in terms of goals we have constructed. For instance, personal and social improvement might be generally accepted as proper goals of a good education, and one form of service-learning might then be justified by evidence that it can more nearly meet these goals than can other forms. This seems a powerful form of justification if unintended meanings are avoided.

For example, such goals are often so vague that we don't really know what they mean until they are spelled out in proposals for their operationalization, whereupon all agreement vanishes. Another possible misunderstanding involves assuming that all educational institutions should or do pursue the same purposes. In fact, elementary, secondary, and higher education institutions are usually expected to achieve very different purposes, as are different kinds of schools (e.g., tech schools and liberal arts institutions). Similarly, the goals of educational institutions at any level change over time as knowledge, sophistication, and interests change. Thus, high schools may take on some goals universities once pursued and some goals may be dropped altogether as they are rendered obsolete. In this sense we may say that education has no purpose in itself. What gives it purpose are the extant moral, political, economic, and social practices, discourses, and norms constructing it on an ongoing basis.

THE PHILANTHROPIST JUSTIFICATION

To justify a particular pedagogy, then, involves specifying currently desirable ends with respect to specific kinds of colleges and universities given the current institutional context of higher education. In fact, the issue at hand arises from a conflict over exactly what the social function of teaching should be in our highly technologized, capitalistic, democratic, and globalized society. Broadly speaking, the clash between what are styled the philanthropic and the civic approaches reflects the clash between neutrality and partisanship, "objective science versus social advocacy, classical versus utilitarian education, and critical thinking versus critical action" (Stanton, Giles, & Cruz, 1999).

THE ENDS

Without pretending to speak for all of the philanthropic persuasion, allow me to suggest that philanthropists generally begin with a comparatively modest conception of educational ends. Beyond providing access to both the joys of education for its own sake and the fuller life that it provides, philanthropists hold that universities fulfill their social responsibility in two ways: first, by helping people to acquire the intellectual tools demanded by contemporary civilized life and second, by concerning themselves with the development of epistemological skills and the self-reflective development of moral values. The philanthropist ideal is neither social transformation nor training in social, political, and economic activism, nor necessarily developing the sort of other-regarding ethic that critical theorists or communitarians of the civic persuasion hold appropriate to their idea of democracy. Rather, it is in the disinterested pursuit of knowledge and the growth of character and wisdom within the individual. From this, it is hoped, society in general will benefit as the critical condition widens with the creation of an educated public (Gutmann, 1987). Education in this sense involves freeing the mind and enabling autonomous, critical, and dialogical thought that is capable of self-determination and is empowered to act as a source of independent social, political, and economic criticism, should the individual so desire (McMurtry, 1991).

Of course, philanthropists are not innocent of the fact that higher education in American society gains only a part of its social significance from the personal satisfaction, self-realization, intellectual autonomy, and wisdom that comes from general learning and the mastery of sophisticated thought. In our current social context, higher education confers increased chances for income, power, and prestige. In our society the allocation of social goods depends to a significant extent upon the habits of thought, attitudes, and special skills that the educated obtain (Blau & Duncan, 1967; Lenski, 1966). However, philanthropists do not generally consider the university the proper venue for deciding how social goods ought to be distributed any more than it is the proper venue for promoting either one religion over another or religious approaches generally over secular approaches to living.

Now, none of the philanthropist's goals as outlined above requires any sort of hands-on pedagogy, let alone any service-learning. In fact, service-learning as defined by proponents disposed to civic action may be positively destructive. Specifically, a focus on civic action may bias what is studied more toward idiosyncratic student interests than toward a discipline-relevant curriculum; it may reduce the amount of disciplinary content conveyed and it may privilege study topics generated more by social and political conflict than by the structure of the discipline. Worse, it may stress problem solving over sound abstract, critical, inductive, analogical, deductive, and ethical reasoning. In light of these dangers, the most that can be said is that certain forms of experiential learning might be helpful for certain purposes under certain circumstances for certain people at certain times. That is, it may be helpful to those with advanced reasoning powers, a mature epistemological understanding, and a rich, sophisticated, and discipline-relevant learning who feel that either their character or their intellect may benefit by some exposure to the mundane problem solving they will encounter daily after leaving the university.

THE CONTEXT

This philanthropic concept of education with its limited role for service-learning arises from experience with modern American democracy. Many argue, for example, that within our society, "to propose a pedagogy is to propose a political vision. In this perspective, we cannot talk about teaching practices without talking about politics" (Darder, 1991). The politics of our democracy is defined by conflicts and compromises among a fluid set of socioeconomic and cultural groups with more or less competing visions of what counts as good teaching, a good life, and a just society (Kliebard, 1994). These competing visions are held more or less strongly at different times by varying arrays of educators, citizens, interest groups, and confederacies. In brief, all of these visions are fundamentally contested in American society and are likely to remain so given the priority of liberty over collectivity, all else being equal (Lane, 1986; Shields, 1952). In this context, philanthropic educators conclude that these visions are best pursued collectively through a continuing debate kept alive by neutrality in the university. Let us consider why.

First, philanthropic educators are convinced that the pressure of opposing visions kept alive by the neutrality of educators enriches the wider debate in which the visions are deployed. For example, adhering closely to the principle that educational institutions should be neutral between competing conceptions of the good life and of what gives life value facilitates social, political, and economic debate by keeping momentarily unpopular or misunderstood or widely unknown conceptualizations in play. In many cases, the contestants themselves are able to grasp the benefit of the polemic, even while they remain unregenerate partisans of their respective personal visions.

Second, many philanthropists argue that continuing neutral and abstract debate over certain terms like *justice* and *the good life* are important and valuable not despite their abstract contestedness but just because of it (Gallie, 1962). Far from contributing to confusion, indecision, and powerlessness, the disagreements play an indispensable role in empowering individuals to participate most fully in social, intellectual, and cultural life. Such essentially contested concepts as justice and the good life, for example, enjoy a range of meanings that only take on a cohesive sense as we develop them in the conflicting discourses into which they are woven. For this reason educational institutions should not discriminate in assisting one doctrine over another but present doctrines neutrally and abstractly so that they are retained as part of the discourse in their most sophisticated form and not trivialized by the pressures and reservations often accompanying political action (Ackerman, 1980; Dworkin, 1985; Gutmann, 1985; Kymlicka, 1989, Rawls, 1988).

Finally, because interests are essentially contested within the American context, it is conceptually impossible to determine precisely an individual's true interests, let alone those of communities or the nation overall. Consequently, debate over interests should be as rich and subtle as possible, and the simple dynamic of debating abstractly and neutrally requires that even initial claims about interests be considerably richer and subtler than they would otherwise be. At a minimum this dynamic includes putting forward views nonconfrontationally, citing and assembling examples, seeking out and responding to rival views, abstractly modifying one's view to meet exceptions, explaining why a particular vision may remain coherent even after modification, and willingly opening one's mind to distasteful and threatening options. Clearly, the richness and subtlety of interest claims are most easily and thoroughly revealed in such an abstract and neutral discourse.

Of course, confrontational advocacy has a proper place in the context of political institutions and most particularly in courts and legislatures, though even in courts and legislatures confrontational advocacy is expected to progress toward abstraction and neutrality when it comes to making policy and writing laws. Educational institutions, being neither partisan nor legislative nor judicial bodies, inherit the task of doing nothing intended to favor or promote any particular comprehensive doctrine and thereby impoverishing the debate over interests and how they may best be served. Not only does such abstract neutrality keep the debate rich and subtle, it allows a continuing reexamination of ideas for strengths and weaknesses and encourages conceptual evolution into perhaps stronger versions of both favored and currently maligned visions.

This philanthropist argument gains power when we consider the homage paid to liberty that is perhaps the hallmark of American democracy. Philanthropic service-learning grounds itself in an educational philosophy maintaining that when universities are earnest in the disinterested pursuit of knowledge and sound thinking, they lay the necessary foundation for individuals to choose those forms of personal engagement in critical and constructive practices that they decide are most productive. Rather than becoming embroiled in ideological and partisan social conflict and presuming to identify (or to help others to identify), promote, or attack ostensible social goods or evils directly, the philanthropic approach seeks to provide the wherewithal for individuals to make these identifications by themselves and to choose the most individually appropriate form of participation for themselves. There is research suggesting, for example, that for some Americans civic and political engagement is irrational, unnecessary, ineffective, and even harmful (Berelson, 1952; Downs, 1957; Edelman, 1988; Neuman, 1986; Olson, 1971). These attitudes should not be denigrated or beleaguered by educational practice but respected as individual life choices and opened for both neutral, abstract consideration and a debate unburdened by the stress of political, social, and cultural competition.

Within the American social context, this bias toward liberty in the university is considered the most desirable approach for several reasons. First, in a neutral educational environment individual conceptions of the good life are allowed to compete, and as they compete, the worthy tend to defeat the unworthy (Hayek, 1960; Kymlicka, 1989). This is not guaranteed. Many factors, of course, influence the survival and success of different conceptions of the good life quite apart from their merit. These factors include peer group pressure, manipulation, ignorance, and cost. Moreover, individuals might suffer from weakness of will and may either fail to play their part in those collective actions necessary to bring about the good life or be incapable of pursuing it on their own even given the opportunity. The claim is just that this sort of educational neutrality is more conducive to the emergence and persistence of the most mutually satisfactory and broadest consensus of the good life.

Moreover, the obstacles of peer pressure, manipulation, and ignorance are increased by engagement with the community, rendering the survival of the most meritorious conceptualizations significantly more problematic. Hence, Gutmann (1987) argues that universities need the "academic freedom of scholars" and the institutional "freedom of the academy" in order to "serve democracy as sanctuaries of nonrepression," fending off the "threat of democratic tyranny" and the oppression of minority views by the majority (pp. 174–175). Freedom from the conflict among interests enables universities to serve society best by educating in a realm where intellectual integrity and the moral principles of nonrepression and nondiscrimination flourish.

Second, educators should favor liberty over promoting particular conceptions of justice or the good life because they will make mistakes (Ackerman, 1980, 1983; Feinberg, 1988). Regardless of how thoughtful and well intentioned, neither educators nor community groups can help but be partial to their own interests in ways they may not recognize. Both are likely to take shortcuts in their thinking derived from their professional socialization, individual histories, individual experiences, religious proclivities, and current positions in the socioeconomic structure. Most importantly, each suffers necessarily from bounded rationality. They necessarily lack perfect knowledge of valuable ways of life and may be unaware of valuable and important conceptions of justice and the good life. These problems would be magnified should the community and the educators be tied together and expected to work in harness. As the research by Milgram (1983), Asche (1951), and others indicates, the pressure to favor certain interests, to take shortcuts, and to focus only on what is immediately known or desired would most certainly increase.

The best educators and most practical communities are acutely aware of this limitation and actively engage and support neutral, abstract scholarship, learning, debate, and research. Moreover, these concerns are precisely why a part of an educator's social function is just to introduce students neutrally and abstractly to a variety of ideas concerning the good life that they would not otherwise encounter. This being true, universities are not the proper loci for experimenting with different conceptions of the good life. Political and economic institutions are established for this purpose, and in those venues reform and political action should be engaged. For these same reasons those forms of service-learning promoting social advocacy should not be allowed to "inhabit the core curriculum" as some promoting the civic version of service-learning suggest (Battistoni, 1997).

Third, if educators intervene by helping individuals or communities to realize their interest in one area, both students and the community may become increasingly dependent upon them for guidance in other areas. Students come to classrooms already socialized into thinking as their parents, clergy, peers, and high school teachers train them to. Nothing is gained if they leave either thinking as their professors instruct or merely resocialized by experiences with selected groups in the community. Marginalized groups are similarly socialized, and university intervention seeking justice among communities similarly undermines the ability to think for one's self, engendering apathy, dependence, and an inability to judge one's own interests well. In brief, the consequence of any avoidable form of partiality or interventionism is the deterioration of the character and ability of both the student and the community (Feinberg, 1980). The best counter to this is to provide strongly, fully, and neutrally the greatest variety of conceptions of the good life, thus providing the greatest scope for deliberation and greatest challenge to the critical faculties of both students and the community.

Fourth, while there is value in experimenting with new and different modes of living and in confronting students and communities who have bad ideas (Lloyd-Thomas, 1983), operationalizing those experiments in the community is best left to those directly affected by the change. In a neutral setting students may detect the right reasons for believing or pursuing certain visions upon becoming aware of other visions and critically evaluating them and grounding their decisions in an assessment of the comparative merits of several options rather than upon socialization, habit, or political pressure. Given that education, students may then compete in the wider society for acceptance of their visions without the aegis of the university and in a context where they will be most directly affected by the results. Instigating action for a semester project and then removing one's self to the security of either the university life or an unaffected home community does everyone a disservice.

Finally, political action by educators raises the prospect of a dictatorship of either the academy or whatever particular community gains political ascendancy with the academy's help. Other communities may be forced to seek only so much of their vision as may be comfortably couched in the discourse and practices of the academy or the newly dominant group. Giroux (1988), for example, a leading light in the theoretical foundation of politicized service-learning, promotes antagonism and the adoption of an oppositional ideology, calling for the transformation of society through a hegemony of the oppressed as opposed to social evolution through debate, cooperation, and compromise. Toward this end, teachers are to become "transformative intellectuals" legitimating their students' "voices in an effort to empower them as critical and active citizens" (p. 32). Furthermore, critical educators "must encourage forms of solidarity rooted in the principles of trust, sharing, and a commitment to improving the quality of human life" (p. 33). These exhortations suggest one of two things. Either, contrary to all experience (both of educators and researchers), there is agreement among the diverse oppressed and marginalized communities currently and historically promoting different visions of what constitutes justice and the good life, or teachers are to weld such a common vision together. In either case, the role of educators seems problematic. For example, how are students or communities to choose among opposing ideologies? If they are to choose freely, what happens if they choose the ideology seen as oppressive by the educator? What if an oppressed community sees the students returning to it or the educator as oppressive just because either is trying to politicize them?

Along this line, Ellsworth (1989) criticizes critical pedagogues such as Giroux for proposing a theory for the "Silent Other" where concepts like "emancipatory authority" imply "the presence of or potential for an emancipated teacher" (p. 307). It is her experience, in other words, that civic sorts of pedagogies quickly become mechanisms for giving voice to the political predilections of the professor or the university, that they assume that certain kinds of democratic outcomes are inherently superior and thus politicize learning, thereby biasing it in ways destructive of the disinterested pursuit of knowledge and the development of sound reasoning.

CONCLUSION

Civic sorts, however, consider this approach irresponsible. First, it leaves to accident and individual choice the ends to which the acquired talents, abilities, skills, and knowledge will be used. Worse, it may be abused as a tool of private advantage and material success. Rather, education should mold itself into an instrument of social justice. Consequently, universities should be involved in both the advocacy of political doctrines and the practice of social action. They should participate in the partisanship and propaganda of social and political faction. In brief, education should be politicized. Accordingly, teachers must choose between the exploitative dominant ideology and the exploited. The educational profession is advised to advance social revolution by aligning itself with the unemancipated, making them conscious of their true interests and informing them of the fundamental sources of their enslavement. To the extent that neutrality is a value at all, it is as either a strong or weak version of a consequentialist neutrality. That is, educational neutrality consists either in having equal effects on all conceptions of the good life or in insuring that all conceptions of the good life do equally well.

This attitude derives from the twist civic sorts generally give to the definition of service-learning. For example, "service-learning combines traditional classroom and laboratory experiences with significant experiences in field placements where pertinent social issues are being played out" (Bonar et al., 1996, pp. 14–15). Again, "service-learning is more of a program emphasis, representative of a set of educational, social, and sometimes political values, rather than a discrete type of experiential education" (Stanton, 1990, p. 65). In brief, for civic sorts "service-learning pedagogies stand apart from much of traditional education in that these pedagogies do not seek, nor claim, value neutrality" (Godfrey, 1999, p. 364). Rather, service-learning is an opportunity for affecting the power struggle among multiple and conflicting political interests. For the reasons given above, philanthropists view this approach as destructive of the proper social and intellectual role of universities and ultimately of the democratic context itself.

REFERENCES

Ackerman, B. (1980). *Social justice in the liberal state.* New Haven, CT: Yale University Press.

Asche, S. (1951). Effects of group pressure upon the modification and distortion of judgments. In H. Guetzkow (Ed.), *Groups, leadership and men.* Pittsburgh, PA: Carnegie Press.

Astin, A. W., & Sax, L. J. (1998). How undergraduates are affected by service participation. *Journal of College Student Development, 39*(3), 251–263.

Barber, B. R., & Battistoni, R. (1993). A season of service: Introducing service-learning into the liberal arts curriculum. *PS: Political Science and Politics, 26,* 235–240.

Battistoni, R. (1997). Service-learning and democratic citizenship. *Theory into Practice, 36,* 150–156.

Berelson, B. (1952). Democratic theory and public opinion. *Public Opinion Quarterly, 16,* 313.

Blau, P. M., & Duncan, O. D. (1967). *The American occupational structure.* New York: John Wiley.

Bode, Boyd. (1938). *Progressive education at the crossroads.* New York: Macmillan.

Bonar, L., Buchanan, R., Fisher, I., & Wechsler, A. (1996). *Service-learning in the curriculum.* Salt Lake City, UT: Lowell Bennion Community Service Center.

Boss, J. A. (1994). The effect of community service work on the moral development of college ethics students. *Journal of Moral Education, 23,* 183–198.

Boyte, H. C. (1993). Civic education as public leadership development. *PS: Political Science and Politics, 26,* 763–769.

Boyte, H. C. & Skelton, N. (1997, February). The legacy of public work: Educating for citizenship. *Educational Leadership, 54*(5), 12–17.

Brody, R. A. (1994). *Secondary education and political attitudes: Examining the effects on political tolerance of the We the People. . .Curriculum.* Calabasas, CA: Center for Civic Education.

Chesney, J. D., & Feinstein, O. (1993). Making political activity a requirement in introductory political science courses. *PS: Political Science and Politics, 6,* 535–538.

Counts, G. (1952). *Education and American civilization.* New York: Macmillan.

Darder, A. (1991). *Culture and power in the classroom: A critical foundation for bicultural education.* Westport, CT: Bergin & Garvey.

Dewey, J. (1916). *Democracy and education: An introduction to the philosophy of education.* New York: Macmillan.

Downs, A. (1957). *An economic theory of democracy.* New York: Harper and Row.

Dworkin, R. (1985). *Liberalism: A matter of principle.* London, UK: Harvard University Press.

Edelman, M. (1988). *Constructing the political spectacle.* Chicago: University of Chicago Press.

Ehrlich, T. (1999). Civic education: Lessons learned. *PS: Political Science and Politics, 32*(2), 245–250.

Ellsworth, E. (1989). Why doesn't this feel empowering?: Working through the repressive myths of critical pedagogy. *Harvard Educational Review, 59,* 307.

Feinberg, J. (1980). The interest in liberty on the scales. In *Rights, justice and the bounds of liberty: Essays in social philosophy.* Princeton, NJ: Princeton University Press.

Feinberg, J. (1988). *The moral limits of the criminal law: Vol. 4. Harmless wrongdoing.* Oxford, UK: Oxford University Press.

Gallie, W. B. (1962). Essentially contested concepts. In M. Black (Ed.), *The Importance of Language.* Englewood Cliffs, NJ: Prentice Hall.

Giles, D. E., Jr., & Eyler, J. (1998). A service-learning research agenda for the next five years. In R. A. Rhoads, & J. P. F. Howard (Eds.), *Academic service-learning: A pedagogy of action and reflection.* New Directions For Teaching and Learning. San Francisco, CA: Jossey-Bass.

Giroux, H. A. (1988). *Schooling and the struggle for public life: Critical pedagogy in the modern age.* Minneapolis: University of Minnesota Press.

Godfrey, P. C. (1999). Service learning and management education: A call to action. *Journal of Management Inquiry, 8*(4), 363–378.

Gutmann, A. (1985). Communitarian critics of liberalism. *Philosophy and Public Affairs, 15,* 313.

Gutmann, A. (1987). *Democratic education.* Princeton, NJ: Princeton University Press.

Hayek, F. A. (1960). *The constitution of liberty.* London: Routledge and Kegan Paul.

Kliebard, H. (1994). *The struggle for the American curriculum* (2nd ed.). New York: Routledge.

Kymlicka, W. (1989). *Liberalism, community and culture.* Oxford, UK: Oxford University Press.

Lane, R. E. (1986). Market justice, political justice. *American Political Science Review, 80,* 383–402.

Leighley, J. (1991). Participation as a stimulus of political conceptualization. *Journal of Politics, 53,* 198–211.

Lenski, G. (1966). *Power and privilege: A theory of social stratification.* New York: McGraw-Hill.

Lloyd-Thomas, D. (1983). In defense of liberalism: Rights, consequences, and Mill on liberty. In A. Griffiths (Ed.), *Of Liberty.* Cambridge, UK: Cambridge University Press.

Markus, G. B., Howard, J. P. F., & King, D. C. (1993). Integrating community service and classroom instruction enhances learning: results from an experiment. *Educational Evaluation and Policy Analysis, 15*(4), 410–419.

McMurtry, J. (1991). Education and the market model. *Journal of Philosophy of Education, 25,* 209.

Milgram, S. (1983). *Obedience to authority: An experimental view.* New York: Harper/Collins.

Neuman, R. (1986). *The paradox of mass politics: Knowledge and opinion in the American electorate.* Cambridge, MA: Harvard University Press.

Olson, M. (1971). *The logic of collective action: Public goods and the theory of groups.* Cambridge, MA: Harvard University Press.

Rawls, J. (1988). The priority of the right and ideas of the good. *Philosophy and Public Affairs, 17,* 251–276.

Shields, C. (1952). The American tradition of empirical collectivism. *The American Political Science Review, 46*(1), 104–120.

Stanton, T. K. (1990). Service-learning: Groping toward a definition. In J. C. Kendall and Associates (Eds.), *Combining service and learning: A resource book for community and public service* (Vol. 1, pp. 65–68). Raleigh, NC: National Society for Internships and Experiential Education.

Stanton, T., Giles, D., & Cruz, N. (1999). *Service-learning: A movement's pioneers reflect on its origins, practice, and future.* San Francisco: Jossey-Bass.

Tan, A. (1980). Mass media use, issue knowledge and political involvement. *Public Opinion Quarterly, 44,* 241–248.

Youniss, J., & Yates, M. (1997). *Community service and social responsibility in youth.* Chicago: University of Chicago Press.

CHAPTER 4

A Critique of the Philanthropic Model

Arthur Sementelli

Service-learning has existed in a variety of forms but most recently has developed into an inter- and multidisciplinary bastillion that academics and practitioners have rallied around as a means to engage students, develop community relations, and in some cases help to achieve a civil and just society (Bellah, Madsen, Sullivan, Swidler, & Tipton, 1996; Boyer, 1996; Nasher & Ruhe, 2001; Rehling, 2000; Thomas & Landau, 2002). This rapid adoption and implementation of these service-learning models, often without consideration of the conceptual, legal, and ethical underpinnings, arguably drove the creation of this volume. Specifically, there are two broad camps in service-learning. They are the civic and the philanthropic models. The charge of this chapter is to critique the philanthropic model presented earlier by Dr. Abel. The process of developing this critique uncovered a number of fundamental issues that must necessarily be considered prior to the adoption of service-learning generally and the philanthropic model in particular.

Abel provides a cogent treatise about many aspects of the philanthropic model. Unlike many others, he also highlights some of the problems inherent in the philanthropic model including issues arising from its internal focus, modest conceptions of educational ends, and tendency toward erroneous perspectives that arise from contextual understandings of what is considered to be just and right. If we delve deeper and examine the philanthropic model and its conceptual underpinnings more thoroughly, we then uncover a number of serious issues that must be considered prior to its adoption in an educational context. This relative lack of reflection on the conceptual underpinnings of the philanthropic model does not diminish the value of Abel's chapter, but instead reveals many of the remaining issues that could and arguably should be considered in this volume and in future research.

To enable us to competently critique the philanthropic model we must first understand its philosophical and conceptual foundations. Once these bases have been explored, we can then begin reflecting on how these groundings influence and affect the design, management, and implementation of it. The limitations of these groundings are best understood as the "conceptual baggage" (Ramos, 1984) associated with charitable or philanthropic models. Additionally, a philanthropic model of service-learning (Ward & Wolf-Wendel, 2000) tends to conjure a variety of images that help illustrate how it serves as a mechanism for reinforcing the politics of advantage, undermining American ideals such as equality of opportunity and democratic participation, while subsequently diminishing the learning portion of service-learning. In this chapter, I will argue these are the most serious problems associated with the philanthropic model. To his credit, Abel alludes to some of these issues, though more research and reflection must take place to fully understand the consequences of them, particularly in the context of higher education. My goal, therefore, is to unpack the concepts behind the philanthropic model and its goals and finally to raise questions about its function in higher education.

UNPACKING THE PHILANTHROPIC MODEL OF SERVICE-LEARNING

As noted previously, service-learning has existed in a variety of forms over the years. Throughout the 1990s it grew in popularity, and it has most recently been broadly adopted by a number of fields, including business administration, communications, and others (Bellah et al., 1996; Boyer, 1996; Nasher & Ruhe, 2001; Rehling, 2000; Thomas & Landau, 2002). This rapid expansion in the interest in and implementation of service-learning has often occurred with minimal consideration of its goals, methods, and assumptions. If we instead take that pause, reflect on service-learning as it has been implemented, and examine it within the context of philanthropy, we then discover that it is much older.

The philanthropic model is a conception of service-learning based on the perceived *need* for charity or philanthropy (Boyer, 1990, 1996). Scholars who support this approach ground it in the concepts of altruism and compensatory justice (Battistoni, 1997, p. 151). These conceptual groundings set up a specific type of relationship between those participating in the service-learning and those receiving the benefits of the service. Many go as far as to argue this is the *only* type of service that can effectively and unconditionally involve oneself in the lives of those needing aid (Morton, 1995, p. 26). Such a relationship requires students to serve because they are more fortunate socially and economically than those receiving the service or due to a *ministerial promise* grounded in the notion of being a witness to some specific faith. These relationships hearken back to medieval conceptions of a proper social order, where some nobleman (or clergyman), due to a specific status-based social obligation, provided food and supplies for his serfs as a means to ensure both compliance and loyalty (Bellah et al., 1996; Madsen, Sullivan, Bellah, & Swidler, 1992). This concept, known as noblesse oblige, was central to the function of both feudalism and feudal thought, particularly combined with the religious promise of a better afterlife for the "meek" (serfs) if they comply with their social position. Of course, it is commonly understood that these notions of social order and religious duty were inextricably linked to one another throughout the Middle Ages and each of the Protestant Reformations. This in turn establishes both a religious and a class-based foundation for concepts that are tied to the family of ideas of charity, philanthropy, and to a lesser extent duty.

If one adopts this model of service-learning in education, it typically functions as an additional requirement and not as an experience to build some civic or cultural awareness. The philanthropic model does not require the sort of analytical approaches or reflection that enable students to foster change or build toward some goal, arguably due to the conditions such reflection would place on the nature of their service. When someone implements this type of service-learning approach, it tends to reinforce the status quo and does not foster debate or action about the nature of a problem, leaving questions of structural impacts, decision making, and delivery in the hands of those conducting the service rather than including the recipients in the process (Morton, 1995, p. 21). Instead, it grows from the assumption that service is simply a natural social responsibility of those who can offer assistance grounded in the context of charity. During these times of budgetary crisis throughout the United States, this approach becomes politically and socially appealing for both its simplicity of motives and lack of cost. Such a conception, over time, might garner a greater commitment of resources, while functioning as a means to cope with societal problems without necessarily addressing or removing their underlying causes, making it more elegant and desirable than either the civic or project models critiqued earlier by Abel. The philanthropic model appears much more attractive when one considers the social and political repercussions of fostering change. However, the philanthropic model has its own limitations, making it a less than ideal solution. Rather than fostering the chaos associated with change, it instead creates and supports dependency (Illich, 1990; McKnight, 1989), where the more fortunate in society are guided to help the less advantaged but often only nominally or as a temporary solution.

GOALS OF SERVICE-LEARNING IN THE CONTEXT
OF THE PHILANTHROPIC MODEL

The philanthropic model has an implicit goal of socialization, and Abel points to a number of the dangers associated with socializing people without developed capacities for self-direction. This socialization process is reciprocal since it creates a giver-receiver relationship in which students provide services to disadvantaged people (Perreault, 1997). This giver-receiver relationship exists at the core of the philanthropic model of service-learning, though it might still exist within other models of service-learning as well. It provides tactile, concrete outcomes, and students, through exposure, can become aware of the needs of others and can experience the emotional rewards associated with such participation. It is this type of exposure, according to Rhoads (1997), that can create dialogue across differences. From the philanthropic model's position, this giver-receiver relationship serves as a basis for connecting with a community, often beyond Dewey's basic conception of a "class achieving merit by doing things gratuitously for an inferior class," by including the effects of religious socialization grounded in the notion that "if it is of God, it will succeed" (Morton, 1995, p. 26). However, grounding service-learning in this particular conception of charity raises questions about whether such a model can or should appropriately function in a public sphere, particularly in the United States with our constitutional tradition of a separation between church and state. Additionally, it more clearly raises some of the questions of justice alluded to by Abel in his chapter.

Another goal, implicit in any service-learning strategy, is that of education. The link between actual learning and the philanthropic model in particular is more tenuous, if it exists at all. Abel goes as far as to state that it could be unnecessary, though it might be useful. Other scholars often stretch such a linkage by stating how these concrete outcomes can help students become aware and ultimately become caring individuals (Morton, 1995, p. 26). Educators are often reluctant to adopt service-learning programs generally and particularly those programs relying on the philanthropic model since they tend to be unable to demonstrate clear linkages between participation and outcome measures such as higher test scores, achievement measures, and other indicators of educational success, especially when compared to traditional instruction (Scheckley & Keeton, 1997, p. 33). Such an issue makes the philanthropic model a particularly inferior choice, given its tendency to not raise questions about social justice including racism, sexism, social class, or religion (Marullo & Edwards, 2000), which in turn makes it a poor mechanism to foster debate, reflection, and learning, especially in the context of higher education.

If we look at the philanthropic model as a means to foster the scholarship of engagement as proposed by Boyer (1990), it is found lacking in many areas. Boyer argues that the scholarship of pedagogy, integration, and application are often lost to the scholarship of discovery. Service-learning, then, provides a means to bring these other areas toward an equal footing with the scholarship of discovery. The scholarship of integration, driven by the need to put isolated facts in perspective, requires one to "interpret, draw together, and bring new insight to bear on original research" (Boyer, 1990, p. 19). From this perspective, the philanthropic model, which minimizes interpretation and reflection, serves a perilously limited role when placed in the most favorable circumstances. The scholarship of application, where knowledge is responsibly applied to problems, fares no better (Boyer, 1990, p. 21). Any exercise grounded in the maintenance of the status quo cannot simultaneously be a change agent. One cannot be resistant to change while at the same time attempting to change some inequity. In this sense, the philanthropic model also fails to achieve a second goal of service-learning. The scholarship of pedagogy, where knowledge must be communicated and understood by others, also has limited applications within the philanthropic model. Since teaching arguably is "a dynamic endeavor involving all the analogies, metaphors, and images that build bridges between the teacher's understanding and student learning" (Boyer, 1990, p. 23), and a philanthropic model is driven by the provision of help or relief (Marullo & Edwards, 2000), the philanthropic model can positively contribute to education by demonstrating basic mechanisms of caring and aid, but in limited ways.

Consider the four goals set out by the Commission on National and Community Service:

(1) students learn and develop through active participation in thoughtfully organized service experiences that meet community needs and that are coordinated in collaboration with the school and community; (2) that is integrated into the students' academic curriculum or provides structured time for the student to *think, talk, or write* about what the student did or saw during the actual service activity; (3) that provides students with opportunities to use newly acquired skills and knowledge in real-life situations in their own communities; and (4) that enhances what is taught in school by extending student learning beyond the classroom and into the community and helps to foster the development of a sense of caring for others. (Waterman, 1997, p. 2, italics added)

The philanthropic model of service-learning ultimately meets the first goal and minimally the fourth goal, given that it socializes students into acting on behalf of someone rather than with them. Such a socialization process would not be effective if it were considered, discussed, deconstructed, and challenged. In addition, if the goal of philanthropic service-learning is charity but not change, then students are limited to the so-called joy of helping others (often with mundane tasks that do not require skill) (Harrison, 1987, p. 2), which fails to meet the third goal.

Therefore, strictly based on goal achievement, the philanthropic model appears to be a resounding failure. Structurally, it is unable to meet roughly 50 percent of the designated goals for service-learning nationally. In addition, it fails to meet, even nominally, most of the goals set out by one of its strongest proponents (Boyer). Although it can be loosely tied to educational processes such as immersion and experiential learning, in this context learning is an *obligation* and not a *choice*. As such, it cannot help but stratify, dominate, and marginalize people given its lack of reflection, emphasizing giving rather than the potentially transformative exercise of caring (Kahne & Westheimer, 1996). Additionally, such a set of processes can and often does result in paternalism, "which is the root of a lot of problems" (Morton, 1995, p. 28) and can serve to objectify the clients of service.

EVALUATION OF SERVICE-LEARNING AND THE PHILANTHROPIC MODEL

Service-learning has two major areas where practical social science issues are raised, assessment and implementation. Regarding assessment, there is a generally held belief that systematic evaluation can help improve service-learning. Abel points toward this weakness by illustrating the problems associated with vague goals, changing goals, and overall lack of purpose. Despite such criticisms, little has been done to develop evaluation procedures or even systematic goals for the practice of service-learning (Lipka, 1997, p. 56). Lipka (1997, p. 60) attempts to bridge this gap by arguing for a set of performance measures that include tests of need, voluntary participation, complexity, and reflection. Beyond the identification of performance measures, little else has been done to systematically evaluate service-learning. If we turn our attention toward its implementation, we see a focus on providing "ownership" of the experience (Wade, 1997), fostering "participatory democracy" and "community partnerships" grounded in a context of interdependence, not dependence (Battistoni, 1997, p. 155). This research underscores the need for structure and planning discussed by Pardo (1997) and others, particularly when students are "responsible for planning and executing activities at their field sites" (Pardo, 1997, p. 99). Each of these assessment and implementation issues leads us to the idea that there is an end product to this service-learning experience that can be fostered and measured, both academically and socially.

This end product, however, appears to conflict with the notion of a philanthropic model. Abel, in chapter 3, goes as far as to state that "philanthropists do not generally consider the university a proper venue for deciding how social goods ought to be distributed any more than it is the proper venue for promoting one religion over another." This points us toward the inherent conflict among goals, motives, and objectives for the philanthropic model. If one's goal is to build a community partnership, where individuals are "part of a group that all belong to" (Battistoni, 1997, p. 155), then the philanthropic model appears to be a poor mechanism to meet this end. If the primary intent of service-learning were to enrich student experiences and provide them with potential career options, then grounding service-learning in the tradition of noblesse oblige appears misfocused and ill advised. However, if the goal is to provide a sort of "ministerial citizenship" grounded in Christianity in general and Catholicism in particular (Morton, 1995, p. 26), then such a tradition could help foster the sort of social responsibility that might exist in an ethnically, economically, and socially fragmented society. Additionally, we must realize that such grounding assumes an inability to change social systems and social order (the meek are given the promise of happiness in the afterlife, not in this life) and cannot truly address the multiplicity of causes for such a fragmentation.

Overall, if one tries to place many of the outcomes associated with service-learning within the context of philanthropy, many cannot be achieved. By its nature, service-learning is difficult to assess, implement, and evaluate using traditional methods for research and evaluation (Serow, 1997). Even if we take the broadest goal, "participation in reality" while moving toward a good society (Serow, 1997, pp. 22–23), it requires one to "enjoy in common with others,"[1] which could not occur in the context of the philanthropic model, since it does not work from the position of a common ground. If we approach it as a ministerial relationship, it then fails as an educational tool while succeeding as one of socialization and as a mechanism that reinforces societal differences. We can then see that the philanthropic model does not function well when faced with the goals of reflection, participation, construction of partnerships, and fostering of community partnerships.

ASSUMPTIONS OF THE PHILANTHROPIC MODEL

Now we turn our attention toward the underlying assumptions of the philanthropic model. As introduced earlier, the philanthropic (or charity) model of service-learning relies on the concepts of noblesse oblige, responsibility, privilege, and dependence. Each of these concepts can create undesirable consequences that undermine many of service-learning's objectives. When it is associated with concepts grounded in religion or aristocracy, then service-learning tends not to succeed at the goals of community building, cooperation, and student understanding of what participation in a democracy means. In this section, we will discuss these assumptions and begin to understand how they can undermine the general goals of a service-learning program.

When there are substantial differences among individuals in society, they become divided into the classic categories of the haves and the have-nots. This can result from economic, social, ethnic, or even gender-based differences. Many believe such an inequity is unfair or unjust and must be dealt with in some way. This need, in turn, creates a place for the service of others (Boyer, 1990, 1996). One method seeks to create a civil society as a way to achieve this end by fostering community (civic model). Another seeks to use altruistic behavior to redistribute wealth based on a perceived obligation (philanthropic model). The philanthropic model seeks to redistribute wealth or services using a model of compensatory justice (Battistoni, 1997, p. 51) or charity (Morton, 1995) as a foil against the effects of inequality that serve to dominate, alienate, and marginalize one group in favor of another (Clegg & Dunkerly, 1980).

The use of compensatory justice, however, creates a dependency on the treatment rather than truly addressing the problem (Illich, 1990; McKnight, 1989). Relying on the notions of charity, altruism, or noblesse oblige, it reinforces the differences among those giving and those receiving. In addition, such a relationship based on gratitude, paying back, or being owed (Buckley, 1990) tends to marginalize, stigmatize, and reinforce differences (Abel & Sementelli, 2002). If we take a step backward, realizing that in the United States there is no patrimony, and specifically understand that there is no aristocracy "chained" to the masses (Buckley, 1990, p. 15), any conception of obligation based on class or aristocratic traditions *must* fail, particularly if we embrace the transactional, utilitarian logic many of us hold dear (Mill, 2002; Weinstein, 1998). Even if we as a society attempt to shoehorn a conception of obligation into a social contract as Buckley (1990) argues, it admittedly best functions when understood as a part of a civic *inter*dependency rather than as charity (pp. 18–19).

Furthermore, the philanthropic model tends to support behaviors that undermine the establishment and growth of a good society (Madsen et al., 1992) in which individuals engage in a dialogue across differences. Rhoads (1997) argued for such a dialogue, noting that service and exposure to different groups in a society could help reconcile many of these differences, arguably by making the exposure foster the sort of reflection, questioning, and debate that moves such agenda items forward in a polity. Rhoads also understands that any such reconciliation cannot happen outside of this interaction, reflection, and dialogue about what it means to be a member of a society, ultimately arguing for the development of caring *citizens* (p. 232, italics added), not an obligated or ministerial aristocracy. Such an interaction, reflection, and debate can lead to the development of community similar to that envisioned by Bellah and others (Bellah et al., 1996; Madsen et al., 1992).

Creating a community, however, requires us to create and develop a civic space (Bohman, 1990) where open procedures that encourage debates lead to solutions. Any conception of community then requires us to develop and understand a common identity (Cerulo, 1997) that can be translated effectively into the processes that lead participants to a civic society. This civic space, arguably, cannot function well if there are substantial differences among individuals and if individuals are unable or unwilling to participate. This can often happen when differences (arguably in power, class, and wealth) exist to separate people into artificial categories (Foucault, 1977; Habermas, 1984). I have demonstrated that the philanthropic model of service-learning serves to establish and foster these differences. These differences can limit the creation and development of a civic space. This in turn can result in alienation and domination from the community rather than inclusion and participation in community processes.

If we go as far as to deconstruct the philanthropic model further, we find additional evidence of the unwanted conceptual baggage this model carries (Ramos, 1984). Unpacking the notion of philanthropy itself reveals a number of issues of concern. These issues can become a paramount concern to those who would establish and build a service-learning program. Philanthropy as a concept implies a "practical benevolence towards men in general,"[2] while a philanthropic effort would include any benign practices to promote happiness or an act of benevolence. These conceptions of the term *philanthropy* lack the negative connotations we have identified earlier in the philanthropic model. What, then, are the origins of the negativity in some models? Arguably, the negative connotations associated with the philanthropic model could have happened as the result of a natural evolution of concepts, metaphors, and terms (Blume, Dejong, Kim, & Sprinkle, 1998; Oswick, Keenoy, & Grant, 2002; Pfeffer, 1981; Pondy, 1983) or through the socialization, domination, and evolution of those who use them in a civic space (Baudrillard, 1994; Foucault, 1977; Fox, 1996).

Noblesse oblige is different and has the connotation that noble ancestry constrains behavior by indicating that the privilege of nobility requires some level of decorum or behavior to maintain the integrity of the position.[3] Grounding the philanthropic model in such a concept is problematic. The problem arises from the assumption that both an aristocracy and a peasantry exist in a society. Consequently, such a concept serves to foster the differences between and among those perceived as peasants and aristocrats, or more accurately, the wealthy and the poor. This conception, unlike that of philanthropy itself, runs against the ethic of service-learning in that it creates a mechanism that serves to dominate, alienate, and marginalize one group in favor of another (Clegg & Dunkerly, 1980) rather than fostering the type of civic engagement offered by Boyer (1990, 1996).

This practice of systematically identifying and marginalizing these so-called less fortunate people results in a social and communicative schism that provides a climate for various groups to establish mechanisms for control and ultimately oppression (Gould, 1984; Hearn, 1987; Marcuse, 1965). Such a climate can undermine the equality of citizenship and participation, potentially leading to a breakdown in communicative, social, and societal spaces (Forester, 1983; Habermas, 1984; Mumby, 1988). Furthermore, such a practice tends to support the brutish, contractarian approach to societal relationships proffered by Hobbes (1988, p. 49) and others, while disenchanting those who would most benefit from participation (Morton, 1995, p. 26). If such a system creates these differences among individuals in a society, they ultimately will become unable or possibly unwilling to participate, given fear of reprisal, the inability to see how participation could make a difference, or a lack of movement toward solutions for basic problems (Foucault, 1977; Habermas, 1984). Such outcomes point toward limitations in the philanthropic model, based on concepts (Ramos, 1984) that do more to undermine service-learning's goals than they do to forward them, leading us to question if a philanthropic model can work, particularly in higher education.

CAN A PHILANTHROPIC MODEL FUNCTION IN HIGHER EDUCATION?

Given the issues discussed throughout this chapter, the following conclusions emerge. By most accounts, service-learning generally has been the bailiwick of primary and secondary education, fitting well within the sorts of goals and outcomes proposed by Dewey, Bellah, and others. However, this set of goals, driven by the socialization of individuals into a good society, appears to be in conflict with many outcomes implied in higher education (including the establishment of critical thinking) (Bloom, 1956; Jones, Merritt, & Palmer, 1999; Vygotsky, 1978). If we instead reflect on Rhoads's argument that higher education should inform basic human questions about how to build a community, then a position for service-learning can emerge from higher education's role as a place for critical thinking, reflection, and learning (Rhoads, 1997). This, of course, conflicts with Abel's argument about the philanthropic model that it should claim value neutrality or at least not affect "a power struggle among multiple and conflicting political interests"(see chapter 3).

Such a claim does not allow for a clear place for the philanthropic model of service-learning, particularly in a liberal arts education where a goal has often been to undo many of the socialization processes of primary and secondary education, allowing for critical thinking. If we reexamine how the philanthropic model minimizes critique, interpretation, and reflection while emphasizing the ideas of socialization, obligation, and dependency, it cannot provide a conceptual space for the type of learning that is a goal in higher education. In addition, it tends to perform rather poorly in the context of the application of knowledge, since it does not foster, enforce, or propose mechanisms to take educational skills and use them effectively in a community (Boyer, 1990, pp. 19–21), especially if we consider the sort of low-level services that many programs use, including interventions during natural disasters, famine, and war (Morton, 1995, p. 21). Regarding the question of how to build a community, if we continue to understand the philanthropic model as an add-on to some educational experience, it remains both conceptually and practically unable to foster the more complex understanding of society and societal relationships proposed by Eyler and Giles (1999, pp. 16–18). At best, the philanthropic model is a tool of mitigation or immediate relief, best applied in cases and situations where other models of service-learning have not yet been employed or considered. Since the philanthropic model cannot foster exposure, reflection, and ultimately debate about issues affecting communities, it remains a poor choice if the goals are to "make a difference," educate, or foster change in a society.

NOTES

1. Participation. (1993). In *The Compact Oxford English Dictionary* (2nd ed.). Oxford, UK: Clarenden Press.
2. Philanthropy. (1993). In *The Compact Oxford English Dictionary* (2nd ed.). Oxford, UK: Clarenden Press.
3. Noblesse Oblige. (1993). In *The Compact Oxford English Dictionary* (2nd ed.). Oxford, UK: Clarenden Press.

REFERENCES

Abel, C., & Sementelli, A. (2002). Power emancipation and the administrative state. *Administrative Theory and Praxis, 24*(2), 253–278.

Battistoni, R. (1997). Service-learning and democratic citizenship. *Theory Into Practice, 36*(3), 150–156.

Baudrillard, J. (1994). *Simulacra and simulation.* Ann Arbor: University of Michigan Press.

Bellah, R., Madsen, R., Sullivan, W., Swidler, A., & Tipton, S. (1996). *Habits of the heart: Individualism and commitment in American life.* Berkeley: University of California Press.

Bloom, B. (1956). *Taxonomy of educational objectives: Handbook 1. Cognitive domain.* New York: Longmans.

Blume, A., Dejong, D., Kim, Y., & Sprinkle, G. (1998). Experimental evidence on the evolution of meaning of messages in sender-receiver games. *American Economic Review, 88*(5), 1323–1340.

Bohman, J. (1990). Communication, ideology, and democratic theory. *The American Political Science Review, 84*(1), 93–109.

Boyer, E. (1990). *Scholarship reconsidered: Priorities of the professorate.* Princeton, NJ: The Carnegie Foundation for the Advancement of Teaching.

Boyer, E. (1996). The scholarship of engagement. *Journal of Public Service & Outreach, 1*(1), 11–20.

Buckley, W. (1990). *Gratitude: Reflections on what we owe our country.* New York: Random House.

Cerulo, K. (1997). Identity construction: New issues, new directions. *Annual Review of Sociology, 23,* 385–409.

Clegg, S., & Dunkerly, D. (1980). *Organization, class and control.* London: Routledge and Kegan Paul.

Eyler, J., & Giles D. (1999). *Where's the learning in service-learning?* San Francisco: Jossey-Bass.

Forester, J. (1983). *Critical theory and organizational analysis.* London: Sage.

Foucault, M. (1977). *Discipline and punish: The birth of the prison.* New York: Pantheon.

Fox, C. (1996). Reinventing government movement as postmodern politics. *Public Administration Review, 56*(3), 256–262.

Gould, C. (1984). Private rights and public virtues: Women, the family, and democracy. In C. G. Gould (Ed.), *Beyond domination: New perspectives on women and philosophy* (pp. 3–20). Totowa, NJ: Rowman & Allanheld.

Habermas, J. (1984). *The theory of communicative action.* Boston: Beacon.

Harrison, C. (1987). *Student service: The new Carnegie unit.* Princeton, NJ: Carnegie Foundation for the Advancement of Teaching.

Hearn, J. (1987). *The gender of oppression: Men, masculinity, and the critique of Marxism.* Brighton, UK: Wheatsheaf Books.

Hobbes, T. (1988). *The leviathan.* Amherst, NY: Prometheus.

Illich, I. (1990). To hell with good intentions. In J. Kendall (Ed.), *Combining service and learning* (pp. 314–320). Raleigh, NC: National Society for Internships and Experiential Education.

Jones, P., Merritt, J., & Palmer, C. (1999). Critical thinking and interdisciplinarity in environmental higher education: The case for epistemological and values awareness. *Journal of Geography in Higher Education, 23*(3), 349–357.

Kahne, J., & Westheimer, J. (1996). In the service of what?: The politics of service-learning. *Phi Delta Kappan, 77,* 592–599.

Lipka, R. (1997). Research and evaluation in service-learning: What do we need to know? In J. Schine (Ed.), *Service-learning* (pp. 56–68). Chicago: University of Chicago Press.

Madsen, R., Sullivan, W., Bellah, R., & Swidler, A. (1992). *The good society.* New York: Vintage Books.

Marcuse, H. (1965). Repressive tolerance. In R. Wolf (Ed.), *A critique of pure tolerance* (pp. 81–118). Boston: Beacon.

Marullo, S., & Edwards, B. (2000). From charity to justice. *American Behavioral Scientist, 43*(5), 895–912.

McKnight, J. (1989). Why servanthood is bad. *The Other Side, 25*(1), 38–42.

Mill, J. (2002). *Utilitarianism.* Indianapolis, IN: Hackett.

Morton, K. (1995). The irony of service: Charity, project and social change in service-learning. *Michigan Journal of Community Service-Learning, 2,* 19–32.

Mumby, D. (1988). Communication and power in organizations. In N. J. Nicholson (Ed.), *Discourse, ideology and domination* (pp. 113–127). Norwood, NJ: Ablex.

Nasher, F., & Ruhe, J. (2001). Putting American pragmatism to work in the classroom. *Journal of Business Ethics, 34*(3/4), 317–330.

Oswick, C., Keenoy, T., & Grant, D. (2002). Metaphor and analogical reasoning in organization theory: Beyond orthodoxy. *Academy of Management Review, 27*(2), 294–303.

Pardo, W. (1997). Service-learning in the classroom: Practical issues. In J. Schine (Ed.), *Service-learning* (pp. 90–104). Chicago: University of Chicago Press.

Perreault, G. (1997). Citizen leader: A community service option of college students. *NASPA, 34,* 147–156.

Pfeffer, J. (1981). Management as symbolic action: The creation and maintenance of organizational paradigm. *Research in Organizational Behavior, 3,* 1–51.

Pondy, L (1983). The role of metaphors and myths in organization and in the facilitation of change. In L. Pondy, J. Frost, G. Morgan, T. Dandridge, and S. Bacharach (Eds.), *Organizational symbolism.* Greenwich, CT: JAI.

Ramos, A. (1984). *The new science of organizations: A reconceptualization of the wealth of nations.* Toronto: University of Toronto Press.

Rehling, L. (2000). Doing good while doing well: Service-learning internships. *Business Communication Quarterly, 63*(1), 77–89.

Rhoads, R. (1997). *Community service and higher learning: Explorations of the caring self.* Albany: State University of New York Press.

Scheckley, B., & Keeton, M. (1997). Service-learning: A theoretical model. In J. Schine (Ed.), *Service-learning.* Chicago: University of Chicago Press.

Serow, R. (1997). Research and evaluation on service-learning: The case for holistic assessment. In A. Waterman (Ed.), *Service-learning applications from the research* (pp. 13–23). Mahwah, NJ: Lawrence Erlbaum.

Thomas, K., & Landau, H. (2002). Organization development students as engaged learners and reflective practitioners: The role of service-learning in teaching. *Organization Development Journal, 20*(3), 88–99.

Vygotsky, L. (1978). *Mind in society: The development of higher psychological processes.* Cambridge, MA: Harvard University Press.

Wade, R. (1997). *Community service-learning: A guide to including service in the public school curriculum.* Albany: State University of New York Press.

Ward, K., & Wolf-Wendell, L. (2000). Community centered service-learning. *The American Behavioral Scientist, 43*(5), 767–780.

Waterman, A. (1997). *Service-learning applications from the research.* Mahwah, NJ: Lawrence Erlbaum.

Weinstein, D. (1998). *Equal freedom and unity: Herbert Spencer's liberal utilitarianism.* Cambridge, UK: Cambridge University Press.

CHAPTER 5

A Justification of the Civic Engagement Model

J. B. Watson, Jr.

INTRODUCTION

The civic engagement of ordinary citizens with voluntary associations, social institutions, and government in local communities is a central feature of strong democracies. Further, a fundamental feature of democratic governmental structure is its relationship to civil society, defined as "voluntary social activity not compelled by the state" (Bahlmueller, 1997, p. 3). Through voluntary participation in civil society associations at the local and regional level, citizens pursue activities that potentially serve the public good. Through this rudimentary civic engagement, citizens learn the attitudes, habits, skills, and knowledge foundational to the democratic process (Patrick, 1998). Unfortunately, in 1998 the National Commission on Civic Renewal (NCCR) highlighted the declining quantity and quality of civic engagement at all levels of American life. A number of other studies concur on the decline of involvement in civic activities (Bahlmueller, 1997; McGrath, 2001; Putnam, 1995). This concern about the nature and extent of civic engagement in the United States has impacted the debate on the proper role of higher education in a democracy. Higher education institutions, as transmitters of essential elements of the dominant culture, struggle with the development of mechanisms to socialize the next generation about democratic values. A national debate has emerged on the higher education response to this perceived need for revitalizing constructive democratic engagement, building civil society, and increasing citizen participation in government at all levels. Colleges and universities have responded with a number of civic engagement initiatives, including university-community partnerships, empirical studies of political engagement, community-based (collaborative) research, and the development of new (or expanded) service-learning programs (Jacoby, 2003).

Service-learning and civic engagement are conceptually similar and conceptually distinct ideas; however, not all service-learning pedagogies incorporate civic engagement and not all civic engagement initiatives involve service-learning. The expansion of service-learning programs in higher education has thus led to the development of multiple models of service-learning pedagogy. Additional support for the growth of service-learning initiatives in colleges and universities has been fueled by calls for the reassessment of the contemporary role of higher education (Ehrlich, 2000a; Zlotkowski, 1996, 2002). In contrast to a narrow focus on the delivery of academic courses and degree programs, many commentators have called for a broader systemic assessment of the impact of higher education institutions as agents of social change (Campus Compact, 2003). Clearly, civic engagement broadly addresses the paradoxical role of higher education in the larger society—higher education is part of the larger society and the dominant culture influences higher education. The expanded role of higher education institutions in civic renewal (in the regions and communities they serve) has received increasing national attention and has led to the recent emergence of civic engagement as a dominant model among service-learning practitioners (Billig & Furco, 2002). Many colleges and universities have developed new international exchange programs to incorporate a cross-national worldview in the undergraduate experience. The American Association of Colleges and Universities (AACU) recently issued its *Greater Expectations* report, calling for a new concept of civic learning, linking newly understood concerns about diversity, civic engagement, and student-centered institutions (Musil, 2003). Other national organizations in higher education, including the American Council on Education (ACE), the American Association of Higher Education (AAHE), Campus Compact, the American Association of Community Colleges (AACC), and the Council on Independent Colleges (CIC) have recently called for a reappraisal of the role of the U.S. higher education system in promoting civic engagement. In early 2003, Campus Compact identified 21 higher education organizations currently sponsoring civic engagement initiatives (Campus Compact, 2003). Campus Compact itself is widely regarded as the leading national advocate of service-learning in higher education and has undertaken an ambitious project called "Mapping Civic Engagement in Higher Education."

The persistence of civic engagement as a theme in higher education reform initiatives is particularly noteworthy in a time of limited economic resources and concerns about increasing accountability (Hollander, 2001). This emerging concern with civic engagement includes all types of higher education institutions—community colleges, liberal arts colleges, undergraduate colleges, professional schools, and research universities. Academic faculty and administrators have embraced the debate on civic engagement as a vital part of the mission of higher education (Campus Compact, 2003).

Researchers, policymakers, and higher education leaders disagree, however, on the appropriate indicators of civic disengagement and exactly what available data currently suggest about the impact of postsecondary institutions on civic life (Boyte & Farr, 1997).

Despite this concern, initiatives on civic engagement reflect a belief in the need to reinvigorate the traditional role of higher education institutions as full partners with the communities and regions they serve (Zlotkowski, 2000). An emphasis on civic engagement also has broad appeal as a source of long-term positive impact on communities, as faculty and students serve as agents of social change consistent with democratic principles (Ehrlich, Colby, Beaumont, & Stephens, 2003).

CONCEPTUAL DEVELOPMENT

The civic engagement model of service-learning is based on the premise that "democracy demands equal participation and voice by all citizens" (Battistoni & Hudson, 1997, p. 5). Civic engagement is defined as ". . . those activities which invigorate the public purposes and civic mission of higher education. Civic engagement activities include objectives such as developing civic skills, inspiring engaged citizenship, promoting a civil society, and building the commonwealth" (Campus Compact, 1999, p. 1). Regrettably, a variety of scholars (e.g., Barber, 1992; Battistoni, 2002; Putnam, 1995) have identified a sharp decline in voting, civic participation, and public trust, leading to identification of strategies to strengthen the role of higher education in civic engagement (Ehrlich et al., 2003; Zlotkowski, 2001). Hollander (2001) suggests that the concept of civic engagement entered the current higher education vocabulary in 1994 through the groundbreaking engaged institutions work of AAHE's Russell Edgerton at the AAHE annual meeting. A growing body of work now focuses on civic engagement as an institutional and community partnership strategy to link colleges and universities with civic action and public priorities (Jacoby, 2003; Stanton, Giles, & Cruz, 1999).

The Kellogg Commission (1999) report *Returning to our Roots: The Engaged Institution* highlighted institutions that have redesigned their missions so that teaching, research, and service have a significant community impact. Distinct from community outreach or extension by its emphasis on reciprocity (Mann & Patrick, 2000), civic engagement can generate change in campus cultures for faculty by increasing access to community-based research and creating more egalitarian relationships between students and faculty. Students benefit from enhanced access to diverse off-campus learning opportunities as the focal point of their academic experience.

The *Presidents' Declaration on the Civic Responsibility of Higher Education* advances civic engagement initiatives promoting local campus assessment of an institution's civic mission by underscoring certain new efforts to expand the institution's civic impact on faculty, students, and the community (Campus Compact, 1999). This feature of the declaration represents an advance in the application of civic engagement by allowing higher education institutions to assess the quantity and quality of civic engagement activities in a public forum. Hollander (2001) offers this statement about high-level civic engagement: "While the Campus Compact declaration and similar initiatives have created the impetus for a national discussion on civic engagement, scholarly debate continues to center on the multiple dimensions of the concept. Faculty members are especially skeptical about the academic relevance of community-based work or the political/organizational wisdom of surrendering the image of postsecondary institutions as places uniquely separated from society—mythical places of learning" (p. 2). Despite these concerns, faculty practitioners of service-learning pedagogy continue to apply the civic engagement model in multiple academic disciplines (Campus Compact, 2003; Zlotkowski, 2000). Empirical assessments of service-learning pedagogy are receiving increasing attention in the field, as indicated by the growing number of research-based articles in refereed academic journals and the inception of an annual International Conference on Service-Learning Research (Jacoby, 2003). These developments have fostered new conceptual frameworks for service-learning pedagogy based on the civic engagement model.

STRENGTHS OF THE CIVIC ENGAGEMENT MODEL

The civic engagement model strengthens the linkage between higher education institutions and their communities and calls attention to the role and value of engaged institutions. According to Campus Compact (2003), engaged institutions are systematically committed to revitalizing the democratic spirit and practicing community engagement in all public activities—by students, faculty, and other institutional representatives. Evidence of the interest in civic engagement is reflected in the growth of Campus Compact and the national debate it has spearheaded on the role and scope of civic engagement in higher education. This movement in higher education highlights strategies for the reinvigoration of the public purposes of higher education and the reordering of campus life to fully devote institutions to civic purposes. Holland and Saltmarsh (2000) pointed out the major reason for the reassessment of higher education's role: "Many people now view higher education as disconnected from social concerns and unresponsive to public needs. Although in 1998, the National Commission on Civic Renewal . . . saw a role for individuals, families, neighborhoods, secondary schools, and the media in meeting the challenges of civic renewal, it offered no role for higher education in helping to rebuild the civic life of the country" (p. 1).

Secondly, the civic engagement model renews and alters the focus of higher education institutions on service as the focal point of their mission of teaching, research, and professional service. The civic engagement model suggests that service-learning is a new voice at the table in discussions of reform within higher education. A number of observers (e.g., Ehrlich et al., 2003; Zlotkowski, 1996) have expressed concern about the compartmentalization of the service role of higher education institutions as separate from research and teaching. Faculty criteria for tenure and promotion, for example, typically include service as the lowest-ranking component, after teaching and research. This pattern is common at both teaching-oriented institutions and research universities (Ehrlich, 2000b). Land grant institutions, for example, often concentrate their service-connected activities in their extension division. When service is measured in faculty evaluation, operational definitions emphasize service to scholarly organizations in contrast to public service. Consequently, service is marginalized as an academic activity, and faculty members may perceive the need to perform only a limited amount of service since quality teaching and research are much more highly valued. Diverse types of institutions have created (or revised) faculty reward and evaluation systems to include service-learning and other community service activities of faculty. The Campus Compact's Engaged Institutions initiative highlights higher education colleges and universities that have systematically incorporated service in the major dimensions of institutional activity (Campus Compact, 2003) and profiles 28 exemplary institutions (on its Web site) that have conducted assessments or implemented faculty reward and evaluation systems incorporating service-learning.

A third strength of the civic engagement model is its utility in leveraging the resources of higher educational institutions to address pressing social problems. Universities and colleges represent new social entrepreneurs—a reservoir of resources available to local communities for solving social problems. The principle of reciprocity encourages a truly collaborative relationship with community partners, and university-community partnerships represent a unique approach to civic engagement. Colleges or universities identify local needs that match well with the resources of the institution and create partnerships with local agencies, nonprofits, or schools to address issues of mutual concern. The University of Pennsylvania, for example, established the Center for Community Partnerships in 1992 to marshal the resources of the institution to solve local problems. The center involves students and faculty in a variety of carefully designed programs with the goal of improving the quality of life in West Philadelphia and supporting the university's overall mission of the advancement of knowledge through applied research and civic engagement initiatives.

The civic engagement model of service-learning alters the traditional role of faculty in relation to teaching, scholarly activity, and the mission of their respective institutions. As faculty members apply service-learning pedagogy in the classroom, or pursue work in the growing multidisciplinary area of community-based research, their role is shaped by these experiences. Faculty practitioners of service-learning apply a learner-centered model of teaching versus a teacher-centered model. Checkaway (2002) suggests that "academically-based knowledge is not sufficient to motivate or prepare people to think about issues" (p. 271). A number of studies have highlighted the potential to increase student comprehension and retention of academic concepts through the use of learner-centered approaches versus the traditional lecture format (Eyler & Giles, 1999; Zlotkowski, 2002). Difficulties may arise, however, when faculty choose to emphasize the generation and application of practical knowledge in the classroom and in scholarly work. This work may be seen broadly as service, the least valued element among the long-standing higher education trio of scholarship, teaching, and service. As a corrective to this pattern, Boyer (1996) advocated a new scholarship of engagement, in which service-learning and other forms of civic engagement are intrinsic to the faculty roles of teaching, research, and professional service. Boyer's vision for the "new American college" involved commitment to excellence in teaching and research coupled with a new focus on connecting academic knowledge to action and practice (Boyer, 1996; Coye, 1997). In addition, Educators for Community Engagement (formerly the Invisible College) sponsors an annual gathering of faculty interested in civic engagement. The growth of this group, coupled with the annual recognition of outstanding service-learning faculty by Campus Compact and reports of increased support by academic administrators, has contributed to improved faculty perceptions of service-learning. The work of the Community College Center for Community Engagement (formerly the Community College Campus Compact) has influenced faculty involvement; approximately 50 percent of community college faculty are involved in service-learning (Campus Compact, 2003). Service-learning based on civic engagement benefits faculty members who are motivated to convey the long-term value of their academic discipline to students by demonstrating its civic value. An awareness of civic engagement encourages faculty to conduct research that treats communities as partners instead of subjects or passive recipients of information. The growth of community-based research (sometimes called action research) has given new legitimacy to applied research of this nature. In community-based research, students have the opportunity to work closely with faculty members and learn research techniques immersed in local communities. By applying their research skills to solve community problems, faculty members serve as role models of civic responsibility to students and colleagues. Involvement in community-based research allows close faculty-student collaboration and reduces the traditional boundaries between research universities, small teaching institutions, and community colleges. Some advocates of community-based research argue that it is conceptually distinct from service-learning. When community-based research is focused on civic needs and involves student researchers, however, it clearly meets the definition of service-learning (Stoecker, 2002).

Finally, civic engagement promotes both an ethic of service and increased understanding of the role of citizen for student participants in service-learning. The civic engagement model assumes that service-learning is a transformational experience for students, faculty, and higher education institutions. In particular, service-learning contributes to engaged citizenship and community-building skills for students. Elshtain (1997) suggested three ways in which service-learning (based on the civic engagement model) targets improvements in the democratic process. First, service-learning leads to the formation of democratic skills and dispositions needed for citizen involvement. Community service activities by students call attention to the outcome of shared ends, a propensity to compromise, and the collective dimension of civic goods. Secondly, service-learning activities routinely place students in civic organizations, nonprofits, health/human service agencies, and governmental agencies where they can observe firsthand their role in American democracy and reflect on the potential impact of the weakening of social support systems and associational life. Finally, by creating experiences across ethnic, racial, or socioeconomic lines, service-learning can promote a multicultural perspective and greater understanding of the multiple dimensions of diversity (Elshtain, 1997).

The civic engagement approach is thus concerned with training students with skills needed to build a civil society, including an understanding of democratic citizenship, democratic leadership skills, and the value of a lifelong service ethic (e.g., commitment to volunteering and civic leadership). The importance of understanding collaborative relationships and well-developed critical thinking skills relevant to public policy, central to the civic engagement model, represents an important outcome from student involvement in service-learning. Finally, service-learning based on the civic engagement model promotes and fosters a lifelong service ethic among students in all academic fields and professions (Mann & Patrick, 2000; Zlotkowski, 2000).

CONCLUSIONS

The consequences of the lack of emphasis on civic engagement by higher education institutions was highlighted by Musil (2003): "Too often, civic engagement is not rooted in the very heart of the academy: its courses, that occur offstage and after hours. Such a bifurcation between the work of the classroom and the life of the college prepares students all too well for the larger societal schizophrenic predicament in which adults are to care about community 5:00 P.M. or on weekends" (p. 4).

Through the application of the civic engagement model, service-learning has great potential as a new "voice at the table" of higher education decision-making (Zlotkowski, 1996). Practitioners of service-learning model a learner-centered approach and a nontraditional faculty-student relationship. As a result, new understandings of the nature of teaching, research, and service may emerge to address the perception of service as limited and secondary to other forms of institutional activity. The emerging civic engagement movement in higher education challenges the traditional higher education distinction among research, teaching, and service as separate spheres of activities (Zlotkowski, 2000). Clearly, the civic engagement model of service-learning highlights the need to recognize the public impact of academic research and teaching. Faculty who conduct community-based research or practice engaged teaching through service-learning should be recognized as pioneers in bringing the community back to its rightful role in academic life. The conceptual framework of the civic renewal approach, as well as that of the social justice approach, has the potential to change higher education in unique ways. Ehrlich (2000b) suggested a pivotal role for institutions of higher education in promoting civic engagement:

Campuses should not be expected to promote a single type of civic or political engagement, but they should prepare their graduates to become engaged citizens who provide the time, attention, understanding, and action to further collective civic goals. Institutions of higher education should help students to recognize themselves as members of a larger social fabric, to consider social problems to be at least partly their own, to see the civic dimensions of issues, to make and justify informed civic judgments, and to take action when appropriate.

Service-learning . . . is a particularly important pedagogy for promoting civic responsibility, especially when used with collaborative learning and problem-based learning, two other modes of active learning. Service-learning connects thought and feeling in a deliberate way, creating a context in which students can explore how they feel about what they are thinking and what they think about how they feel; through guided reflection, it offers students opportunities to explore the relationship between their academic learning and their civic values and commitments. (pp. 4–5)

The civic engagement model of service-learning holds great promise to provide faculty in a variety of disciplines and multiple types of higher education institutions with a valuable mechanism to highlight their central roles in promoting and maintaining a civil society. An engaged faculty can work in partnership with communities, businesses, non-profits, and community organizations to address pressing social problems. A partnership with the community can directly impact faculty research and teaching through a scholarship of engagement (Boyer, 1996).

Increasing the role of higher education in civic engagement is not without pitfalls and complexities, many of which may not yet be fully identified. Faculty practitioners of service-learning, however, can add value to their work, focusing on civic renewal. While still recognizing traditional disciplinary boundaries and analytical frameworks, the civic engagement model expands the focus on service to the common good. Structured experiences emphasizing civic obligations, the responsibilities of citizenship, and other democratic processes create a synergy between learning and service. An emphasis on civic engagement does not diminish the academic component of service-learning. On the contrary, the civic engagement model of service-learning holds the potential to cultivate a rich context in which academic and civic culture intertwine (Boyer, 1996).

REFERENCES

Bahlmueller, C. (1997). Civil society and democracy reconsidered. *Civnet's Journal for Civil Society, 1*(1), 1–23. Retrieved March 1, 2003, from http://www.civnet.org/journal/journal_frameset.htm.

Barber, B. (1992). *From classroom to community service: A bridge to citizenship.* Los Angeles: Constitutional Rights Foundation National Youth Service Network.

Battistoni, R. (2002). *Civic engagement across the curriculum: A resource for service-learning faculty in all disciplines.* Providence, RI: Campus Compact.

Battistoni, R., & Hudson, W. (Eds.). (1997). *Practicing democracy: Concepts and models of service-learning in political science.* Washington, DC: American Association of Higher Education.

Billig, S., & Furco, A. (Eds.). (2002). *Advances in service-learning research: Vol. 2. Service learning through a multidisciplinary lens.* Greenwich, CT: Information Age.

Boyer, E. (1996). The scholarship of engagement. *The Journal of Public Service and Outreach, 1*(1), 11–20.

Boyte, H., & Farr, J. (1997). The work of citizenship and problem-solving. In R. Battistoni & W. Hudson (Eds.), *Practicing democracy: Concepts and models of service-learning in political science* (pp. 35–48). Washington, DC: American Association of Higher Education.

Campus Compact. (1999). *Presidents' declaration on the civic responsibility of higher education.* Providence, RI: Campus Compact. Retrieved March 1, 2003, from http://www.compact.org/presidential/plc/plc-declaration.html.

Campus Compact. (2003). *Mapping civic engagement in higher education.* Retrieved

March 1, 2003, from http://www.compact.org/mapping/civic terminology.html.

Checkaway, B. (2002). Renewing the civic mission of the American research university. *The Journal of Public Affairs, 6*(1), 265–293.

Coye, D. (1997). Ernest Boyer and the American college. *Change, 29*(3), 20–29.

Ehrlich, T. (Ed.) (2000a). *Civic responsibility and higher education.* Phoenix, AZ: Oryx Press.

Ehrlich, T. (2000b). *Measuring up 2000: The state by state report card on higher education.* Retrieved March 1, 2003 from http://measuringup.higher education.org/2000/articles/ThomasEhrlich.cfm

Ehrlich, T., Colby, A., Beaumont, E., & Stephens, J. (2003). *Educating citizens: preparing America's undergraduates for lives of moral and civic responsibility.* Indianapolis, IN: Jossey-Bass.

Elshtain, J. (1997). The decline of democratic faith. In R. Battistoni & W. Hudson (Eds.), *Practicing democracy: Concepts and models of service-learning in political science* (pp. 9–14). Washington, DC: American Association of Higher Education.

Eyler, J., & Giles, D. (1999). *Where's the learning in service-learning?* Indianapolis, IN: Jossey-Bass.

Hollander, B. (2001, March 23). *Exploring the challenge of documenting and measuring civic engagement endeavors of colleges and universities: Purposes, issues, and ideas.* Paper presented at the Campus Compact Advanced Institute on Classification of Civic Engagement, Providence, RI. Retrieved March 1, 2003 from http://www.compact.org/advancedtoolkit/pdf/holland_paper.pdf

Hollander, E., & Saltmarsh, J. (2000, July–August). The engaged university. *Academe: Bulletin of the American Association of University Professors, 86*(4), 29–31.

Jacoby, B. (Ed.) (2003). *Building service-learning partnerships.* San Francisco: Jossey-Bass.

Kellogg Commission on the Future of State and Land-Grant Universities (1999). *Returning to our roots: The engaged institution. Third report.* Washington, DC: The National Association of State Universities and Land-Grant Colleges.

Mann, S., & Patrick, J. (Eds.). (2000). *Education for civic engagement in democracy: Service-learning and other promising approaches.* Bloomington, IN: ERIC Clearinghouse for Social Studies/Social Science Education.

McGrath, M. (2001). *National Civic Review: Vol. 89, No. 4. Fostering civic engagement in America's communities.* Hoboken, NJ: Jossey-Bass.

Musil, C. (2003). Educating for citizenship. *Peer Review, 5*(3), 4–8. Retrieved September 15, 2003 from http://www.aacu-edu.org/peerreview/pr-sp03/pr-sp03feature1.cfm.

National Commission on Civic Renewal. (1998). *A nation of spectators: How civic disengagement weakens America and what we can do about it.* College Park: University of Maryland.

Patrick, J. (1998). *Education for engagement in civil society and government* (ERIC Digest No. 423211). Bloomington, IN: ERIC Clearinghouse for Social Studies/Social Science Education.

Putnam, R. (1995). Bowling alone: America's declining social capital. *Journal of Democracy, 6*(1), 65–78.

Stanton, T., Giles, D., & Cruz, N. (1999). *Service-learning: A movement's pioneers reflect on its origins, practice, and future.* Indianapolis, IN: Jossey-Bass.

Stoecker, R. (2002). Practices and challenges of community-based research. *The Journal of Public Affairs, 6*(1), 219–239.

Zlotkowski, E. (1996, January–February). A new voice at the table: Linking service-learning and the academy. *Change,* 21–27.

Zlotkowski, E. (2000). Civic engagement and the academic disciplines. In T. Ehrlich (Ed.), *Civic responsibility and higher education* (pp. 309–322). Phoenix, AZ: Oryx Press.

Zlotkowski, E. (Ed.) (2001). *Successful service-learning programs: New models of excellence in higher education.* Bolton, MA: Anker.

Zlotkowski, E. (2002). Social crises and the faculty response. *The Journal of Public Affairs, 6*(1), 1–18.

CHAPTER 6

A Critique of the Civic Engagement Model

Robert J. Exley

INTRODUCTION

Civic engagement definitely represents a fundamental goal for higher education. The Association of American Colleges and Universities' recent report *Greater Expectations: A New Vision for Learning as a Nation Goes to College* eloquently affirms this when it states: "Throughout its history, the United States has asked much of higher education: to prepare leaders, train employees, provide the creative base for scientific and artistic discovery, transmit past culture, create new knowledge, *redress the legacies of discrimination, and ensure continuation of democratic principles*" (Association of American Colleges and Universities, 2002, p. iii; emphasis mine). There can be no debate regarding the importance of this issue. However, to assume that the civic engagement model of service-learning is the panacea for fixing all current social ills is simply wrong. In fact, I agree with Watson's premise that not all service-learning involves civic engagement, and not all civic engagement involves service-learning. Furthermore, I would like to point out that the role of higher education is far greater than promoting civic engagement. Watson also notes that multiple models for service-learning have evolved over the past decade, and significant emphasis is being placed on the concept of civic engagement. But, to simplify the service-learning debate into one or two models is difficult for me. In fact, I have doubts as to the veracity of his arguments for the conceptual premise of the civic engagement model as the dominant methodology for service-learning, and I am not convinced that the evidence fully supports the suggested strengths he purports.

This response will address the broad premise of civic engagement as the dominant model of service-learning and also argue the purported strengths of this model of service-learning. As Watson has pointed out, numerous authors have over the last decade addressed the potential (and in some cases real) benefits of service-learning for both the student's learning and for society (Butler & Hawley, 1997; Delve, Mintz, & Stewart, 1990; Zlotkowski, 1998, 2002.) An examination of this plethora of writings reveals a broader view of the models for service-learning than that of the civic engagement model. A review of the writings reveals the existence of multiple models of service-learning, with the important issue of reciprocity with one's community as one of many key factors.

As the term *civic engagement* has come to the fore in the discussions of service-learning, the purest definition of service-learning—that of an academically anchored partnership—has become adulterated to the point that the learning of core discipline knowledge is being placed in jeopardy. The educational attractiveness of service-learning has always been its ability to keep the student's learning at the core of the experience. In fact, the most effective rationale for the service experience has always been its power to assist the student in mastering course content. Its beauty has been the near-magical ability—via carefully conducted reflective teaching—for it to produce serendipitous learning as well as individual human development within the students as they serve their communities. Simply put, a well-crafted service-learning experience does foster increased engagement of students in the society around them but not at the expense of their learning the fundamental content of the specific course they are enrolled in at the time. I fear that the current emphasis on civic engagement will result in a service rather than learning indoctrination and promote a learning experience that will focus on predetermined behavioral outcomes of accepted democratic actions (e.g., increased voter participation or volunteering with a local nonprofit) rather than a thought-provoking intellectual and visceral education experience that prompts a student to carefully examine his/her role in a democratic society—an examination that begins with the student's educational interest and challenges the student to see how his/her personal, private goals and dreams are connected to community. Finally, if one listens carefully one might hear that the civic engagement model of service-learning is the model pedagogy with no downside, a pedagogy to serve as the preferred means for higher education to produce the mythical citizens, inferred by the *Greater Expectations* report, who are highly patriotic, contributing members of society. This, too, is simply not the case, and prior to delving into this further, I want to quickly point out one alternative concept regarding models of service-learning and remind us of the essential attributes of service-learning.

CONCEPT

Keith Morton in his work *Models of Service and Civic Education* (1993) revealed four distinct philosophies of practice in the realm of service-learning. Although a decade old now, these four basic models can easily be conceptualized as resting on a continuum of civic engagement if one so chooses. They are as follow:

- Liberal Democracy: Programs emphasize the relationship between persons and the state. The student participants are seen as our future leaders, and civic engagement for students would include formal experiences with nonprofit organizations, public agencies, or other sites with the explicit goal of enhancing the leadership and involvement of students in the operations of the state.

- Participatory Democracy: Programs emphasize the importance of "citizen problem solving." The long-term goal for students is to build their capacity as individual participants in the process of self-government. As for civic engagement, the ideal level of involvement for these students includes current, active tasks producing immediately measurable results. One example could be the clean up of an inner-city neighborhood and the building of new park equipment for the children.

- Social Justice: Programs emphasize first-hand experiences of injustice. Students are viewed as essential components of the fabric of society, and experiences must be structured to acquaint them with social injustice in a manner that makes it a personal issue. A primary goal is to bring about a more equitable distribution of society's wealth. The civic engagement of students would include direct leadership and involvement in social activism. An example would be the students who organize and lead a protest of some sort to address environmental racism.

- Service as Citizenship: The service itself defines citizenship. The individual's relationship to the community is critical, and the primary program challenge rests in connecting students to placement experiences that will sustain their commitment to service over a lifetime. The civic engagement work of students within this context is less predetermined and allows the student greater leeway to match his/her interests, and the discussion of democracy and community remains in more general terms than that of the formal state.

In my experience, the operational model of service-learning is a function of the personal beliefs and educational philosophy of the faculty member using service-learning. It is possible for one college or university to have multiple models of service-learning occurring at the same time with varying levels of civic engagement. It is important for the institution to value such diversity within its faculty because this diversity of thought and inquiry is exactly what generates the rich learning opportunity for students upon which the higher education experience is based.

ESSENTIAL ATTRIBUTES

Good service-learning begins with sound, academically anchored partnerships. The nature of the partnership between the college and any community agency must be based on a shared commitment to the student's education. Thus, the first essential attribute is to include the active practice of reciprocity and for this to occur, the service and learning must be worthwhile for both the student and the community. However, to honor reciprocity, the service assignment must be driven by community needs. It is essential for community agencies to identify the needs of their constituents and the service opportunities for students. In turn, the student must realize that the community will teach him/her valuable lessons. This is much more than doing good; this is respecting one another and learning the importance of seeing the world as others see it, and it requires an active, ongoing dialogue with the members of the community.

The second critical attribute is an appreciation for the complexity of human development. Service-learning occurs in different stages—beginning with serving and moving to enabling, then to empowering. It also moves from observation to experience to leadership. How effective a student is at moving through these stages is directly related to his/her level of personal development. Thus, our shared responsibility is to assist the student with his/her movement through these critical stages with an appreciation for the broader impact of that same student's personal journey to maturity. The movement is rarely, if ever, a direct linear path; instead, the path of development is usually one of loops and curves. As such, faculty members must become experts in more than their disciplines— they must gain a working knowledge of human development theory.

The third attribute that must be included is that of meaningful service. The service tasks become meaningful and worthwhile when the student's critical thinking ability is challenged. This can be accomplished not only through assignment of a complex or challenging task, but also by how well we assist the student with understanding and seeing the need for the task in the context of the service site's mission and goals.

A fourth key attribute is the inclusion of diversity in the experience. A priority is placed on involving as broad a cross section of students as is possible in serving in diverse settings with many populations within the community. One example of this is the faculty member who instructs her students to select a service placement where they normally would never be involved. This inclusion of diversity will nearly always produce cognitive dissonance and affective challenges for the students. The resultant uncertainty provides a rich learning opportunity for the student and the faculty member through the use of reflective teaching strategies—the final key attribute.

The fifth key attribute is the integration of reflective teaching strategies.

Service-learning must include a faculty-led reflection component that addresses the issues of democracy and civic engagement. It should include intentional, systematic reflection about the service experience to accomplish rational harmony in community service experiences. Faculty members must develop the skills necessary to teach their students how to harvest the learning available through their service experience. Without this process, we run the risk of the student never truly learning from the experience. The developmental psychologist William Perry (1970) labels true learning as that which includes *accommodation*—the process of consciously processing new information to fit into one's present thinking structure. Perry's scheme of cognitive development provides a means for justifying the use of reflection when teaching.

His theory proposes three stages or levels of cognitive development. They are dualism, relativism, and commitment. Dualistic thinking is characterized by the view that all information is either right or wrong and the authority is the expert. In this stage, things are either black or white, with no in-between or shades of gray. Relativistic thinking is characterized by a progression in one's thinking processes, where the context of the issue and one's personal decision making come into play. This stage includes movement from the either/or thinking of dualism to the acceptance that (1) knowledge is pervasively uncertain, as ideas are of equal value and there is no one answer; (2) knowledge is contextual, and judgments should concern better or worse rather than right or wrong; and (3) a person's values and life will emerge as he/she makes commitments and applies contextual criteria to identify issues. Finally, the commitment stage is an almost existential level where one's experiences with commitment define one's identity. In other words, I hold certain values and beliefs because of the cognitive processes I have utilized to make my decisions, rather than my values being based on my failure to consciously process the issues (Rodgers, 1980).

It is precisely the inclusion of these key attributes that make service-learning the powerful pedagogy that it is. Although many individuals are utilizing service-learning in one way or another, the complete combination of all essential elements may be rare, and this leads to some existing weakness in the claims of many. With this as background, I will now address what Watson, in chapter 5, describes as strengths of the civic engagement model.

STRENGTHS-RESPONSE

Watson uses the following Campus Compact definition for civic engagement, "those activities which invigorate the public purposes and civic mission of higher education. Civic engagement activities include objectives such as developing civic skills, inspiring engaged citizenship, promoting a civil society, and building the commonwealth" (see chapter 5). I will thus use this as a baseline for examining the strengths that he notes.

The first purported strength from the previous chapter is: "The civic engagement model strengthens the linkage between higher education institutions and their communities and calls attention to the role and value of engaged institutions." To support this claim, Watson reviews the growth of Campus Compact over the past decade. The growth of the Compact membership is indeed striking. However, the level of active participation by faculty members and students within each institution that is a member of the Compact remains modest for the most part, especially if one would apply a strict definition for service-learning to include the accepted key attributes. For example, Miami-Dade Community College has one of the nation's most respected service-learning programs. Yet, from a total faculty of approximately 750, fewer than 100 faculty members actively use service-learning, and collectively they engage less than two percent of the student enrollment at any given time.

Also, if one would use the civic engagement model of service-learning with an emphasis on achieving an increase by students and faculty in completing predetermined civic skills as the measure, one might find even less support for this purported enhanced linkage. It simply remains difficult to find data that support greater involvement by faculty and students in the democratic processes of voting, running for local office, and/or participation in community forums to solve local issues, as one example. The opportunities to find solid evidence for the vague terms *promoting a civil society* and *building the commonwealth* are even more difficult.

I do agree with Watson's statement that the model will call attention to the "role and value of engaged institutions." This is a noteworthy motivation for a college president to support the civic engagement model of service-learning. A major part of a president's responsibility and work is to promote the image and reputation of his/her institution. He/she, in a public institution, must also work the political system for support—fiscal and otherwise. Therefore, it is a wise president who quickly sees the value of having faculty and students involved in educational activities that promote the college's visibility and positive contribution to community.

The second strength Watson claims is that "the civic engagement model renews and alters the focus of higher education institutions on service as the focal point of their mission of teaching, research, and professional service." Again, the data simply are not there to support such a claim. This strength as a possibility makes sense, but it is simply not a reality at this time. In fact, I am not sure if service should be the focal point of an institution of higher learning's mission. As I reflect on the opening comments of the *Greater Expectations* report, I am struck by the critical nature of what might be called the knowledge work expected of higher education. In part the report states that higher education is expected "to prepare leaders, train employees, provide the creative base for scientific and artistic discovery, transmit past culture, create new knowledge . . ." (Association of American Colleges and Universities, 2002, p. iii), and I have no desire for higher education to place these very important responsibilities in any lesser role than they have historically held.

I do agree with Watson that pockets of change are occurring within the academy as a few institutions work to make service of more importance within the rank and tenure systems. Portland State University is one prime example of this work. And Zlotkowski's work with the American Association of Higher Education (AAHE) certainly provides evidence that various discipline-groups are willing to support community-based action research.

A third strength, Watson states, for the civic engagement model "is its utility in leveraging the resources of higher educational institutions to address pressing social problems." And while I agree with Watson's statement, I also believe the jury is still out regarding the practicality of such a statement. Colleges and universities are not bottomless reservoirs of resources to solve all social ills. One has only to look at the rapidly falling support for public higher education across the nation for evidence of this fact. The single greatest resource of any institution is its faculty, their knowledge, their abilities, and their hearts. I am concerned by the inference that college and university faculty members are prepared and willing to fundamentally change not only how they do their scholarly work (teaching and research) but who they are as professionals.

Watson accurately states, "The civic engagement model of service-learning alters the traditional role of faculty in relationship to teaching, scholarly activity, and the mission of their respective institutions." For those few faculty members who fully embrace the model, I believe this is true, but I remain concerned that we are not fully appreciative of what this means. In fact, one of the most significant weaknesses of the civic engagement/social justice model of service-learning is our lack of consideration for its power.

Watson comments on a final strength when he purports that "civic engagement promotes both an ethic of service and increased understanding of the role of citizen for student participants in service-learning." Furthermore, he says, "The civic engagement model assumes that service-learning is a transformational experience for students, faculty, and higher education institutions." This may not be the case.

Jones (2002), in "The Underside of Service-Learning," puts it well when she says, "my experience as a faculty member teaching service-learning courses suggests that not all students are as gracefully transformed or engaged in the opportunity to be 'developed' as the literature might imply. Instead, there is some likelihood of service-learning experiences actually reinforcing negative stereotypes and assumptions that students bring with them to the class environment" (p. 10). I cannot agree with her more.

I contend that the "underside of service-learning" exists because of a failure to take seriously that with which we are experimenting. It is a very powerful tool and we must never underestimate it. It is powerful because it relies on a most basic of all things—human relationships. Healthy and productive relationships represent one key indication of any individual's level of personal development.

Relationships are brought to the forefront in service-learning—especially service-learning that is civic engagement/social justice oriented. Through service-learning activities, relationships of a very particular merit form between students and faculty members, students and community members, and students and other students. In addition, students are placed in cognitive situations where their prior belief structures cannot help but be challenged. It is critical that during these times of challenge students do not become disoriented and struggle in their attempts to deal with the cognitive and affective overload of new information. During these times they are very reliant on people of influence in their lives. However, students are not the only ones undergoing developmental challenge.

Each participant, including the faculty member, remains a work in progress, so to speak. The faculty member's cognitive development may or may not allow for the student to challenge his/her authority in a productive manner. According to Perry, the final stage of development is that of commitment characterized by an appreciation for the complexity of life rather than by a simplification of the issues to either 'for' or 'against.' In too many cases, service-learning advocates are unable to allow students to disagree with them, and in so doing they fail to acknowledge the power they have over their students.

The goal of the experience (for example, to create student activists who lead a demonstration) becomes more important than the development of the students' ability to commit to a cause because they individually believe in the cause—not because a person of influence in their lives believes in the cause. Higher education in general is very good at moving students from the dualistic stage of thinking into the relativistic thinking arena. However, we are not so good at assisting students to move into the commitment stage.

Some service-learning faculty members may believe so ardently in their chosen cause(s) that they prevent rather than foster effective student learning. On the one hand, the dualistic-thinking student with predetermined attitudes can harden even further his/her ideas and biases if the faculty member cannot allow him/her some space in the dialogue. Too much challenge too quickly will result in entrenchment. On the other hand, the dualistic-thinking student with the underdeveloped cognitive functioning characterized by the idea that the faculty member is always right will ardently agree but not have any substantive change in his/her maturity level. This latter student is the one who drifts from position to position in his/her thinking based on the latest person of influence in his/her life. Of the two, the latter may represent the greater risk for service-learning, resulting in great harm.

Jones (2002) addresses this challenge when she speaks of the students who "get it" and those who do not. In either case the impact is deeply personal and far-reaching on the students involved in the service. Speaking of those who fail to get it, Jones says, "They quickly find themselves in an overly stimulating environment that challenges them in a way they are ill-equipped to process. The kind of learning heralded by service-learning educators does not occur as students move through the process of completing the course, clinging tenaciously to previously held understanding and stereotypes" (p. 11).

Perry's theory of cognitive development describes this phenomenon as assimilation of information rather than accommodation, and true learning requires accommodation. Rodgers (1980) completed an extensive analysis of the literature related to the process whereby an individual integrates new information into his/her scheme of thinking, and he states the following: "If a person's attitudes toward, reactions to, and feelings about the challenges he has experienced are facilitated with support, feedback, and integration, then the probability of achieving accommodation is increased" (pp. 18–19).

The use of effective, comprehensive, and carefully planned reflective teaching is thus critical to a student being able to get it. This carefully crafted component of instruction can only occur when the faculty member fully comprehends the impact education, and in particular service-learning, has on the student. In Jones's words, "I do not want to dispute the positive outcomes associated with service-learning. I do, however, want to propose that the complexities that emerge be identified, addressed, and incorporated into the practice of service-learning. Importantly, I also want to acknowledge that this process is not an easy one, for students or faculty alike; it may result in what the title of Robert Kegan's book suggests: the experience of getting *In Over Our Heads*" (p. 12). She goes on to comment on the importance of understanding the multiple dynamics that come into play during a service-learning experience. In short, she raises the good question of whether we are paying enough attention to these dynamics.

Hadley and Graham's (1987) work regarding how students perceive the pressures of a college classroom provides insight from a developmental point of view. They state, "If an individual is functioning at one particular intellectual developmental level, that person's cognitive level plays an important role in shaping his or her view of the classroom setting"

(p. 389). They posit that Perry's scheme can accurately predict how a student interprets the learning environment.

In their study, individuals who were at the higher levels of cognitive development perceived the environment to include greater amounts of innovation, student involvement, and teacher support than did those who were at the dualistic levels. The authors state, "The low tolerance for ambiguity and flexibility in the classroom displayed by dualists is reflected in their need for clarity and specificity in completing classroom tasks" (p. 391). By its very nature, a service-learning course includes more ambiguity and flexibility than the traditional lecture-based class. This, in part, explains the difficulty of this work and why some students get it and others do not. In fact, the students who experience difficulty in getting it are most likely students functioning at the dualistic level.

It is self-deceptive for us to conclude that we do not influence the lives of our students. In fact, every aspect of how we conduct ourselves and our classrooms combined with what we share of our personal philosophies and beliefs (through both our words and deeds) significantly impacts students. We cannot hide behind the mask of objectivity and pretend that all we do is provide information and content knowledge, especially if we use service-learning. Vogel (1999) believes that we serve as "companion and guide" for our students, and offers this poignant description of the responsibilities and opportunities we have when we accept the role:

We need to ask ourselves what we would expect from a guide if we were climbing a dangerous mountain peak. I would want someone who knew the territory—who would not be misled when we came to forks in the path. I would want someone who understood the seasons, weather-conditions, and human nature and someone who could make reasoned decisions about when to begin and when to take refuge in a sheltered area. The guide should be able to make wise decisions about what we need to carry with us and what we should leave behind. My guide would need to be wise: to know when to take risks and when prudence was the better course.

I would not want my guide to hurry me unduly or to pamper me unnecessarily. I would expect that person to challenge me to develop greater skills in and understanding of climbing; I would be expected to carry my weight and to be responsible to the total group of climbers. The guide I would choose would hold me and my companions accountable so that we might all reach our destination safely.

All these things being equal, I would also hope my guide would have a love of nature and the gift to see beauty along the way, a sense of humor that would lighten an otherwise serious and dangerous climb, and an awareness that the quality of the journey is at least as important as reaching our destination.

Much is required of those who agree to guide others: knowledge and wisdom, skills and understanding of how to engage others in the process of learning, and the ability to trust and be trusted. The teacher must also be able to discern when to push and when to comfort, when to chastise and when to praise, when to challenge and when to hold back, when to encourage risk and when to protect. (pp. 123–124)

Once we, as faculty members, acknowledge the power of the service-learning course—the impact of the service, the academic content, and the personal relationships involved—it becomes obvious the inherent danger of underestimating it. To deal with potential for both great good and great harm, we must simply accept that each of us remains within the developmental process daily.

CONCLUSION

Service-learning, and in particular the civic engagement model of service-learning, is an extremely powerful teaching strategy. It continues to gain support and acceptance throughout the academy of higher education. However, this continual increase of acceptance and use also demands a corollary increase in the examination of its rigor and impact. In short, the fundamental weakness with the pedagogy is our lack of understanding of, and perhaps even a lack of appreciation for, the complexity of this process.

Jones (2002) again states the concern eloquently:

The underside of service-learning, then, is not just about students' inability to get it (which is rarely from unwillingness or recalcitrance, instead having to do with cognitive capacity, self-knowledge, and interpersonal maturity) or to process new experience, but also about *our inability to anticipate comments, understand where students are in their developmental process, and acknowledge complex issues.*

Service-learning may also take us as faculty and educators into new territory for which we too may be ill-equipped. Reflection on our own background, our developmental readiness, and where we stand in relation to power, privilege, and community service encourages discernment on the complex issues that emerge in service-learning. (p. 15, emphasis mine)

One example of a faculty member who gets it regarding how critical it is to prepare oneself for service-learning courses by engaging in one's own service experience is Pinto-Torres. In her essay "From Ideology to Piano Playing" (1998), she discusses her three-year journey from novice to experienced practitioner with service-learning. In particular, she writes about the gradual dawning of understanding that finally culminates in her engaging in a service activity of her own. She begins by saying, "These three years have been both the most challenging and the most rewarding in my life as a teacher. I have come to see the classroom not as the locus of learning, but as a springboard (launching pad?)" (p. 23). After a series of different course sections and various renditions of service-learning, she finally came to a realization that something was missing. "I realized that no matter how many hundreds of hours my students contributed to helping others, I was evading the question I had posed initially: 'What can I do to help solve the problems of my community?'" She goes on to write:

Finally, it occurred to me that I should do something that I love, and know how to do well, for the people that I want to help. So I decided to offer free piano lessons to the children of migrant farm workers in Homestead, Florida. From the very first telephone contact, I began to understand more profoundly what my students experience. I felt their "first-day jitters," the feeling of being out of one's comfort zone, the excitement of meeting new people, being in a different environment, doing a non-routine job, and wanting to please. Reflection sessions became livelier. I could truly relate to what my students were saying! (p. 25)

Does the civic engagement model of service-learning have merit? Yes!

Is it the only model that can make a difference? I don't believe so. Nor do I believe that it is the panacea for the social ills that we face in our communities. It is one, just one, effective means for providing high-quality educational experiences for our students.

REFERENCES

Association of American Colleges and Universities. (2002). Greater expectations: A new vision for learning as a nation goes to college. *Peer Review, 5*(2), 13–16.

Butler, D. Q., & Hawley, M. D. (Eds.). (1997). Service-learning: "Community as classroom" gains currency across country [Special issue]. *Journal of Public Service and Outreach, 2*(1).

Delve, C. I., Mintz, S. D., & Stewart, G. M. (Eds.). (1990). *Community service as values education.* New Directions for Student Services. San Francisco: Jossey-Bass.

Hadley, T., & Graham, J. W. (1987). The influence of cognitive development on perceptions of environmental press. *Journal of College Student Personnel Development, 28*(5), 388–393.

Jones, S. R. (2002, September–October). The underside of service-learning. *About Campus, 7*(4), 10–15.

Morton, K. (1992). *Models of service and civic education.* Providence, RI: Camus Compact Occasional Paper.

Perry, W. G. (1970). Forms of intellectual and ethical development in the college years: A scheme. Austin, TX: Holt, Rinehart, & Winston.

Pinto-Torres, L. (1998). From ideology to piano playing. In B. Exley & D. Johnson (Eds.), *Teachers of life–learners for life: Faculty stories in service-learning from Miami-Dade Community College* (pp. 23–26). Miami, FL: Miami-Dade Community College.

Rodgers, R. F. (1980). Recent theories and research underlying student development: Student development in higher education. *ACPA, Student Personnel Series, 27,* 10–95.

Vogel, L. J. (1999). *Teaching and learning in communities of faith: Empowering adults through religious education*. San Francisco: Jossey-Bass.

Zlotkowski, E. (Ed.). (1998). *Successful service-learning programs: New models of excellence in higher education*. Bolton, MA: Anker.

Zlotkowski, E. (Ed.). (2002). *Service-learning and the first year experience: Preparing students for personal success and civic responsibility* (Monograph No. 34). Columbia: University of South Carolina, National Resource Center for The First-Year Experience and Students in Transition.

CHAPTER 7

A Justification of the Communitarian Model

Frank Codispoti

INTRODUCTION

Service-learning is not an end in itself. It is a pedagogy for educating students and, as such, requires justification. All models of service-learning are based on the premise that one goal of a college education is to cultivate positive ethical habits and behaviors, particularly toward the less fortunate members of society. It is the thesis of this chapter that service-learning can be part of the process by which colleges and universities achieve the vital mission of educating citizens for collective self-government. Self-government is, I will argue, the essence of democracy and must be understood as such. Such understanding is not natural and does not automatically develop in American popular culture, which associates liberty with freedom from government and pursuit of self-interest, rather than associating it with shaping our collective lives. The habits of self-government are natural, but must be nurtured, cultivated, and trained. This is the vital mission of education in a democracy. It is not a new mission for higher education in the United States, but the historic mission for which colleges and universities were once founded and developed. This mission has been replaced in recent generations, much to the detriment of both the nation and higher education. The mission must be restored and renewed for both to be healthy.

In this chapter I argue that a communitarian model is best able to justify ethical training as part of higher education and particularly service-learning as a component of that training. The argument will be developed by first examining and evaluating the alternatives to the communitarian model: the philanthropic model and the civic model. After that I will elaborate a theoretical basis for a communitarian model. Then I will discuss the application of the communitarian model in the classroom and examine some of the impediments to its acceptance, with responses to those impediments. Finally, I will identify and respond to some of the criticisms that can be made of the communitarian model.

THE PHILANTHROPIC AND CIVIC MODELS

The philanthropic and the civic models of service-learning both seek to create a change in the attitudes of students. The philanthropic model exposes students to those who are considered less fortunate and engages the students in service activities with the goal of developing a lifelong habit of philanthropy (Lisman, 1998, pp. 45–57). This approach, which is designed to counter the perceived selfishness of the young and to moderate their materialism, has the advantage of doing little to disturb or change the academic world the student inhabits. It therefore places few demands on faculty or students to change their academic activities or the content of courses.

The philanthropic model best supports a voluntary, extracurricular approach to service-learning. The advocate of the philanthropic model hopes that those who have benefited from their status in society will learn to give back to the less fortunate. By providing service to those in need, the student will learn philanthropy. If service-learning is brought into the classroom in the philanthropic model, it is probably as an optional element tacked on to an appropriate course. Under such circumstances, the use of service-learning is determined by the individual professor and student. It is not central to the responsibilities of the professor or the requirements for students. This structure is likely to lead to an unstable status for service-learning in the university. University administrators will adopt service-learning when they believe students are displaying particularly selfish attitudes or there is a need to develop better relationships with the community of which the university is a part. Individual faculty members who are committed to changing attitudes will incorporate service-learning into their classrooms, while those without such commitments will not. Students who are already predisposed or open to the value of philanthropy will be far more likely to choose service-learning as an option than will those who are not predisposed to such an activity. Service-learning will, therefore, have a very limited impact. Further, because service-learning is not central to the teaching mission of the university, it will place a burden on those who choose to use it. Service-learning projects take a great deal of time for a professor to arrange and monitor, time that is unlikely to be rewarded very heavily in merit, promotion, and tenure decisions—decisions that tend to turn on research productivity. For the student, service-learning adds to the burden of activities that one must complete before graduation. Getting the same academic credit as one's peers who do not spend the considerable amount of time required for service-learning creates a disadvantage that is only partially compensated for by any extra weight given to applications for employment or graduate school.

The philanthropic model also leaves service-learning vulnerable to the criticism that it interferes with course work rather than contributing to it, because the time spent on service-learning is time lost to teach and learn academic material. Philanthropic service-learning activities do not further the comprehension of important concepts or ideas because they are not integrated into the academic work of a class. This situation further devalues such activities in the weighing of rewards and increases the likelihood that service-learning will be abandoned when resources are short or the university feels less inclined to worry about the development of philanthropic habits among its students.

The civic model seeks a more ambitious transformation of students' attitudes than does the philanthropic model. While the philanthropic model is intended to respond to perceived student selfishness, the civic model is responding to perceived political apathy and cynicism. Advocates of the civic model want their students to become active and concerned citizens. They seek to have their students develop more than a sense of duty to help the less fortunate. Advocates of the civic model want students to develop a sense of duty to modify the forces causing the conditions afflicting the lives of such people. Essentially, they want students to become active in creating social justice (e.g., Elshtain, 1997; Lisman, 1998; Mendel-Reyes, 1997; Robinson, 2000). They often mean by this a redistribution of resources and also opportunities to eliminate, or at least reduce, the conditions they identify as causing the need for the service their students provide. As Zivi (1997) demonstrates, an attitudinal transformation of this magnitude cannot be achieved without an academic component to the process. Students must have their attention drawn to the conditions that affect people's lives. The effects of the socioeconomic system must be studied and the linkages between the conditions students see in their service-learning projects and the system must be clarified. Students must learn to question assumptions and explanations that they have accepted all their lives concerning people not like themselves.

A fundamental problem for the civic model is its obvious ideological preferences. The desire to correct social injustices is the product of a liberal or radical ideology. As such, its appeal is limited to those who agree with such positions. In fact, it is likely to be openly opposed by conservative scholars on the grounds of bias. Even those who are not sympathetic to a conservative ideology are likely to be uneasy with education that can be portrayed as indoctrination.

The basic motivating force behind both the civic and philanthropic models of service-learning can be characterized as the desire to inject an ethical dimension into college education. Ethics concerns the question of how we ought to live. Much of American higher education relegates ethical questions to the periphery of education, if it gives such questions attention of any kind. However, ethics was once a central dimension of education, or at least that is the claim of many who advocate service-learning (e.g., Barber, 1998; Boyte & Kari, 2000). There is a nostalgic or even romantic element to these claims—which does not mean, however, that ethical considerations should not be infused or reinfused into higher education. To do so requires a more radical view of what should be done than either of the two models discussed so far. The communitarian basis of service-learning provides that view.

THE COMMUNITARIAN MODEL OF SERVICE-LEARNING

Communitarian theories of citizenship assume that humans are social creatures, not self-interested individual egoists who see their main concern in politics as protecting their liberty and property. In the introduction to a volume advocating the mission of teaching civic responsibility for higher education, Colby, Ehrlich, Beaumont, Rosner, and Stephens (2000a) argue that "a morally and civically responsible individual recognizes himself or herself as a member of a larger social fabric and therefore considers social problems to be at least partly his or her own" (p. xxvi). The recognition of oneself as "a member of a larger social fabric" is at the core of the definition of a social creature. The need to make individuals aware of this status through socialization and education does not negate the idea that it is natural to humans to be social, only that it is obvious. To assert that citizens are people "who share common values and are responsible for each other" (Boyte & Kari, 2000, p. 40) is to assume that humans are capable of and inclined to take such a stance toward others. This concept does not require that we demonstrate that individuals never behave in a self-interested manner. Rather, it requires that we believe that social action is important enough for individuals that society can be constructed on the basis of such activities. To assert that citizens are "[P]roblem solvers and co-producers of public goods" (Boyte & Kari, 2000, p. 40) is to assume that there are significant and continuing public problems to be solved and public goods to be produced. It is further to assume that individuals have the capacity and the will to dedicate significant amounts of time to such projects. Every public project makes a claim on individual resources in the form of taxes, time, or both. Public projects place restrictions on the use and availability of property or time that might be owned and used by individuals in private activities or for services that might be provided on an individual basis for profit. Some public projects may enhance our private activities, but, if that is their only appeal, such projects can be left to professionals whom we pay, either in the private sector or in public life directed by representatives we select. The latter arrangement frees us to live our private lives. It is only if we value public action that we would choose it over private activity. We will do so if we perceive liberty not in the negative terms of freedom from government but in positive terms of controlling our common lives. From this perspective democracy is the process of self-government, not a method for ensuring protection from government. If we are, in fact, social creatures, we will see our lives in this context and perceive democracy in these terms.

Only if we are social creatures does it make sense to speak of being "members of a community who share common values and are responsible to each other and for their community" (Boyte & Kari, 2000, p. 40). Rights-bearing citizens need only voluntary interaction that is mutually beneficial and the creation of a minimal government that can provide the order necessary for each citizen to enjoy his or her private life. Such citizens would be responsible only to and for themselves. From this perspective values are private matters. To claim that citizens are responsible to each other is to make an ethical claim that can only be sustained if we are social creatures. That humans have the capacity and will to be ethical creatures is the major implication of the assumption that humans are social creatures. If we do not have a natural ability to be ethical, concern for others can be achieved only through power, not through reason or education. The same argument applies to responsibility for one's community. A description of obligations would collapse into a discussion of which rights we must forgo for the good of others, and we would return to the concept of citizens as rights-bearers.

Fully to understand the relationship of citizens as members of communities who share values related to higher education, we must analyze the concepts of community and shared values. However, there is hostility to the communitarian element of citizenship as an element of training citizens for self-government even from some of the advocates of service-learning. For example, Barber (1998) bases his opposition to communitarianism on his belief that it stands for ascriptive associations in which a citizen of a community is "the clansman: the bondsman tied to community by birth, blood, and bathos" (pp. 23–24). However, as Fowler (1991) makes clear in his survey of the use of the term *community* in American political thought, this is not the only meaning of the term: "The concept of community invariably invokes the notion of commonality, of sharing in common, being and experiencing together" (p. 3). Thus, some sense of unity and commonality is essential to the belief that humans are social creatures. The concept of democratic community that I wish to describe as a basis for democratic citizenship is one based not on ascriptive connections but on a characteristic that humans have in common and that must lead them to create communities. This is the theory of community developed by Tinder (1980, chapter II), who argues that humans are inquirers:

A human being transcends every social role in which he finds himself, and he does so by questioning and criticizing—by raising doubts concerning society as a whole. He does this not only because of the enduring inadequacies of society but also because he is a being in search of being, his own being and that of others. One searches through social criticism and political controversy; one searches through science and art, through philosophy and religion; one searches in daily life and conversation. To search in these ways is to inquire, and to do this by virtue of one's nature is to show that one is essentially an inquirer. The implications for community are easily seen: if community unites people in their essential being, community must be in the nature of inquiry. (p. 17)

What Tinder makes clear is that, while inquiry is a process by which we transcend society, it is also a communal, that is, social activity. "We inquire, however, in two different ways. We inquire about, and we inquire with; we inquire about various objects of inquiry, and we inquire with fellow inquirers" (p. 24). It is the latter that constitutes community. We must inquire with others because we learn and experience very little on our own. Second, we need others to challenge and critique our own inquiry. Third, and most importantly, the will to inquire is the will to share with others. There is no greater source of skepticism concerning the self-interest concept of human nature than the communication argument of collective reflection and joint action occasioned by inquiry. Inquiry is our way of overcoming separation, not a method of increasing or enforcing it. The subject of our deepest inquiries concerns the mutual character of our shared lives.

Several important implications stem from this concept of community. First, it is a proposal for how we should live our lives together based on a claim about human nature. It is not a description of ascriptive relationships. Second, it implies that we should shape our common lives, wherever and with whomever we share them, so as to recognize and nourish this basic characteristic of our being. Tinder's concept can be contrasted with individualism's concept of human nature that is the basis of the rights-bearing view of citizenship. Further, Tinder's concept does not deny or subvert the importance of the individual. Rather, the individual deserves respect and dignity as a fellow inquirer whose experiences and feelings must be taken seriously, rather than as a solitary creature who needs the maximum freedom from interference by others.

Tinder's definition of community is also an open concept that does not base community on the identification of certain individuals or groups. Instead, community is often identified with exclusively defined groupings that designate some people as insiders and others as outsiders. The exclusive nature of some definitions of community is the basis of Barber's objection mentioned above. Any concept of community that denies the essential equality of humanity violates basic values that are essential to American and Western culture. Community as inquiry is also open in the sense that it is never a finished process. "It is of the human essence to ask after, but not to possess, the truth" (Tinder, 1980, p. 26). Answers to questions must always be treated within the community as tentative and open to change. This outlook does not mean that individuals can never commit themselves to any beliefs because, no matter how skeptical one wishes to be, inquiry must begin by taking some things for granted, by making assumptions. Inquiry cannot progress without accepting some things as true. Just as important, humans must act. Boyte and Kari (2000) criticize communitarian concepts of citizenship on the grounds that they "tend to separate ideals like community, the common good, and deliberation from the messy, everyday process of getting things done in a public world of diverse interests" (p. 41). The insight in this criticism comes from a recognition that a commitment to inquiry can lead to a permanent postponement of action. Yet this view also explains why we are always seekers after truth rather than possessors of it. We live in time and cannot wait for certainty before we act. An awareness of this fact justifies temporizing our commitments and being open to others. Additionally, action must be purposeful and goal oriented. It must have a basis and a framework. Action without community is as destructive as community without action, if not more so. This characteristic also justifies other basic values. If we are all inquirers, we must all be heard and our contributions to the task must be respected. Freedom of speech, religion, and press are all essential elements of inquiry. Tolerance is also a basic value of inquiry, though its meaning is contested. Inquiry takes place through reasoned discourse and argument. Any such discourse requires values such as honesty and self-reflection. While others might be cited, it is beyond the scope of this essay to list every value that arises out of the concept of community based on inquiry.

Boyte and Kari (2000) contrast the concept of civil society, which they identify with the communitarian concept of citizenship, with the concept of commonwealth, which they identify with the work-centered concept of citizenship. They argue that democratic citizenship in the United States has been historically identified as "the work of common citizens joined in projects which shaped communities and, ultimately, the nation," (p. 44). The point Boyte and Kari wish to make is an important one, namely that democratic citizenship is an active role. However, the activities of citizens can take many forms. Barber (1998) has pointed out that the tendency has been to define civil society as either the private sector of the rights-bearing definition of citizenship or as the boundaries of an ethnic or religious community (pp. 16–33). In either case, the concept is flawed by the identification of civil space with private space (p. 34). Barber offers a concept of civil society that meets the needs for a space in modern societies to recognize and engage in activities that are social and common in nature, yet are not coercive, where voluntary, cooperative associations engage in activities that are neither for-profit and market driven nor official, government-created services. Public interest groups, schools, churches, voluntary associations, social movements, and the family are among the associations that inhabit civil society (p. 49). Barber also includes the media, when they are not focused on profit but on informing the public. I would add political parties to this category. Not all groups can be included. Barber includes only those associations that are "open and inclusive (and thus include the right of exit as well as free entry) and must enforce some degree of equality among their members" (p. 53). He goes on to explain that "democrats realize that in speaking of civil society they are speaking not of any old kind of society, but of one that stipulates public and democratic conditions" (p. 53). It is within civil society that the "public work" extolled by Boyte and Kari can take place. But this work and the associations that define it must be perceived themselves as civic in character rather than as private. In the modern age, civil society that existed in an earlier era of American history has disappeared, and groups motivated by a concern for the common good or promoting social and democratic values have been lumped into the private sector. The result of this categorization is that such activities are labeled as just one more form of private-interest activity, no different from corporate lobbies or businesses. No wonder that citizens come to think of themselves as outsiders to the public sector, which is identified with official government organizations, and to see government in cynical terms. No wonder that young people do not associate activities that benefit society as separate from politics. Civil society must be consciously nurtured and developed. Citizens must be aware of it as a separate arena in which they can act.

If we combine the elements developed in this section, we get a definition of citizenship in a democracy. A democratic citizen is a self-consciously active, ethical, and civic member of an open and inclusive community in which democracy is understood as self-government actualized through collective inquiry and as action carried out in civil society as much as through representative government. Democratic citizenship must be learned and cultivated. The civic mission of higher education is to contribute to this process.

Community is not just a set of skills or attitudes that can be learned. The development of community requires that the process of education be changed to incorporate the environment and values of community in place of the individualistic values that currently permeate college education in the United States. While it is beyond the scope of this chapter to develop a full critique of the educational environment in colleges and universities, such critiques are widely available (e.g., Barber, 1992; Colby, Ehrlich, Beaumont, Rosner, & Stephens, 2000b, pp. 26–27). A major point these critiques make is that college education in the United States is not, as many of its practitioners would claim, value neutral. Rather, it is based on and furthers an ideology of self-interested and materialistic individualism. Such an approach relegates all ethical questions to a secondary status.

A key element in the philosophy of higher education is the claim to value neutrality. Values, morals, or ethical standards cannot be validated from within the materialist epistemology of science. Therefore, the argument goes, science says nothing about such subjects and is neutral towards them. Whether this claim is true philosophically, it is not true when applied to the effects of scientific learning on students or even scientists. As Tinder points out, humans inquire after being. They seek the ground for their own existence and, in doing so, treat what they learn about the world as evidence in the inquiry. The social scientist teaches the student, consciously or inadvertently, that he or she is a particular type of creature with particular needs, thought processes, capabilities, and ends. Students learn that the relationships they can forge with others are shaped by the type of creatures involved. If nothing else, the social scientist tends to teach that the world, that our social condition and relationships, should be taken as givens. If one studies the social world as one studies the physical world, one is taking the stance that certain regularities and stable relationships can be identified and understood. If there are no such regularities, the scientific approach is not possible. As a consequence, one takes the patterns and regularities one finds as stable patterns to be explained. This point cannot be taken too literally. Science looks for reasons for change as well as stability. More importantly, if one finds the causes of a particular pattern, one can propose changing the causes and thus changing the effects. However, a basic conservatism follows from always asking what exists, while ruling out of bounds the question of whether it should exist. The implication for the student is that he or she should find his or her place within the existing social and political world.

A basic element of this phenomenon is related to the influence of the social-scientific approach to the understanding of citizenship and democracy. Because the scientific approach seeks to explain phenomena through identifying and specifying the effects of other phenomena, the basic concept of the study of politics is power. Any cause can be understood as an application of power and to explain effects is to explain dynamics of power. Additionally, social-scientific approaches to society inevitably begin from individualistic and materialistic views of human beings. Scientific analysis breaks the world into separate units of activity and searches for the observable relationships among them. Humans must be conceptualized in this way for science to deal with them. Even if humans are spoken of as part of groups, the forces that create the groups must be investigated and explained. In his letter written to a group of clergymen from the Birmingham city jail, Martin Luther King, Jr., claimed, "I am cognizant of the interrelatedness of all communities and states. I cannot sit idly by in Atlanta and not be concerned about what happens in Birmingham. Injustice anywhere is a threat to justice everywhere. We are caught in an inescapable network of mutuality tied in a single garment of destiny" (1998, p. 483). The idea of such connections among human beings makes no sense from the viewpoint of a social scientist because such a "network of mutuality" cannot be detected, let alone measured in material terms. King was, of course, speaking as a religious person of the common destiny Christians believe all humans share.

There is a more subtle sense in which the social sciences influence how citizens perceive and act toward each other. The social sciences use methods of data gathering and analysis that emphasize the treatment of humans as objects to be studied for the purpose of determining what causes their actions and what actions they take to affect others. The phenomena studied are treated as instances of the interaction of conscious and/or incidental forces that explain outcomes of interest. An example is the study of elections. Some of the relevant questions asked concerning such events are: Why did a specific candidate win? Why did the candidate win by a particular margin of victory? Why did voters vote for each candidate? Why did some citizens vote while others did not? These are the exact questions a candidate would ask about past campaigns to maximize his or her chances of winning a current campaign. Students who are taught to ask these questions and to use the methods that provide answers to them will, according to the current approach to higher education, either become a member of the next generation of scholars asking similar questions or seek employment in which they will use this knowledge and these skills to help others attempt to manipulate citizens (or consumers) for their own ends. Those ends will inevitably and predictably be defined by self-interest.

The effects of this situation have not gone unnoticed. In the 1970s and 1980s a perception developed that an alarming number of bright, well-educated people, particularly professionals, were acting in unethical ways in carrying out their responsibilities. The response was to develop ethics courses in professional schools. What is missing from this approach is the understanding that ethics is not just a subunit of public administration, or any other profession, but is at the core of the subject. Why actions should be taken, and toward what ends, must be explored before any other questions can be asked. Practical questions are bound to crowd out ethical questions if such practical questions and how to answer them dominate the education and training of professionals, which they are bound to do so long as social science epistemology dominates education. Lilla (1981) argues that teaching ethics as just one more subject, instead of making it part of the basic education of citizens, will create skilled sophists instead of ethical professionals. The same argument could be generalized to any citizen.

The importance, content, and effects of teaching in American higher education have been dramatically affected by the adoption of a scientific epistemology among scholars. Students receive an education in which subjects are taught as narrow enclaves of knowledge and skills, only tangentially related to each other. Education is a smorgasbord of courses that fulfill requirements in various general subject areas, rather than a coherent series of experiences that relate to each other by illuminating various aspects of a unifying set of basic questions. The world is taught as fragmented, walled-off sets of facts set forth by experts. Students are left to unify these sets on their own, and it is only natural that they do so by relating them to personal goals and ambitions. Education is something to be made use of to further one's career.

The adoption of a scientific epistemology in the study of humanity was intended to deliver a value-neutral education to college students. The scholar as social scientist was not to affect the political, social, or economic values and ethics of society. Instead, he or she was to provide a neutral description of how the world worked so that society could achieve its chosen ends more effectively. Science would tell us how to do things, but not what to do or when to do it. However, as we have seen, this is not the case. An education based on a scientific epistemology does indeed affect what students do and when they do it. Scientists themselves, not understanding this phenomenon, have dramatic impacts of which they are unaware and for which they take no credit or blame.

For this reason, colleges and universities do not counteract, and may even foster, the selfishness and political apathy that advocates of service-learning wish to overcome. What is needed is an approach to education that is communal at its base and therefore supports and even requires service-learning.

A classroom that focuses on community as a goal must be a communal classroom. Rather than focusing on the mastery of material by solitary individuals, the classroom focuses on collective deliberation, analysis, and evaluation to solve problems and answer questions raised by the subject matter of the discipline. If community is a part of the human condition because we inquire together, inquiry in collective processes must characterize the educational process. Paul and his colleagues at the Foundation for Critical Thinking (*Critical Thinking,* 1992) present an example of a systematic approach to learning that emphasizes the need to ask questions and solve problems collectively. The presentation of all subjects as modes of thinking, the use of Socratic dialogues, critical group analysis of reading materials, and critical exercises make up the educational process for Paul.

While Paul and his colleagues do not present this approach as a way to develop community, it is an approach that easily lends itself to that goal. Collective interaction designed to discover, interpret, and see the significance of a subject matter develops the skills necessary for collective activity. Paul's proposed educational process does not sacrifice intellectual rigor. Rather, it is based on the premise that intellectual rigor requires active learning and that active learning involves interaction between a teacher and students and among students. Students must be constantly working through the concepts, ideas, and discoveries of the discipline as a class. They learn to think like a chemist, mathematician, philosopher, or historian by practicing the reasoning skills of the relevant discipline. The key point for our purposes is the cooperative and collective nature of the enterprise.

The classroom is, however, not an isolated community. The students are being initiated into the community of historians, chemists, or the like and, more broadly, into a body of inquirers that stretches across space and time. Creating a sense of community with the scholars who are or have been engaged in answering the same questions and attempting to resolve the same issues as the class material develops a second community. The development of concepts, ideas, facts, and theories within the classroom can be enhanced by tracing the contributions of the relevant scholars and developing a sense of identity with them. This historical aspect of the discipline need not be a significant part of every course, but it should be a significant element of the curriculum.

There is a third community to which students belong, the community of the university or college they attend. While there are many aspects to this community, the relevant one for this chapter is the community of academic inquirers, meaning students and faculty. This community is brought together through the introduction of cross-disciplinary course work. The analytic power unleashed by categorizing knowledge into disciplines must be balanced by efforts to reintegrate knowledge. Students must learn the basic fact that human knowledge is actually a whole. Such integration can take place in many ways, and certainly it need not be a part of all or even most of the course work students undertake. In the current circumstances, however, it is left to the student to grasp the relevance of various fields of knowledge and their interrelationship. The student is expected to comprehend how the knowledge gained in one subject illuminates the questions and issues of other subjects. It is unreasonable to expect such a high level of intellectual activity on the part of students without their being made conscious of the connections through their course work. Making such connections requires cooperation among faculty in building a sense of community that serves as a model for students.

The inclusion of cross-disciplinary courses, therefore, is essential to a curriculum built on the concept of community.

Finally, students must come to understand themselves as part of the larger community beyond the campus. That larger community can and should be framed in international and national terms, but it is important that it be understood also in local terms. Regardless of the size or complexity of the world, people live in certain places, and they can best develop the sense of community in a concrete sense by exploring and interacting with that community. It is here that service-learning becomes important.

The reason that service-learning is central to developing a sense of human community at the local level is related to an important element of the entire subject of community. Using community as the framework for understanding human relationships inevitably raises questions concerning the proper nature of such relationships. It raises questions of ethics. If students are part of an intellectual community, they must learn and practice traits of honesty so that communication can be trusted. They must learn respect for the positions of others so that there is free and open discussion. They must learn intellectual integrity so that they are willing to live with and act upon their beliefs as to what is true. They must learn intellectual humility so that they do acknowledge the limitations and fallibility of their own reasoning. In every form of community the relationships among the members and the proper nature of that relationship are factors that must be explored and developed. The same is true for relationships in the larger community beyond the campus. Without prejudging the answers that will be given to questions concerning those relationships, it is necessary for each student to participate in exploring the possible answers to questions regarding equality, liberty, distributions of resources, and social and political justice, among others. In the communities discussed in this chapter, the student is not simply told the "correct" nature of communal relationships and ethics. People do not strengthen their ability to be ethical beings by learning correct answers. Rather, they learn through participating in the community and, in the process, by analyzing and evaluating these relationships. They learn to recognize and think about the ethical dimensions of questions just as they learn to recognize other questions. The student must also participate in the local community to understand the lives and the needs of the community. There is no better way to do this than through the activity of service-learning.

THE ELEMENTS OF COMMUNITARIAN SERVICE-LEARNING

The communitarian approach to service-learning requires a communitarian approach to higher education. Service-learning should be integrated into a college curriculum that is communitarian in nature. Teaching styles and content should be consciously designed to teach students that they are part of larger communities, not that they are solitary individuals who are being taught alongside other solitary individuals. Classes in such a curriculum should use pedagogies that are cooperative, communal, and in which learning is an active, shared experience. Discussion, experimentation, case studies, presentations, Socratic dialogue, and analysis and evaluations developed in group settings should all be elements of the predominant teaching style in such a curriculum.

The best class setting for service-learning is a cross-disciplinary, even multidisciplinary course. Such a course could be developed in two places in an undergraduate liberal arts curriculum. It could be part of the general education requirements for students in the first two years of their education. The current tendency to reinforce the difference among the disciplines could be counteracted by courses that teach, for example, the main theoretical postulates of modern science in a common course. As a vehicle for tying these elements together, a common problem or question could be examined from the various scientific approaches. Some problems, such as medical questions or environmental questions, would lend themselves to field learning in the form of service-learning in hospitals, nursing homes, or the like that could illustrate how the problems and questions of the course relate to real people and how answering or solving problems can have real benefits.

At the other end of the curriculum, a senior course, perhaps even a two-semester course, intended as a culmination of a student's undergraduate work, could focus not on a subject in a single discipline but could be the basis for a common attack on an issue involving several disciplines. Students majoring in the various disciplines represented in the course could bring the skills and knowledge they have developed to the study of the common problem. Research on various aspects of the problem aimed at contributing to a common understanding and perhaps solutions would provide a focus for the course. Again, service-learning opportunities related to the common problem could be an opportunity for learning and analysis as well as service. In addition, service-learning could include the common development of solutions to problems by a class, rather than limiting service-learning to individual experiences. This past semester, for example, students in an urban geography class on our campus studied the downtown area of Nacogdoches and wrote a report that they submitted to the city and that may become the basis for new city policies. Service-learning should not be limited to individual effort and it need not be aimed at aiding specific individuals.

A strong impediment to the implementation of the communitarian model in the classroom is its heavy demands on teachers and students. The communitarian model will not work in a lecture-style classroom in which students are passive learners. Large classes are particularly difficult to use for this purpose. This problem argues for using service-learning in upper-division classes, which are likely to be smaller.

A second impediment to the use of the communitarian model is the requirement that professors and students rethink the subject matter and their relationships to each other. Professors must learn to comprehend their subject matter as a contribution to a community, and they must make connections in their teaching to community issues and concerns. Such a shift in perspective and practice represents a major adjustment in a profession in which specialization has become the norm and is only likely to take place when a commitment to such a change is made by a department, college, or even an entire university campus.

Students must overcome inhibitions to speaking in class and to having their work critiqued and questioned by fellow students. They must also cease to think of other students as competitors in a race for grades. Individual grading will not disappear, but striking the right balance between concern for the individual reward of grades and the collective rewards that follow from cooperation and contributions made to the class is difficult and will have to be worked out. Seeking this balance is a fundamental problem for our society as a whole, which places such a strong emphasis on individual achievement and reward. Responding to this problem is an ethical issue in that an awareness of the need to balance these values in the classroom will help prepare students to balance them after they leave college. Such a focus on ethical behavior is in sharp contrast to the current situation in which harmony between ambition and the community is ignored.

I would also not wish to minimize the difficulties of developing a course in which service-learning experiences are integrated into the subject matter. Unlike experiments in science classes, service-learning opportunities that mesh well with a class may be hard to find. One must assume that experience and time will help improve fit. Service-learning in the form of reports and projects that are conducted by an entire class may be an alternative to individual placements, but they may be more difficult to control.

The element of action is missing from the discussion to this point. Citizenship is likely to remain an abstraction unless students can become involved in civil society directly. They must experience citizenship to become citizens. Anne Colby and her colleagues (2000b) state: "As a whole, the research indicates that if used well these student-centered, or active pedagogies can have a positive impact on many dimensions of moral and civic learning as well as on other aspects of academic achievement" (p. 136).

The proposal that developing democratic citizens be the guiding mission of higher education must not be a romantic plea for a return to an earlier time. Although American higher education took civic education as its mission in the nineteenth century, society and colleges were very different places to which we shall not return. People no longer live in small towns or rural areas where they know all of their neighbors. We no longer expect to live in the same places for our entire lives. The concept of community was easier to teach to students who lived in nineteenth-century America because it resonated in their own experience. The concept of community adopted in this chapter is one of community as a state of existence and a stance toward the world. This type of abstract concept can more easily be taught to individuals who must carry it with them to different physical locations and live among various groups of people during their lives. The issue that must be addressed is what characteristics service-learning must possess if it is to be part of civic education. I would offer the following characteristics as a minimal list.

Service-learning must involve real situations. Civic education requires that students struggle with the complexities and uncertainties of real life so that they can learn to be realistic and so that their learning can be maximized. At the same time, the situations must be on an appropriate scale so that the students can make a real contribution. The goal of a real situation is not to discourage students but to have them learn from experience that they can be effective. Situations must also be real so that students have to work with people who have a genuine stake in the outcomes. Students should get used to the passion, commitment, stubbornness, and worry that people display when things matter. Resolving issues and taking action in such situations is more difficult but definitely more rewarding.

Service-learning must involve collective action. Civic action is public action and public action is collective action. In general, American education tends to be individual, which is poor preparation for working with others. Whether a service-learning project involves other students, members of the broader community, or both, it should help raise awareness of the need to work with others. It should also increase students' skills and confidence in acting in such environments.

OBJECTIONS TO THE COMMUNITARIAN MODEL

The most basic objection to the communitarian model is that it replaces a value-neutral education with one that places ethical issues in the forefront of education by emphasizing the importance of human relationships. This criticism is likely to be leveled both by supporters of the philanthropic model of service-learning and by those who are skeptical of the value of service-learning. My response to this objection is twofold. The first response is that any justification for service-learning will not be value neutral because service implies evaluation. Service is always justified by its contribution to changing the attitudes of students to encourage them to make positive contributions to others, whether it be as philanthropy or social change. These changes are, by definition, changes in ethical standards.

The second response is that the criticism is based on the assumption that college education is currently value neutral. However, the value neutrality claim of the social sciences in particular disguises an individualistic, self-interested, and materialistic philosophy that is compatible with the basic assumptions of the social-scientific epistemology (Bender, 1997). There is a significant literature arguing that it is a fallacy to believe that students can be taught a basic approach to how the social world works without including assumptions about how one ought to act in that world (e.g., Sullivan, 2000). The fundamental questions to be answered are what view of human nature and human relationships a college education will support and whether that support will be consciously chosen or will be an unintended consequence of the educational process.

A second objection to the communitarian model is that it requires too great a change from current higher education practices. I have not tried to hide the fact that this model is difficult to incorporate into one particular class; instead, I have argued that this model works best as part of a broad, general strategy for higher education. The individual professor who attempts to use this approach without the strong support of his or her colleagues, department chair, or dean is likely to be undertaking work that will require a great deal of time and bring little reward. In fact, the professor will be violating the well-established rules for emphasizing research to achieve tenure and promotion. Further, the individual will find his or her class so out of step with the experiences students have in other classes that it will be hard to achieve the changes in outlook and understanding that are central to this approach.

Without doubt, the communitarian approach requires significant commitment and also substantial reform of higher education. However, the reforms of higher education that have been proposed for many years by critics such as Boyer (1987, 1990) are more compatible with a communitarian position than the individualistic position that is now the norm of higher education. While this process is not easy, that does not mean it should not be undertaken. A recent report for the Carnegie Foundation for the Advancement of Teaching describes how several American colleges and universities of various sizes and missions have adopted curricula that are designed with a focus on civic education (Colby et al., 2000b). A communitarian approach is compatible with and no more radical than these changes.

CONCLUSIONS

For service-learning to become a major pedagogy in college education, it must follow logically from a theory of education that justifies and requires its presence. Service-learning emphasizes the development of ethical consciousness and reasoning and is a method for developing such qualities. A philanthropic model is too weak to provide a justification for service-learning. It remains wedded to an individualistic, self-interested concept of human nature that does not elevate ethics to an important concern. A civic model of service-learning overcomes this problem by infusing the educational process with a mission to make students advocates for a liberal or radical definition of social justice. Such an approach can have only a limited appeal and is bound to come and go in popularity, never establishing itself as a foundational part of the educational curriculum.

The communitarian model requires radical change in our understanding of higher education. It requires a renewal of the commitment of faculty and administrators to the goal of undergraduate education as a primary activity, complete with a reward structure that reflects such a commitment. This is a great hurdle to overcome, but the civic model also proposes this type of change for higher education. The communitarian model is broader in scope than the civic model and more inclusive in the ethical positions it permits into the discussion, and, as such, it is better able to serve as a basis for undergraduate education and as a basis for service-learning than either the civic or the philanthropic models.

REFERENCES

Barber, B. J. (1992). *An aristocracy of everyone: The politics of education and the future of America*. New York: Ballantine Books.

Barber, B. J. (1998). *A place for us: How to make society civil and democracy strong*. New York: Hill and Wang.

Bender, T. (1997). Politics, intellect, and the American university, 1945–1995. *Daedalus, 126*(1), 1–38.

Boyer, E. (1987). *College: The undergraduate experience in America*. New York: Harper & Row.

Boyer, E. (1990). *Scholarship reconsidered: Priorities of the professoriate*. Princeton, NJ: Carnegie Foundation for the Advancement of Teaching.

Boyte, H. C., & Kari, N. N. (2000). Renewing the democratic spirit in American colleges and universities: Higher education as public work. In T. Ehrlich (Ed.), *Civic responsibility and higher education* (pp. 37–59). Phoenix, AZ: American Council on Education and Oryx Press.

Colby, A., Ehrlich, T., Beaumont E., Rosner, J, & Stephens, J. (2000a). Higher education and the development of civic responsibility. In T. Ehrlich (Ed.), *Civic responsibility and higher education* (pp. xxi–xliii). Phoenix, AZ: American Council on Education and Oryx Press.

Colby, A., Ehrlich, T., Beaumont E., Rosner, J, & Stephens, J. (2000b). *Educating citizens: Preparing America's undergraduates for lives of moral and civic responsibility.* San Francisco: Jossey-Bass for the Carnegie Foundation for the Advancement of Teaching.

Elshtain, J. B. (1997). The decline of democratic faith. In R. M. Battistoni & W. E. Hudson (Eds.), *Experiencing citizenship: Concepts and models for service-learning in political science* (pp. 9–14). Washington, DC: American Association for Higher Education.

Fowler, R. B. (1991). *The dance with community: The contemporary debate in American political thought.* Lawrence: University of Kansas Press.

King, M. L., Jr. (1998). Letter from the Birmingham city jail (16 April 1963). In K. Dolbeare (Ed.), *American political thought* (pp. 482–489). Chatham, NJ: Chatham House.

Lilla, M. T. (1981, Spring). Ethos, "ethics," and public service. *Public Service, 63,* 3–17.

Lisman, C. D. (1998). *Toward a civil society: Civic literacy and service-learning.* Westport, CT: Bergin & Garvey.

Mendel-Reyes, M. (1997). Teaching/theorizing/practicing democracy: An activist's perspective on service-learning in political science. In R. M. Battistoni & W. E. Hudson (Eds.), *Experiencing citizenship: Concepts and models for service-learning in political science* (pp. 15–34). Washington, DC: American Association for Higher Education.

Paul, Richard. (1992). *Critical thinking: What every person needs to survive in a rapidly changing world* (Rev. 2nd ed.). Sonoma, CA: Foundation for Critical Thinking.

Robinson, T. (2000). Service-learning as justice advocacy: Can political scientists do politics? *PS: Political Science and Politics, 33*(3), 605–612.

Sullivan, W. M. (2000). Institutional identity and social responsibility in higher education. In T. Ehrlich (Ed.), *Civic responsibility and higher education* (pp. 19–36). Phoenix, AZ: American Council on Education and Oryx Press.

Tinder, G. (1980). *Community: Reflections on a tragic ideal.* Baton Rouge: Louisiana State University Press.

Zivi, K. (1997). Examining pedagogy in the service-learning classroom: Reflections on integrating service-learning into the classroom. In R. M. Battistoni & W. E. Hudson (Eds.), *Experiencing citizenship: Concepts and models for service-learning in political science* (pp. 49–68). Washington, DC: American Association for Higher Education.

CHAPTER 8

A Critique of the Communitarian Model

Christina Murphy

INTRODUCTION

The renewed attention to the issue of community in political thought generated by such social theorists as Lawler (2002), MacIntyre (1997), Sandel
(1996, 1998), Selznick (1992), Taylor (1989), and Walzer (1984) has carried
over into debates about the purpose and value of education in American
society. Professor Codispoti, in chapter 7, is correct in discussing current
educational debates in terms of two political philosophies of the individual and society—liberalism and communitarianism. He is correct, too, in
arguing that these philosophies represent divergent views of how individuals should be educated to function within society. What Codispoti
calls the civic model of education and of service-learning, I shall call the
liberal view, largely because this perspective emerges in contemporary
times from traditional liberal philosophies that have been honed during
the political and social conflicts of previous centuries. Moving beyond
Codispoti's somewhat tame perspective, I shall extend the critique of the
liberal views of education and citizenship to consider three major premises: (1) liberal defenses of education—especially of the general education
curricula within which a number of service-learning programs are em-
bedded—rest upon outdated concepts of individualism and autonomy in
relation to community and social action; (2) such outdated views are
largely ineffective as an advocacy model for redefining the role of service-
learning programs within general education; and (3) communitarianism
offers a better advocacy model than liberalism, because communitarianism is rooted in broader understandings of the concepts of community

and social contexts while emphasizing the balance between individual rights and social responsibilities in educating citizens for collective self-government. Where Codispoti and I disagree most is in our understanding of how the political and philosophical insights of communitarianism can or should be translated into educational and civic practice, especially in terms of service-learning.

LIBERAL VS. COMMUNITARIAN IDEALS

Codispoti does not go as far as I shall in arguing that a failed liberalism has compromised the power of service-learning to establish a dynamic role in education and has, instead, relegated service-learning to quasi-service courses in support of either civic education or a marketplace agenda. Recent efforts to reincorporate or reconfigure service-learning courses into social advocacy courses have only intensified this conflict by failing to move beyond liberal ideas of individualism and autonomy into the more broadly defined communitarian ideas of educated citizens as public problem solvers. Once more I shall disagree with Codispoti, who, in my opinion, does not focus upon the fact that communitarianism must move away from a liberal tradition that argues for sustaining cultural structures and toward a different model or paradigm of culture itself as a community of communities. Codispoti's essay, in my view, is a nostalgic (if not wistful) expression of longing for an educational model that would broaden the focus of academic classes and help students realize the interconnectedness of civic knowledge and academic preparation. He contends that communitarianism does and should provide such a model, yet he offers few specifics on how this transformation can or will occur. In this regard, his views also fail to incorporate communitarian understandings of the impact of social institutions on ethical decision making in the workplace. Clearly he states that such an incorporation should occur, but he does not provide a clear mechanism or persuasive argument for the way in which political theory can become social and educational reality.

Let me also add that I disagree with Codispoti in terms of how communitarianism depends on the nature of social creatures in a civil society. Codispoti's view depicts "concerned members of communities who share common values and are responsible to each other and for their community." He adds that this rendering of citizenship is also regularly associated with the ideas of "civil society." Two issues here that weaken the impact of this argument and thus the effectiveness of communitarianism as either a political or educational philosophy are (1) that communitarian members must share common values and must demonstrate both concern and social responsibility toward the community as a whole and (2) the deflating (if not destructive) identification of communitarianism with ideas of civil society. In essence, I find Codispoti's interpretation to be

representative of the problems detailed by Jardine (1998) who states that
the term *communitarianism* has been only vaguely defined in contemporary political analyses: "To some, the term implies a backward-looking
nostalgia for an idealized communal past that would restore old social
hierarchies and limit individual freedom; to others, it sounds suspiciously
like a kind of closet socialism that would replace the market economy
with centralized regulation in the name of community" (p. 27).

In a similar vein, I find Codispoti's arguments for a communal redefi-
nition of academic instruction and thus, by extension, for the development
of more and more extensive interdisciplinary courses and majors to be
outdated at best. Codispoti presents these ideas as if they were new or
radical suggestions, but, in reality, such collaborative and interdisciplinary
efforts have been proposed and undertaken in academics since at least the
1980s. In fact, the predominant educational paradigm of the 1980s was
social constructionism, which argued for a decentering of the teacher as
the authority figure in education and for a renewed focus upon the classroom as a community of students and teachers working collaboratively
as inquirers into social and academic issues (Gergen, 2001). In essence, the
types of classrooms and classes that Codispoti calls for as a new response
to the demands and benefits of communitarianism not only already exist
but have been tried in academics for two decades or more. During this
time, of course, academicians have not seen the type of revolutions in
attitude or educational experiences that Codispoti predicts would take
place if such communal and interdisciplinary courses were in place. In
fact, ironically, the rise in apathy toward social, political, and ethical issues
that Codispoti decries has intensified as social constructionism has reshaped American education from the traditional teacher-centered classroom to the socially constructed communal classroom of teacher and
students as peer learners, or what Codispoti would call peer inquirers.
Thus, since communitarianism has restructured many aspects of American higher education but has not produced the type of revolution in educational, social, and ethical attitudes that Codispoti and other advocates
of communitarianism would like to see, it is difficult to conclude that the
arguments made for this type of revolution actually have a great deal of
relevance in reality, though they may have great appeal in the abstract.

REDEFINING THE COMMUNAL AS COMMUNITY:
CONCEPTS AND CONCERNS

Codispoti's definition of communitarianism is presented a bit sketchily
as an expression of social or communal inquiry. Drawing upon the ideas
of Tinder (1980) in *Community: Reflections on a Tragic Ideal,* Codispoti claims
that "it is the need to engage in such inquiry that characterizes human
beings." He adds that "in fact, the subject of our deepest inquiries concerns

the mutual character of our shared lives, which is the subject matter of ethics." Key terms in this definition are *inquiry, shared lives,* and *ethics*— all of which focus upon community solidarity in terms of what values are shared by members of a group or community. Another concept rooted in both Tinder's and Codispoti's arguments is the degree of participation individuals will seek within communities, especially in terms of voluntary organizations and the role such organizations play in the greater good or social commonwealth of their lives (Tinder, p. 82). Here we find a major problem in the argument that Tinder and Codispoti present. Codispoti would have us believe that education in and of itself will be sufficient to unify the goals and the ethics of group participants. In other words, if individuals come together through the educational process—and especially through the activities of service-learning—they will be challenged to "incorporate the environment and values of community in place of the individualistic values that currently permeate college education in the United States." Such a stance presupposes that communal interaction will automatically lead to a communal sharing of values. I find this assumption to be faulty because it neglects to take into account the power and influence of special interests and special-interest groups within communities. While Codispoti and Tinder would argue that an important object of the process of setting goals for a community is to bring individuals together to clarify their values and express their views, they seem to assume that rationality will be the key to community and communal harmony.

In contrast, Blakely (1979) believes that the fragmentation of special interests in communities requires new models to restore the value of co-operation. Blakely contends that such new models are needed to "explore the conceptual bases for social action in relation to concrete experiences" (p. 20). Fundamentally, making the connection between experiences and social action is the most complex aspect of communal interaction and cooperation. Merely placing students in situations that call for communal responses to social action will not be sufficient to produce the type of engagement that Codispoti seeks. Further, I do not find Codispoti offering us the exploration of conceptual bases that Blakely argues for. In fact, I find his arguments to be substantially devoid of a broad understanding of human motivations for social actions. I agree with Tomm (1998) that saying individuals are social or communal by nature is not sufficient to conclude that they will be inclined to act in socially responsible or ethical ways toward each other. If this were true, then all that would be needed for particular social changes to occur would be acculturation (Bereiter, 1994). In fact, this is a concept that has been called into question—if not fully rejected—by theorists who find that such a view does not explain the variety of responses that individuals have to the acculturation process—not the least of which is a higher emphasis upon individualism than a communal or communitarian view might wish for or conclude (Phillips, 1995).

My deepest concerns with the view of communitarianism that Codispoti proposes center precisely in this idea of centralized regulation in the name of community. Part of the justification for such a restrictive view is a very proscriptive idea of human nature. I am tempted to say it is an idealistic view, but the truth is that it is a poorly reasoned view based upon an argument from a faulty analogy. For example, Codispoti states that "the habits of self-government are natural, but must be nurtured, cultivated, and trained." He does not provide proof or argumentation for such a broad statement as "the habits of self-government are natural." Instead, he moves from this premise to other equally broad and unsubstantiated premises about human nature. Further, he also draws false assumptions from the premises he asserts. For example, while it may be accurate for Codispoti to assert that "it is natural to humans to be social," it is incorrect reasoning by faulty analogy to then assume and assert that humans are naturally political. Yet this is the line of reasoning and the major premise from which Codispoti makes a host of claims about the individual, the community, the purposes of education and politics in the socialization process, and the nature of human actions as virtuous or nonvirtuous choices.

From such flimsy assumptions Codispoti goes on to construct a philosophical schema and justification for communitarian views both as a support for communitarianism as a political ideal and as a model for the value and purpose of service-learning:

To assert that citizens are people "who share common values and are responsible for each other" is to assume that humans are capable of and inclined to take such a stance toward others. This does not require that we demonstrate that individuals never behave in a self-interested manner. Rather it requires that we believe that social action is important enough for individuals that society can be constructed on the basis of such activities, rather than on the more limited relationships prescribed by the rights-bearing definition of citizenship.

Codispoti's argument is rooted in assumptions about human virtue that may be theoretically attractive but pragmatically unattainable. It remains to be seen if society and its institutions can be structured on the basis of an assumed or imagined sense that humans naturally seek communal bonding and thus experience a resulting sense of responsibility for others. Certainly, not all theorists would agree with this premise. For example, Jardine (1998) points out that the end result of the technological progress and economic prosperity of contemporary life has been alienation, not communal bonding. Further, "modern individuals are subjected to systems of technical examination and psychological manipulation unimaginable in premodern societies" that, in turn, set the stage for unlikely scenarios that contrast starkly with the highly positive communitarian vision:

Similarly, the modern rights and liberties that have freed individuals from the (frequently harsh) hierarchical authority of the past seem to have resulted in profound feelings of insecurity and alienation—so much so that in the twentieth-century whole nations have voluntarily—indeed, enthusiastically—submitted to tyrannical control as a way of escaping such disorientation. (p. 29)

Living now in what Jardine calls "the third industrial revolution" (p. 29), we find ourselves more removed from social and political involvement than ever before and less trustful of impulses or organized efforts toward group identification and unity.

SERVICE-LEARNING: COMMUNITARIAN IDEALS OF EDUCATING FOR CITIZENSHIP

The philosophical territory into which Codispoti enters becomes even more dubious when he turns his attention to service-learning and the educational initiatives and rationales that would support service-learning. As one might expect, Codispoti places more emphasis upon what he sees as the ameliorative social aspects of communitarianism than he does upon providing a justification for the educational benefits of this philosophy. In fact, Codispoti's main line of reasoning about the relationship of service-learning to the public good can be found in the following critique of communitarianism offered by Stone (1998):

The main features of this world view are a Rousseauean-styled belief in political participation as an end in itself; a deep fear of egoism and economic inequality; a belief in the need to submit the natural inclinations of individuals to a socially constructed "common good"; the conviction that the American problems associated with individualism result exclusively from the misarrangement of "the large structures of the economy and state"; and a fervent belief in the unifying, equalizing and redemptive powers of the state. Coterminous with these beliefs is an animus toward liberal thinking, especially classical liberal thought, and toward the liberal public order of unregulated markets and rights-based, limited government. (pp. 83–84)

Certainly one can question the value and the actual pragmatics of structuring the service-learning experience around, in Stone's phrasing, "the need to submit the natural inclinations of individuals to a socially constructed 'common good'" (p. 84). The two terms of this equation remain difficult to define or to implement. In the complex of human emotions and cognition, can one really talk about natural inclinations beyond the level of simple instincts? And in the complex of competing and conflicting social, political, and economic forces, can one really talk about a socially constructed common good? And even if these barriers were overcome and these issues resolved, how would one construct a service-learning program that would combine natural inclinations and a socially constructed common good?

Needless to say, Codispoti is long on the theorizing but short on the details with regard to these questions. First, he must shift the definition of *liberty* from "the negative terms of freedom from government" to "positive terms of controlling our common lives." Then he must argue that "from this perspective democracy is the process of self-government, not a method for ensuring protection from government." From here, it is but a small philosophical maneuver to claim that "to fully understand the relationship of citizens as members of communities who share values related to higher education, we must analyze the concepts of community and shared values." To support the interrelationship of the two, Codispoti must claim that citizenship is more than a communal experience; it is also a process of inquiry. The shared values emerge from this process almost as a parody of a popular saying: Those who inquire together, stay together. Even more, they stay together to form a community of shared values that is sustained through the process of inquiry—or, as Codispoti, quoting Tinder, presents it, "if community unites people in their essential being, community must be in the nature of inquiry" (see chapter 7).

To give Codispoti his due and to find a measure of significance within the communitarian philosophy, it may well be beneficial to conceptualize service-learning "as an element of training citizens for self-government." Certainly Codispoti's view aligns with that of Stanton, Giles, and Cruz (1999), who state that "growing up in a turbulent time caused many pioneers [of the service-learning movement] to ask serious questions about society and ultimately about their education" (p. 38). The turbulent times to which Stanton, Giles, and Cruz refer are the decades of the 1940s, 1950s, and 1960s; however, their point is relevant to contemporary times and the conflicting messages and meanings for both education and society to be found there. Stone (1998) would argue, though, that the legacy of turbulent times can be "a tenaciously held and largely misconceived world view" (p. 83).

Thus, we arrive at the conundrum raised by Codispoti's essay and by communitarian views of service-learning. Are people social, communal, and political by nature; do they seek virtuous action through a process of inquiry that results in a desire for egalitarian and just self-government; and can an educational system design and also deliver a service-learning program that will result in the actualization of these communitarian ideals? My answer would be: doubtful. I answer this way precisely because I believe that communitarianism, as espoused by Codispoti and those of his persuasion, does represent "a tenaciously held and largely misconceived world view."

COMMUNITARIAN PARADIGMS: SOCIAL CONTEXTS AND PROGRESSIVE VISIONS

Is anything salvageable from Codispoti's version of communitarianism, particularly as it relates to service-learning education? The impulse toward a virtuous vision of common humanity is indeed an appealing outlook, as is the impulse toward educating individuals to desire to achieve a unity of purpose within their communities and thus, in essence, create self-government via a community of communities. Certainly this concept was what Dewey had in mind with the revolutionary ideas of progressivism as far back as 1938. The disappointing aspects of this approach then and now, though, are its distortion of terms, its heavy sentimentality, and its reworking and adoption of the liberal views it claims to eschew. McClay (1998) best describes these disappointing aspects of communitarianism:

The communitarian "movement" has arisen as an effort to address the evident deficiencies of modern liberalism, and to push our political thinking beyond its fixation on the sovereign autonomy of rights-bearing individuals. There is much that is commendable in such an effort. But the communitarianism we have been getting so far suffers from a fatal defect: it is much too closely bound to the very liberalism it would correct. As a result, it tends to use the language of "community" as a form of mood music, a pleasingly imprecise way to soften our image of all organizations, including those that are decidedly not families or communities, such as universities, business corporations, or nation-states. The problem with such discourse . . . is that it is not only inaccurate but pernicious. It serves to dismiss or devalue the elements of genuine community where they exist, while distorting our speech about other kinds of organizations with imprecision, sentimentality, and coercive unctuousness. (p. 101)

Etzioni (1996) provides a similar critique in calling for the need to understand communitarianism within social histories and contexts:

Communitarian tracks and traces can be found throughout the ages. However, it was only in the 1990s that communitarian thinking became a widely known public philosophy, a social force. This was achieved by expanding the communitarian thesis to include not only the emphasis on the common good and social bonds but also the notion of balance between the communal and the personal, between individual rights and social responsibilities, and the notion of pluralism bounded by a core of shared values. And systematic efforts were made to take the message from academia to wider circles of those who influence opinion, political and community leaders, and the public at large. These efforts allowed communitarian

thinking to emerge as an influential public philosophy and, above all, to become
something of a social movement. (p. 40)

As communitarianism increasingly has taken on the call and the con-
tours of a social movement, its influence upon social institutions, especially upon education, has become both strong and controversial. A
primary challenge to the value of communitarianism as a movement for
reform within both society and education is this: "to determine the direction in which a specific communitarian society needs to move" (Etzioni,
1996, p. xix). Obviously, this point is of great relevance to the program-
matic design and pedagogical value of service-learning. To argue, as communitarians do, that individuals should be communal and socially
responsible and can be educated to these roles is also to raise the question
of what type of community and society shall be created to encompass
these values. It is not enough to argue, as Codispoti does, that we should
create service-learning programs that will educate students to embrace
social action and social responsibility in forging a new sense of community. It is also necessary to define what type of community we are advocating in the process. And here may well lie the rub, as Etzioni (1996) has
pointed out in stating that communitarians are often charged with "trying
to put a human face on conservative ideals" (p. xix). Consider this statement from Himmelfarb (1995), for example: "It is not enough, then, to
revitalize civil society. The more urgent, and difficult, task is to remoralize
civil society" (p. A9). Etzioni (1996) argues that such reasoning leads to
the charge that communitarians are "attempting to put a false normative
hue on liberal secular ideals" (p. xix).

The concept of shared values that Codispoti and other advocates of
communitarianism espouse would seem to suggest the idea of a community of communities when applied to social groups and social advocacy since, after all, not everyone can be expected to share the same values.
Even an attempt to educate students to particular shared values is problematic in terms of who shall determine which values are worthy of acceptance and emulation. Further, such a goal takes on a highly exhortatory
nature, and educational objectives based upon exhortation seldom achieve
the desired results, especially in the long run. If exhortation were an effective means for social improvement, nearly all religious movements
would have had greater success in molding the social order to their particular value schemes. Instead, it seems to be that exhortation works best
when it supports the one aspect of human character to which communitarians grant only limited status: self-interest. Codispoti does not provide
a convincing rationale for how exhortation will move those to be educated
through service-learning programs from self-interest to shared values and
social commitment. This is a major flaw in his argument and perhaps in
the philosophy of communitarianism itself.

Certainly there is merit to the premise that "a core of shared values enhances the ability of a society to formulate specific public policies" (Etzioni, 1996, p. 87). This seems to be a concept that Codispoti embraces in his claim that his concept of community is one of "community as a state of existence and a stance toward the world." While Codispoti does not directly state his allegiance to moral education, in my view he is certainly among those who advocate educational systems and processes that will instill moral virtue and its resultant commitment to civic investment and improvement. Such a concept is intellectually appealing; the question is how this goal is to be achieved. Much more is needed than an admixture of morality and apprenticeship learning to create the dynamic impact needed within service-learning to create the civic transformation Codispoti seeks.

For example, Etzioni (1996) states that the development and the extent of human virtue "depends on three conditions: first, on the internalization—rather than merely or mainly reinforcement—of values, on making them an integral part of self; second, on the evolution or development of social formations needed to undergird the given values; and, third, on reducing the inevitable contradiction between full order and full autonomy by making the main social formation more responsive to human nature" (pp. 165–166). Perhaps education, especially through service-learning programs, can provide the seedbed for the internalization of particular values within the self as part of a process of self-identity and self-determination. Certainly service-learning programs can provide the opportunity to become more broadly aware of a range of values and perspectives as well as of cultural and socioeconomic backgrounds. Codispoti sees this aspect of service-learning in its capacity to educate for multicultural awareness to be a major advantage of educational programs that place students within actual communities "in different physical locations" and thus enable students to "live among various groups of people during their lives." The problem is, though, how does one distinguish this experience from study abroad, let's say? Both experiences would be enriching in broadening perspectives and understandings. However, how does one move from the experience to the next phases of the development of human virtue that Codispoti and communitarians seek? In other words, how does one—or how does an educational program—move beyond the quality of the experience as a learning venture to an experience that translates into a commitment to community, social responsibility, and civic action?

ETHICS AS SOCIAL ACTION: COMMUNITARIAN PERSPECTIVES

Not surprisingly, Codispoti and many of the other communitarian writers are short on the specifics of how this can be achieved. At best Codispoti can advocate for an inclusive pedagogy of ethics. In this regard he is an advocate of education for character development. Codispoti would find little argument in contemporary educational circles for his views that ethics cannot be taught in isolation if society seeks to educate individuals who will act in ethical ways. Nearly all educators would agree with this premise since the experience of education has historically been identified with transformation and opportunity; however, many might disagree on the issue of how educated students contribute to the betterment of the community and solve community problems. Those who would seek to address these concerns and to structure programs that would achieve these aims would need to operate from an agenda—especially from a belief system that defined civic responsibility. Perhaps they would be operating from the modality that Etzioni (1996) describes—a communitarian paradigm that "applies the notion of the golden rule at the societal level, to characterize the good society as one that nourishes both social virtues and individual rights" (p. 4). However they were to proceed, though, they would still need to have a clear sense of the relationship of education to virtuous human conduct and also a clear understanding of how one influences the other in achieving the outcome of the betterment of society and the individual.

Even if, as a number of theorists contend, communitarianism in its contemporary manifestation is no more than a reworking of conservative values in an era perceived to be one of liberal excess, there is a necessary historicity to this process of reworking values. As Etzioni (1996) points out:

A good, communitarian society . . . requires more than seeing the whole; it calls on those who are socially aware and active, people of insight and conscience, to throw themselves to the side opposite that toward which history is tilting. This is not because all virtue is on that opposite side, but because if the element that the society is neglecting will continue to be deprived of support, the society will become either oppressive or anarchic, ceasing to be a good society, if it does not collapse altogether. Once the communitarian checklist (what is lacking, and to what extent?) of a particular society is drawn up, the specifics required for its return to equilibrium must be examined. (p. xx)

Eyler and Giles (1997) point out that service-learning has now moved in its history and maturation from being primarily a "practitioner enterprise" to an "educational philosophy and pedagogical approach" whose primary aim is to instill a greater capacity for "critical reflection" in students (pp. 57–58). No doubt this guiding principle is central to the philosophy of communitarianism, which also seeks to instill a greater capacity for critical reflection in those who participate in service-learning programs. For communitarianism, the focus of that critical reflection should be upon social responsibility, which is perceived to be a function of a moral and virtuous understanding of the relationship of humans as communal and interdependent beings. Communitarianism resonates with the current thinking on service-learning in asserting that the best learning takes place in real settings versus the general type of educational knowledge that is "largely abstracted from experience" (Denise & Harris, 1989, p. 20).

EDUCATION AND SOCIAL RESPONSIBILITY: COMMUNAL VALUES AND COMMITMENT

Though communitarianism does support a number of fundamental principles of service-learning as an educational philosophy and experience, the question still remains of what aims communitarianism can achieve within this educational model. Codispoti seems to feel that a radical transformation of the student, the educational experience, and the community can be achieved through a communitarian approach to service-learning. He writes:

Service-learning must involve real situations. Civic education requires that students struggle with the complexities and uncertainties of real life so that they can learn to be realistic and so that their learning can be maximized. At the same time, the situations must be on an appropriate scale so that the students can make a real contribution. The goal of a real situation is not to discourage students but to have them learn from experience that they can be effective. Situations must also be real so that students have to work with people who have a genuine stake in the outcomes. Students should get used to the passion, commitment, stubbornness, and worry that people display when things matter.

While finding merit in some aspects of Codispoti's argument, I would still contend that it is a flawed methodology because it depends too heavily upon assumptions about human nature, character, and actions that seem more idealistic than realistic and more theoretical than practical. Certainly the communitarian argument that each individual self is encumbered by its social roles and cannot be understood apart from those roles is a compelling argument in many ways. Where the difficulty resides in implementing this view, though, is in the merit of the opposite argument regarding how much individuals can be expected to embrace social roles and social responsibilities for which they do not feel an inherent identification. In other words, to what extent can they be compelled to act in a manner that others (the community) may regard as virtuous? Ultimately, as well, how can education function to promote virtuous actions, especially through service-learning within community settings that draws upon the immediate experience of real situations and upon the critical reflections of the participants? Answers to some aspects of these questions may be found in communitarianism; however, Codispoti does not provide them to us in his essay nor point us in profitable directions for the types of critical reflection that both communitarianism and service-learning endorse.

Part of the reason for this deficiency is that Codispoti is arguing for the lesser of evils, or at least the lesser of limited perspectives. For example, he finds the civic and the philanthropic models to be deficient in their understanding of long-term goals. The philanthropic model encourages students to embrace philanthropy, and the civic model encourages students to seek social justice. While there are advantages to both approaches and possible ethical outcomes, the main problem for Codispoti is that both have "the advantage of doing little to disturb or change the academic world the student inhabits" and thus both models place "few demands on faculty or students to change their academic activities or the content of courses." In supporting communitarianism, Codispoti must argue that this model has the greatest potential for transforming academic practice; however, his argument is not convincing because it does not address the major obstacles to the types of wholesale collaboration and of communal instruction that have not transformed education during the last quarter of the twentieth century in the ways that communitarians would seek. Similarly, Codispoti recognizes the enormous obstacles represented by the rewards system in academics in which research is often rewarded as the highest level of achievement in merit, tenure, and promotion decisions. Curricular innovation and creative teaching may find a measure of support within academics, but even Codispoti acknowledges that any teacher who undertakes such a transformation of his or her pedagogy does so at some risk and also must have broad institutional support to have any hope of being successful. Codispoti states:

The individual professor who attempts to use this approach without the strong support of his or her colleagues, department chair, or dean is likely to be undertaking work that will require a great deal of time and bring little reward. In fact, the professor will be violating the well-established rules for emphasizing research to achieve tenure and promotion. Further, the individual will find his or her class so out of step with the experiences students have in other classes that it will be hard to achieve the changes in outlook and understanding that are central to this approach.

Codispoti goes on to point out that the reforms he advocates are similar to the calls for educational reform presented by Boyer (1987, 1990) and are best served by a communitarian agenda. Aside from the fact that a number of Boyer's premises about restructuring the faculty rewards system have lately been called into question (Diamond, 1994), some theorists,

chief among them Lenker and Moxley (1995), contend that what will re-
structure the rewards system is not the type of curricular reforms Codispoti advocates, but instead, the challenge that will truly "transform the
academic reward system lies ahead in the networked, electronic community" (p. ix). In other words, the Internet will have the greatest impact
upon creating a communal academic enterprise. Interestingly, though, the
type of communalism created may or may not reflect communitarian values or a refocusing of ethical commitment to the social community. Once
again, we return to the consummate dilemma of communitarianism as a
philosophy—that is, communal action in itself cannot guarantee an ethical
response or commitment from the participants.

In this regard, I find it to be of paramount importance that Codispoti
states he draws his views of community from Tinder (1980), who argues
that humans are inquirers who search for the ground of their essential
being in all activities of life (p. 17). In *The Political Meaning of Christianity:
An Interpretation* (1990), Tinder argues for a prophetic stance that involves
a questioning attitude toward all forms of established authority, together
with a recognition of Christianity as a means of addressing the broader
ills of mass society, especially the breakdown of community and the pervasive alienation of the contemporary world. In this regard, Tinder is similar to other communitarians who argue for a rejection of contemporary
liberalism and a return to a more conservative view of society and politics.
The reason for this change is the argument that liberalism has failed to
provide a true sense of community and has offered, instead, only the
temporary alliances generated by fads, likes, dislikes, and fleeting causes.

My concern with Tinder is not that his work is often and largely an
advocacy of Christian values in the guise of an advocacy for political
reform. Instead, I am interested in the fact that Codispoti draws from a
minor communitarian philosopher while never once referencing Etzioni,
who is the acknowledged founding father of communitarianism. In *The
Spirit of Community* (1994) and *The New Golden Rule: Community and Morality in a Democratic Society* (1998), Etzioni has moved the typical debate
of liberalism versus communitarianism beyond the conventional black/
white dichotomies and has called for a new balance between individual
rights and social responsibility. I sense that Codispoti may be calling for
the same type of balance in the institutional reforms he advocates, but
there is no clear expression of how that balance is to be achieved. Certainly, and clearly, he calls for a restructuring of the rewards system in
academics so that more emphasis can be placed upon reworking traditional pedagogy into communal pedagogy. Aside from arguing that this
cannot be done alone but must be an institutional commitment, he does
not tell us how to get to that commitment in the current academic climate.
I sense he would prefer an academy that is persuaded by reason to embrace higher ideals and ethical stances; however, in contemporary times,

the academy is being reshaped more into a corporate entity and culture than into a bastion of ethical ideals and actions.

CONCLUSION

To state, though, that the concepts Codispoti advocates may be difficult to achieve is not a sufficient reason in itself to refute the power or the appeal of many aspects of communitarianism. The greater concern is that Codispoti's views of what communitarianism can bring to academics and to contemporary life are repetitions of previous nineteenth-century debates between individualism and collectivism—or, more precisely, between human individuality and the human social nature. In many ways, these concepts derive from Hegel's philosophy (Williams, 2000), and the complexities of how self-interest and communal interests can be navigated by individuals as they form groups and group alliances may represent an eternal problem. I do not argue with this complexity or seek to minimize the significance of the questions communitarianism raises for consideration. Instead, I argue that the application of communitarian ideas to academics—particularly as Codispoti has presented those ideas—is unlikely to achieve the goals and the ideals Codispoti claims. Fundamentally, I would contend that these types of changes will not occur without a radical transformation of human nature itself. Although certainly education can achieve this on a small scale with some individuals, the communitarian model Codispoti describes is no more likely or unlikely to achieve this goal than the philanthropic or civic models that he dismisses as inadequate. Each will reach those who find their goals persuasive, and each will generate aspects of the transformations of heart and mind that Codispoti envisions as essential to restoring a sense of community to contemporary education and society. As for the radical transformation of the political, social, and educational systems that Codispoti also sees as essential, that outcome is unlikely to occur. Essentially, service-learning is being asked by Codispoti to carry too great a load within a philosophy that does not offer a viable means of radical transformation of institutions. Absent such a broad option of change, the case Codispoti makes for the communitarian model is no stronger than the case he makes against the philanthropic and civic models of service-learning.

REFERENCES

Bereiter, Carl (1994). Constructivism, socioculturalism, and Popper's World 3. *Educational Researcher*, 23(7): 21–23.

Blakely, E. J. (1979). *Community development research: Concepts, issues and strategies.* New York: Human Sciences Press.

Boyer, E. (1987). *College: The undergraduate experience in America.* New York: Harper & Row.

Boyer, E. (1990). *Scholarship reconsidered: Priorities of the professoriate.* Princeton, NJ: Carnegie Foundation for the Advancement of Teaching.

Denise, P. S., & Harris, I. M. (1989). *Experiential education for community development.* Westport, CT: Greenwood Press.

Dewey, J. (1938). *Experience and education.* New York: Collier Books.

Diamond, R. M. (1994). The tough task of reforming the faculty-reward system. *Chronicle of Higher Education,* p. A14.

Etzioni, A. (1994). *The spirit of community.* New York: Touchstone Books.

Etzioni, A. (1998). *The new golden rule: Community and morality in a democratic society.* New York: Basic Books.

Eyler, J., & Giles, D., Jr. (1997). The importance of program quality in service-learning. In A. S. Waterman (Ed.), *Service-learning: Applications from the research* (pp. 57–76). Mahwah, NJ: Lawrence Erlbaum.

Gergen, K. J. (2001). *Social construction in context.* London: Sage.

Himmelfarb, G. (7 February 1995). Re-moralizing America: Beyond social policy. *Wall Street Journal,* p. A22, A26.

Jardine, M. (1998). Are communitarians "premodern" or "postmodern"? The place of communitarian thought in contemporary political theory. In P. A. Lawler & D. McConkey (Eds.), *Community and political thought today* (pp. 27–38). Westport, CT: Praeger.

Lawler, P. A. (2002). *Aliens in America: The strange truth about our souls.* Wilmington, DE: Intercollegiate Studies Institute.

Lenker, L. T., & Moxley, J. M. (1995). *The politics and processes of scholarship.* Westport, CT: Greenwood Press.

MacIntyre, A. (1997). *After virtue: A study in moral theory.* South Bend, IN: University of Notre Dame Press.

McClay, W. (1998). Communitarianism and the federal idea. In P. A. Lawler & D. McConkey (Eds.), *Community and political thought today* (pp. 101–107). Westport, CT: Praeger.

Phillips, D. C. (1995). The good, the bad and the ugly: The many faces of constructivism. *Educational Researcher, 24* (7), 5–12.

Sandel, M. J. (1996). *Democracy's discontent: America in search of a public philosophy.* Cambridge, MA: Harvard University Press.

Sandel, M. J. (1998). *Liberalism and the limits of justice.* Cambridge, UK: Cambridge University Press.

Selznick, P. (1992). *The moral commonwealth: Social theory and the promise of community.* Berkeley: University of California Press.

Stanton, T. K., Giles, D. E., Jr., & Cruz, N. I. (1999). *Service-learning: A movement's pioneers reflect on its origins, practice, and future.* San Francisco: Jossey-Bass.

Stone, B. S. (1998). Universal benevolence, adjective justice, and the Rousseauean way. In P. A. Lawler & D. McConkey (Eds.), *Community and political thought today* (pp. 83–100). Westport, CT: Praeger.

Taylor, C. (1989). *Sources of the self: The making of the modern identity.* Cambridge, MA: Harvard University Press.

Tinder, G. (1980). *Community: Reflections on a tragic ideal.* Baton Rouge: Louisiana State University Press.

Tinder, G. (1990). *The political meaning of Christianity: An interpretation.* Baton Rouge: Louisiana State University Press.

Tomm, K. (1998). Co-constructing responsibility. In K. J. Gergen & S. McNamee (Eds.), *Relational responsibility : Resources for sustainable dialogue* (pp. 129–138). London: Sage.

Walzer, M. (1984). *Spheres of justice: A defense of pluralism and equality.* New York: Basic Books.

Williams, R. R. (2000). *Beyond liberalism and communitarianism: Studies in Hegel's philosophy of right.* Albany: State University of New York Press.

CHAPTER 9

A Synthesis of the Theoretical Stances

Sherry L. Hoppe

INTRODUCTION

Although many faculty (especially those of the liberal arts ilk) may see service-learning as superfluous and intrusive in their curriculum, others see the merits of linking classroom pursuits with the broader aspects of life. For those who have yet to see that connection (and perhaps just as importantly, for those who *have* embraced the practicality of service-learning), an understanding of theoretical roots may serve as a stimulus for defining the basis and justification for service in the learning process. Thus, the preceding six chapters, delineating the merits and criticisms of the civic, philanthropic, and communitarian theories underpinning service-learning, warrant synthesizing for those who want to discern the differences and similarities as they consider and plan service-learning programs.

The synthesis of the theoretical stances of service-learning must first begin with an acknowledgement that these stances drive multiple definitions of service-learning—from simple community service and public service to practical applications outside the college's walls of knowledge acquired *within* those ivy-covered walls. Speck (2001), after citing three definitions elucidating the above, posits the existence of two common threads: (1) separation and (2) integration and engagement. The very words Speck uses imply difference, not commonality, but he aptly ties the differences together. Students, according to Speck (2001), study in an environment absent a real-world context. Their studies *could*, however, serve as the means to integrate them into public life if the students were required to engage in relationships and work in the larger community outside the institution.

Speck's (2001) common threads tie together the theoretical foundations of the three models presented in chapters 3–8. Abel, in chapter 3, posits neutrality regarding social issues as the proper basis for the philanthropic model and contrasts it to the civic model's dependence on partisanship. Sementelli, in chapter 4, poses a contrast between neutrality and altruism as the basis for the philanthropic model. In chapter 5, Watson asserts that the civic theory emanates from both a civic renewal and a social justice approach. Exley, in chapter 6, expands that twofold approach to include two additional philosophies: liberal democracy and participatory democracy. In chapters 7 and 8, Codispoti and Murphy pick up the liberal view of the civic approach as they contrast it to the communitarian approach. Murphy, though, criticizes Codispoti's stance as being too nostalgic about idealized communities of the past and asserts that communitarianism must move service-learning away from the traditional liberal approach of sustaining cultural structures and more toward embracing a new paradigm of culture defined as a community of communities.

With such diverse and overlapping theories, how can the most appropriate foundation for service-learning in a particular institution be formulated? This chapter's synthesis attempts to summarize in some detail the essence of each theory, beginning with the short descriptions in the preceding paragraph, followed by an assessment of the strengths and weaknesses of each philosophical base with implications for translating the theory into practice in service-learning classrooms and experiences.

PHILANTHROPIC APPROACH

As noted above, Abel, in chapter 3, asserts that the philanthropic model must place neutrality regarding social issues at its core, while Sementelli argues that current scholarship grounds the philanthropic model in the concepts of altruism and compensatory justice. Althaus (1997) adds another dimension to this disagreement with a focus on different levels of service in service-learning. Kahne and Westheimer's differentiation (as cited in Althaus, 1997) between students who engage in direct service and those who engage in social activism and advocacy illustrates the similarity between charity and change. Althaus (1997) believes charity and change, while seemingly dichotomous, are really just alternative forms of serving and learning. Althaus asserts one must simply determine the relationship of change and charity to a framework of morality, politics, and intellectualism. The concepts, according to Althaus, intertwine and cannot be ranked in terms of value.

Building on Althaus's (1997) premise, one might be able to blend charity, social change, altruism, social justice, and compensatory justice into a theoretical stance for philanthropic service-learning. First, though, defining some of the above attributes is important:

Charity: the liberal giving of gifts to the poor based on love and goodness

Social change: the impetus to address the ills of society through addressing systemic causes

Altruism: giving based on an obligation to pay back

Compensatory justice: the obligation of the fortunate or well-off to help the less fortunate or disadvantaged

Social justice: bringing about a more equitable distribution of society's wealth

Can one take these definitions as the basis for the philanthropic approach and still maintain the neutrality deemed essential by Abel in chapter 3? He insists that the best way to develop community is to provide an educational environment in which students are allowed to grapple with issues and come to their own conclusions. Abel grounds this view in liberalism, asserting that educational institutions have the responsibility to be neutral in presenting competing conceptions of the good life. This neutrality extends to determining what gives life value and thus to social, political, and economic positions. These positions should, according to Abel's liberalistic approach, stem individually from neutral and abstract debate. Going a step further, Abel asserts that determining precisely an individual's true interest is conceptually impossible, as is ascertaining the true interests of communities or nations. Abstraction and neutrality, then, will lead to service in the form of personal engagement chosen individually—not based on someone's preconceived notion of social good. Clearly, Abel's self-described "bias toward liberty" allows considerable leeway in determining what constitutes the good life and what an individual wants to contribute to help others attain it.

Sementelli takes a different stance, asserting that the philanthropic model of service-learning begins with a perceived need for charity. This position advocates altruism over neutrality as the basis for the philanthropic model and goes even further by requiring the existence of a relationship between the student participating in service-learning and those who are the recipients of the benefits of the service. Such a relationship, according to Sementelli, must be based on the recognition by the students that they have social and economic benefits not available to those they are serving and that they have an obligation to serve those less fortunate than they. (Sementelli thus comingles the above definitions of altruism and charity.) Dating back to feudal times, this concept of noblesse oblige places a burden of service on those born into social status and wealth. While less dramatic in the twenty-first century, the basis of the philanthropic model as described by Sementelli defines a giver-receiver relationship as its core motivation. He is quick to note, though, that grounding service-learning in such a charitable approach may fit religious socialization needs but raises questions about appropriateness in public institutions.

Sementelli also questions the effectiveness of the philanthropic model in other ways, including its minimization of interpretation and reflection. If the primary goal of the philanthropic model is to provide assistance to disadvantaged individuals, Sementelli challenges its usefulness beyond that provision of help or relief. He uses his assessment that the philanthropic model achieves only two of the four goals set out by the Commission on National and Community Service to further diminish its value. Acknowledging that students can learn and develop through thoughtfully organized service experiences that meet community needs, Sementelli expresses concern that the philanthropic model fails to integrate service-learning into the students' academic curriculum. He also fears that the philanthropic model falls short on providing structured time for students to think, talk, or write about what they experienced in the service-learning activity. Moreover, he avows that philanthropic-based service-learning fails to provide students adequate opportunities to use newly acquired skills in real-life experiences in their own communities. At the same time, he affirms that the philanthropic model does make some effort to socialize students into acting on behalf of someone else.

What, then, is the value of the philanthropic approach in service-learning? Do its shortcomings outweigh its altruistic benefits? If the goal of service-learning is to provide service to those needing it and to create in students a sense of their responsibility to do so, the model has merit. However, if the goal is to create opportunities to explore that responsibility in terms of liberal learning—to reflect on the justice or lack thereof in the world and one's role in influencing justice—then a model based on civic responsibility may be a better choice. If one must choose between a relationship based on gratitude or paying back and one based on civic interdependency, service-learning faculty in the twenty-first century may determine that charity is paternalistic and marginalizes those it seeks to help. A society built on equality should support service-learning based on civic responsibility that leads toward recognition that all share in that responsibility and benefit from its acceptance. The philanthropic model fosters differences and limits civic growth, leading away from community building rather than toward inclusion and participation. It may provide social welfare, but it fails to address needed change in the social systems and social order that create the need for charity in the first place. Redistribution of wealth because of a perceived obligation for the philanthropy is a short-term fix for society's injustices.

CIVIC APPROACH

Battistoni (1997) succinctly summarizes the difference between the civic view and the philanthropic view in noting that the first "emphasizes mutual responsibility and the interdependence of rights and responsibilities," focusing "not on altruism but on enlightened self-interest" (p. 151). He adds that "the idea is not that the well-off 'owe' something to the less fortunate, but that free democratic communities depend on mutual responsibility and that rights without obligations are ultimately not sustainable" (p. 151).

The conflict between the civic approach and the philanthropic one is further delineated by Speck (2001), who avers that the more radical civic model assumes four underlying factors: "(1) the American social order is fragmented, lacking a sense of community, (2) lack of community has produced injustices of various kinds, (3) higher education is deeply implicated in the perpetuation of injustice, and (4) higher education must be radically transformed to meet its obligation to produce citizens who can promote justice in a democratic society" (p. 5). Speck contrasts these assumptions to the more simplistic basis of the philanthropic model, which he describes as an additive approach, whereby a community or public service component is simply added to the standard classroom activities.

Speck's fourfold assumption supports the premise of Watson in chapter 5 that the civic theory emanates from both a civic renewal and a social justice approach. Further examination of this theory almost inevitably leads one to John Dewey, whose theory of democratic education was a move away from the aristocratic theory of education and society advocated by Plato (Harkavy & Benson, 1998). Watson's failure to address this theoretical underpinning is a notable absence, since most discussions of service-learning begin with an acknowledgement of Dewey's contributions to civic education. Speck noted that "those who advocate the civic approach to service-learning insist that the academy must be transformed to fit the impulse that drove John Dewey to promote 'knowledge as a tool for creating a just society'" (2001, p. 6). Speck declares such knowledge moves citizens to participate fully in the decision making of politics with the ultimate outcome of eradicating social evils.

Harkavy and Benson (1998) delineate this knowledge base as: (1) actively responding to the challenge of the environment through reflective thought; (2) learning through participation in the formulation of purpose preceding activity; and (3) improving human welfare as the fundamental purpose of knowledge. According to Harkavy and Benson, while Dewey did not originate all of these propositions, his theory of instrumental intelligence and democratic education advanced and integrated them. Dewey held that the American public school system was "radically antithetical to American democratic ideals" (Harkavy & Benson, 1998, p. 16). Admitting that Dewey's writings did not specifically address service-learning, Harkavy and Benson assert he believed that real-world problem solving requiring informed judgment and action would advance both democracy and learning. Combined with Dewey's advocacy for an ethical democracy in which relations would be determined by "equity of justice, not the inequality of conferring benefits" (Dewey, 1908, as quoted in Morton & Saltmarsh, 1997, p. 142), one can safely assume that Dewey would have found the civic approach to service-learning more palatable than the philanthropic approach.

Despite Watson's failure in chapter 5 to credit Dewey's contributions to the civic theory underlying a significant approach to service-learning, he does adopt many of the attributes of Dewey's philosophical stance. He supports Elshtain's (1997) premise that service-learning can help reverse the decline in democratic processes and asserts that civic renewal promotes collaborative relationships and critical thinking skills in the development of public policies. He adds to this process the development of an understanding of democratic citizenship and a service ethic that results in civic leadership, all of which would meet Dewey's goals for an ethical democracy and lead toward Dewey's pursuit of "the equity of justice." It also supports the second of Watson's two bases in chapter 5 for civic theory: social justice and civic renewal. Unfortunately, Watson never discusses those bases in a theoretical framework—he simply cites and touts the model of civic engagement that undergirds movements such as *Greater Expectations,* the National Commission on Civic Renewal, *Mapping Civic Engagement in Higher Education,* and numerous others. He makes the case for a strong conceptual framework, but he utterly fails to provide any theory as a foundation for service-learning based on civic engagement. Watson, in this writer's opinion, misses the opportunity to position the civic approach effectively.

A civic approach to service-learning might seemingly mirror a definition of social justice that surrounds a social construction of reality. Framing social justice in the context of individuals who begin with separate interests but become engaged in determining equitable distributions of opportunities and rights can move one back toward the noblesse oblige of the philanthropic model, acknowledging "privilege and non-privilege in the social order" as described by Butler (as cited by Watson). One can move further in that direction when considering Couto (as cited by Watson) in respect to "the haves and the have-nots" as the basis for civic engagement from a social justice perspective. Yet a careful analysis of the theoretical base of civic learning would refute such a comparison. Unfortunately, Watson never makes this distinction, leaving the reader to seek an analysis of the overlapping yet contrasting theories elsewhere.

Although Watson fails to support his advocacy with historical or theoretical bases, he does clearly and strongly support service-learning based on civic engagement. In contrast, Exley's chapter 6 begins with queries about the efficacy of the civic approach. Despite his questions, he does believe that a fundamental goal of higher education is civic engagement—he just maintains that it is not the panacea some envision. Specifically, he declares that using civic engagement as the model for service-learning must go beyond just social justice and civic renewal. Is it necessary that philosophies underlying service-learning embrace both liberal democracy and participatory democracy? Relationships between the individuals and the state are critical, as is building the capacity of individuals for self-government. Exley apparently believes that social justice alone—defined as bringing about a more equitable distribution of society's wealth—is an inadequate basis for service-learning. Otherwise, an extended approach to the philanthropic theory might suffice. Service must, according to Exley, define citizenship. Service-learning must connect students to experiences in their communities in a way that builds a lifetime commitment to such service.

Exley also makes an important point in his assertion that each individual faculty member's personal beliefs and educational philosophy will provide the bases for the use of a unique combination of models and definitions of service-learning. He notes that a given university might have multiple approaches to service-learning based on faculty interest and philosophy. He supports such diversity and freedom strongly, but others might advocate a common theoretical base if service-learning is to be tied directly to an institution's mission and values.

Even though he identifies diverse approaches to civic-based service-learning, Exley is quick to note that such approaches all have weaknesses. His first concern is that practitioners might underestimate the power of service-learning to overly influence developing minds to adopt the positions of their instructors. According to Exley, faculty members with too strong a propensity to social justice may not allow for dissenting opinions. A second concern arises from a failure to operate from a clear theoretical foundation. If Exley bases this concern on Watson's chapter, it is well founded. However, the civic approach is well grounded in theory, beginning (as noted above) with Dewey's philosophy. The third weakness noted by Exley, a failure to prepare for the experience, would be applicable to service-learning regardless of the theoretical base and would appear to be a weakness only if a course failed to address the three questions posed by Exley (the questions relate to the philosophical base for a service-learning course, the content and its emphasis on reflection, and the need to ensure that service-learning is an integral part of the course rather than just an add-on assignment). The final weakness identified by Exley is merely a repetition of his premise that the power of a faculty member may have a personal impact on students. In this writer's opinion, Exley fails to make his case for weaknesses of the civic approach to service-learning because his reasoning is too broad based and could easily encompass all or any of the three major theories discussed in the preceding chapters.

Speck (2001) counters much of Exley's argument against the civic approach to service-learning, referring to Dewey's promotion of knowledge as a means of creating a society that is just and equitable. Knowledge, according to Speck, moves citizens toward full participation in political decision making and thus toward eradication of social evils. Empowerment to change democratic society and to oppose oppression is possible in a classroom where "equals meet and form communities based on mutual respect to support each other as they identify with communities outside the classroom—communities broken and bleeding because they have been oppressed and treated unjustly. In meeting in the classroom to provide a staging area for the offense against injustice, students and professors create a community that practices the values they will promote in the new society" (Speck, 2001, p. 7). Speck uses his words to support the civic approach to service-learning, but his advocacy might just as easily be applicable to the communitarian model, thus leading to this book's third and final option for a philosophical basis for service-learning.

COMMUNITARIAN MODEL

When reading Codispoti's chapter on the communitarian model, one sometimes finds it difficult to distinguish it from the civic model—not surprisingly, considering Speck's (2001) advocacy noted above as being dually applicable. Codispoti seemingly bases his view of the communitarian model on democratic citizenship as it relates to an open and inclusive community. While this concept has merit, Murphy's chapter 8 challenges this basis as being too liberal. She alleges that a liberal-oriented education is premised on "outdated concepts of individualism and autonomy in relation to community and social action." She contends that service-learning cannot be effectively defined in such a context and that communitarianism offers a better choice as students are prepared for self-government because it provides a balance between the rights of individuals and their social responsibilities.

Hepburn (1997) grounds community service in this balance between individual and community, quoting Dunn's statement in 1907 that "The best of your life comes from participation in the life of your community . . . giving to and receiving from the community's life" (Hepburn, p. 1). One of the first American educators to "propose practical educational experiences to teach interdependence within the community and personal responsibility in the community" (Hepburn, p. 1), Dunn espoused that community life began in school. He saw the individual's life as inextricably tied to the community's life, and this writer sees in his philosophy a clear basis for service-learning grounded in all aspects of community life—not just civic but also social. Even Dewey (1908, as cited in Hatcher, 1997) could conceivably have been as strong an advocate for the communitarian model as for the civic model. Hatcher (1997) draws upon Saltmarsh (1996) to describe "Dewey's contribution to the pedagogy of community service-learning and challenges service-learning educators to go beyond the limits of Dewey's 'pragmatic communitarianism' to pursue social justice as an integrated and essential aspect of community service-learning" (Hatcher, p. 23). Despite Dewey's prediction that the machine age would eventually destroy community and perhaps even threaten democracy, he still avowed the sanctity of individual capacities and the association of citizens one with another as the means for promoting humane conditions (Hatcher, p. 23).

What, then, is the definition of communitarianism? Murphy alludes to a "community of communities." She challenges Codispoti's definition of "concerned members of communities who share common values and are responsible to each other and for their community" as too sketchy, yet her definition is more elusive and obtuse. She objects to his requirement for common values and social responsibility toward the community as a whole and complains that he is being nostalgic in his picture of an "idealized communal past." She references Jardine's (1998) statement about this nostalgia and its affinity for a "kind of closet socialism." She also opposes communitarianism on the basis that it stems from "centralized regulation in the name of community." With all of Murphy's objections to what communitarianism is *not*, the reader is still left wondering what it is. We can discern that it is a move away from liberalism. We can decipher its commitment to communal individuals who are socially responsible. And we can consider Etzioni's (1996) position that "communitarians are often charged with 'trying to put a human face on conservative ideals'" (see chapter 8). We can also be informed by Codispoti's assertion that individuals are social creatures who are all members of a larger social fabric. Codispoti extends his description of social creatures as "members of a community who share common values and are responsible to each other and for their community" (see chapter 7). All of this leads Murphy back to a community of communities that is applied to social groups and social advocacy, but she is quick to note that the shared values noted by Codispoti and other advocates of communitarianism may not be achievable.

Interestingly, it also leads her to an approach close to the civic theory discussed in chapters 5 and 6, because she expands her community of communities to social responsibility and civic action. The paradigm Murphy borrows from Etzioni "applies the notion of the golden rule at the societal level, to characterize the good society as one that nourishes both social values and individual rights." Individual rights in the community lead one to civic education, and this requires a contribution to the community and one's fellow students, according to Codispoti. Murphy clearly ties communitarianism to a "reworking of conservative values in an era perceived to be one of liberal excess." She cites Etzioni to define what is required of a communitarian society: not just the capacity to see the whole but a commitment to be socially aware and active. She also draws on Eyler and Giles (1997) in asserting that the guiding principle for communitarianism is "to instill a greater capacity for 'critical reflection' on social responsibility" (see chapter 8). The relationship of humans as communal and interdependent beings thus forms the basis for communitarianism, according to Murphy. She remains unconvinced, though, that service-learning can force on students the kind of social roles and social responsibilities this requires. Real situations and critical reflections of service-learning participants may enhance their learning, but Murphy questions whether they can be compelled to adopt virtuous actions if they do not have the requisite theoretical base and philosophical stance to give them the propensity and commitment to serve their communities.

IMPLICATIONS OF THE THEORIES FOR SERVICE-LEARNING APPLICATIONS

Morton and Saltmarsh (1997) argue that community service is "a modern concept emerging out of the collision of capitalism and democracy at the turn of the century" (p. 137). They extend this concept by asserting that the collision is generated from "a crisis of community and a profound rethinking of the meaning and practice of charity, which resulted in the definition of three 'paths' of service: the nonprofit human service organization; a strong federal government and active citizenship supported by democratic education; and the creation of alternative communities which reject many of the values of capitalism and democracy in favor of more humane or spiritual values" (p. 137). Morton and Saltmarsh's comments form the basis for an argument that the philanthropic, civic, and communitarian models have intersecting points. Taking their definition of service-learning, "the integration of community service with intentional, structured learning" (p. 137), it is possible to apply the term *community service* to charity, to public affairs, and to communities. Indeed, Morton and Saltmarsh declare that in the 1930s community service had extended to three different sectors: nonprofits, education and public policy, and countercultural responses.

Is it necessary, then, for a university to have a single theoretical basis for its service-learning programs? Would it be possible to formulate a theoretical base that is broad enough to encompass the essence of the philanthropic, civic, and communitarian approaches? Would this not give faculty the academic freedom they desire to incorporate service-learning into courses based on a combination of the discipline subject matter and the professor's own philosophy? I believe the answer to each of the above questions is a resounding *yes*. Students gravitate toward or consciously choose majors based on their own beliefs, values, and aspirations. Thus, a nursing major (and likewise a nursing faculty member) might well embrace a philanthropic-based service-learning program while a history or political science student or faculty member might see more applicability in the civic approach. Likewise, a social work or sociology professor or student likely would see the merits of a communitarian approach.

In essence, if one takes the position that an individual student or professor should be able to define his or her own community for applying concepts learned in the classroom, one could even find room for all three approaches to operate simultaneously on a college campus. Taken to the extreme, one might even detect leeway to allow individual students to choose from one of the three approaches regardless of the discipline. This would certainly make a faculty member's integration of classroom learning and service-learning more complicated. In addition, Furco's (2001) premise that the theories of constructivism and experiential education form the roots of service-learning might seem to argue against the above multiple theoretical base approach. However, he cites a number of experts in defining service-learning as "a teaching strategy that enhances students' learning of academic content by engaging them in authentic activities in which they apply the content of the course to address identified needs in the local and broader community" (p. 67). This definition lends itself to a discipline-related approach.

CONCLUSION

Regardless of the theoretical base or the single/multiple approach discussed above, service-learning has the potential for addressing a crisis of community in the twenty-first century that is as problematic as the one defined by Dewey, Addams, and Day in the early 1800s. According to Morton and Saltmarsh (1997), this crisis was one of "social, political, intellectual and moral fragmentation" (p. 139). Addams, Day, and Dewey saw the "fragmentation of a unified American culture by the combined forces of industrialization, urbanization, and immigration, and by the increasing centralization of political and economic power in the hands of a private, industrial elite" (p. 139). While some might argue that the crisis has changed today by the political and social forces accompanying globalization, technology, and social welfare, few would argue that a crisis of community does not exist today and that fragmentation is at the root of it. Questions of equality, justice, and citizenship in a democratic society are fertile ground for service-learning regardless of the philosophical basis. Dewey's shift in defining *charity* from an assumption of a superior and inferior class to a definition based on the well-being of society as a whole as being more "constructive and expansive" (Morton and Saltmarsh, 1997, p. 142) may preclude a noblesse oblige component of service-learning theory, but it leaves the door open for a charitable or altruistic base for practical applications of learning. Dewey's aim of charity as "general social advance, constructive social reform" (as quoted in Morton and Saltmarsh,

1997, p. 142) and his basis for relationships "in an ethical democracy" as being determined by "the equity of justice, not the inequality of conferring benefits" (as quoted in Morton and Saltmarsh, 1997, p. 142) are not antithetical to a multitheoretical approach. Charity and justice combined, then, could form the basis of a service-learning model that adds practicality to learning while preparing students for citizenship *and* community life. The goal of service-learning should be an informed and unbiased study of social and civic issues, resulting in a commitment to participation in solving those issues for the benefit of individuals and the good of society as a whole.

REFERENCES

Althaus, J. (1997). Service-learning and leadership development: Posing questions not answers. *Michigan Journal of Community Service-Learning, 4*, 122–129.

Battistoni, R. (1997). Service-learning and democratic citizenship. *Theory into Practice, 36*(3), 150–156.

Elshtain, J. (1997). The decline of democratic faith. In R. Battistoni & W. Hudson (Eds.), *Practicing democracy: Concepts and models of service-learning in political science* (pp. 9–14). Washington, DC: American Association of Higher Education.

Etzioni, A. (1996). *The new golden rule: Community and morality in a democratic society.* New York: Basic Books.

Eyler, J., & Giles, D., Jr. (1997). The importance of program quality in service-learning. In A. A. Waterman (Ed.), *Service-learning: Applications from the research* (pp. 57–76). Mahwah, NJ: Lawrence Erlbaum.

Furco, A. (2001). Advancing service-learning at research universities. In M. Canada & B. Speck (Eds.), *Developing and implementing service-learning programs* (pp. 67–78). New Directions for Higher Education, no. 114. San Francisco: Jossey-Bass.

Harkavy, I., & Benson, L. (1998). De-Platonizing and democratizing education as the bases of service-learning. In R. A. Rhoads & J. P. F. Howard (Eds.), *Academic service-learning: A pedagogy of action and reflection* (pp. 11–20). New Directions for Teaching and Learning, no. 73. San Francisco: Jossey-Bass.

Hatcher, J. (1997). The moral dimensions of John Dewey's philosophy: Implications for undergraduate education. *Michigan Journal of Community Service-Learning, 4*, 22–29.

Hepburn, M. (1997). Service-learning in civic education: A concept with long, sturdy roots. *Theory into Practice, 36*(3), 136–142.

Jardine, M. (1998). Are communitarians "premodern" or "postmodern"? The place of communitarian thought in contemporary political theory. In P. A. Lawler & D. McConkey (Eds.), *Community and political thought today* (pp. 27–38). Westport, CT: Praeger.

Morton, K., & Saltmarsh, J. (1997). Addams, Day, and Dewey: The emergence of community service in American culture. *Michigan Journal of Community Service-Learning, 4*, 137–149.

Saltmarsh, J. (1996). Education for critical citizenship: John Dewey's contribution to the pedagogy of community service-learning. *Michigan Journal of Community Service-Learning, 3*, 13–21.

Speck, B. (2001). Why service-learning? In M. Canada & B. Speck (Eds.), *Developing and implementing service-learning programs* (pp. 3–13). New Directions for Higher Education, no. 114. San Francisco: Jossey-Bass.

PART III

Related Issues

CHAPTER 10

The Ethics of Classroom Advocacy

C. F. Abel, J. G. Lacina, and C. D. Abel

What is the ethical status of classroom advocacy? Is it right or wrong morally for a teacher to promote the idea that some particular action or some particular choice or some particular proposition is right, good, or true? This question is of central concern to the debate in this volume, as the civic education approach to service-learning considers classrooms to be proper venues for advocating and nurturing activist and confrontational forms of good citizenship. Thus service-learning experiences are designed by civic education activists to socialize students into certain values, habits, and dispositions that promote partisan ideals and alter dispositions, attitudes, and behaviors in ways conducive to issue advocacy. It is assumed that service-learning practiced in this way enhances a student's educational experience, sustains democratic culture, strengthens democratic institutions, and advances social justice (Barber & Battistoni, 1993; Boyte, 1993; Chesney & Feinstein, 1993; Ehrlich, 1997). For others, the mission of producing political activists is the antithesis of education, and the central classroom mission is not to advocate activist ideals, values, attitudes, and beliefs but to develop within the student a capacity for judicious self-direction. Once developed, this capacity is thought to empower students to mold the relationships they have with others in ways that they personally value, perhaps including partisan political activity and perhaps not. Thus, this philanthropic approach is distinguished from the civic education approach by its neutrality regarding social issues and its placement of the student in the role of assistant observer as opposed to trained partisan advocate. In brief, one approach advances and the other abhors classroom advocacy, and both claim the moral high ground.

Which approach, then, is morally correct? Toward answering this question it is helpful to take it as one of applied ethics. That is, it is helpful to look at the question as involving a controversy among significant groups of people over what practices are to be considered obligatory in a moral sense rather than merely conventional or merely matters of political, economic, or social policy. Thus, it is a controversy over the proper application of some normative principle or set of principles. The problem is that there are rival normative principles, some of which when applied to the same situation yield opposed conclusions as to what we should do. Consequently, resolving the issue necessarily involves arriving at some set of principles as determinative for choice that are understood as having merit by people holding rival normative principles and then applying those principles to the civic and philanthropic approaches in turn. This, of course, requires that we consult several representative schools of thought on what constitute proper normative principles in order to distill a set of principles that are useful to teachers in that they are commonly acceptable to the several representative schools. Briefly, such representative schools of thought include virtue-based ethics (holding that ethical choice depends upon acquiring a good character), duty-based ethics (holding that there are clear duties we must fulfill regardless of our character), and consequentialist ethics (holding behavior should be evaluated morally according to its impact upon others). Upon distilling out such a set of principles, we will first evaluate the civic and philanthropic approaches against those principles and then consider some arguments for advocacy in the classroom that might be made in addition to those made by champions of the civic approach.

REPRESENTATIVE ETHICAL PRINCIPLES

A familiar rule that seems always popular is "do unto others as you would have others do unto you." But in a university setting this is not too helpful. Most simply, the statuses and roles of professor and student are not commensurate, and it would be unfair to treat students as one would a colleague. Should I then treat students as I would have wanted to be treated when I was a student, or should I treat them as I now understand it is best to treat students? Do I spoon-feed or do I challenge, do I suffer fools or do I demand that they act less foolishly, do I reveal the truth (i.e., the scholarly consensus) or do I inveigle them to discover it themselves? Do I act as friend or as disciplinarian or as avatar? Being uncertain about how I would actually like to be treated as a student, I am uncertain about how I should in fact treat them.

As an aid in such situations, Socrates suggested that in evaluating the professional conduct of doctors, lawyers, and engineers, for example, it seemed appropriate to require that they seek not their own advantage but instead the benefit of those whom they serve (Plato, trans. 1941, p. 241). On the other hand, such a dictum seems less appropriate to chemists, biologists, and physicists who are often expected to act primarily in the interest of their own or another's research interests. The problem for professors is that they seem to occupy a third professional status wherein they clearly have some professional relationship to students but might conceive of their responsibilities as those of a master to an apprentice rather than as those of a physician to a patient or a lawyer to a client.

To resolve this sort of problem, Socrates and Rawls (1971, p. 3) suggested that certain individual or institutional characteristics, qualities, or dispositions inclined people to act properly toward others in ambiguous situations. Hence, they proceeded to identify certain character traits (virtues) that once developed and displayed would contribute to the realization of a good life for both the self and others. According to this approach, ethical behaviors and choices depend upon developing within a person or structuring into a society's institutions, specific habits of character. Individuals would then act ethically (justly), as their behavior would be regulated (habituated) into just actions and choices either through internal moral development (perhaps a la Piaget) or through social and institutional pressure.

A number of such virtues have been identified. Plato (trans. 1941, pp. 510–511), for example, suggested both four cardinal virtues (wisdom, courage, temperance, and justice) and a discrete number of secondary virtues (fortitude, generosity, self-respect, good temper, and sincerity). Rawls suggested that all social and political institutions be so contrived as to ensure that all social goods are equally distributed unless an unequal distribution redounds to the benefit of everyone but particularly to the benefit of the least well off. In a similar vein, Aristotle (trans. 1984) argued that ethical or virtuous behavior ensued from the regulation of one's passions by reason. Thus, for him, the cardinal virtue was reason, and the development of that ability was the proper task of educators. Following Aristotle, medieval theologians argued that emotions should be regulated as much by faith, hope, and charity as by reason, and MacIntyre (1984) argued that the virtues that were the most desirable were grounded in and emerged from within a particular society's social traditions. For our purposes, the important point is that according to this approach, adults are responsible for instilling virtues in both the young and the society's educational institutions through a moral education; and this education is not to proceed by training or indoctrinating them to a set of proper behaviors according to wise or temperate or just rules but rather by developing wise, temperate, and just students.

Not everyone, however, agrees that ethical behavior is grounded in the moral insights of virtuous individuals or institutions. Rather, they are of the opinion that we are under certain clear obligations as human beings regardless of our personal virtue. These deontological theorists (from the Greek *deon* or *duty*) suggest that we have a number of clear duties that emerge from a variety of sources. Many, following Pufendorf (1927), for example, hold that we have clear obligations to God, to ourselves, and to others. Concerning our duties to others, Pufendorf argues that they are of two kinds. First, there are duties that are universal and absolute, such as treating others with dignity and respect, promoting the good of others, and not wronging others intentionally. Next there are duties that emerge from various types of agreements that we make with others (what he calls conditional duties), the most important of which is the duty to keep one's promises. In a similar vein, many follow Locke (1963) in arguing that certain obligations follow from certain laws of nature that mandate a respect for the life, liberty, property, and health of others. Still others, following Kant (trans. 1985), argue that there is a single, self-evident principle of reason (the categorical imperative) that directs how we should behave regardless of our virtue or personal desires. We should act in recognition of the inherent value of each individual by treating people with dignity and never using them as mere instruments for our personal ends.

Unfortunately, there are those who are uncomfortable with appealing to wisdom or to gut intuitions or to long lists of virtues and duties. All of these, they argue, lead regularly to contradictory behaviors or confusion when applied to concrete situations. They would rather appeal to experience. To them, an action is morally right if the consequences of that action are more favorable than unfavorable. Competing consequentialist theories specify which consequences for affected groups of people are relevant. Ethical egoism, for example, holds that an action is morally right if the consequences of an action or choice are more favorable than unfavorable to the agent performing the action. Hobbes (1994) takes this approach in arguing that as all of our actions are selfishly motivated, we are better off living with moral rules than without them. Absent moral rules we are necessarily condemned to a nasty, brutal, and short existence wherein each of us plunders everyone else. So for purely selfish reasons it is better to agree upon and to enforce certain ethical ways of behaving (hence social contract theory). Ethical altruists, on the other hand, argue that an action is morally right if the consequences of that act or choice are more favorable than unfavorable overall (i.e., considering the consequences to everyone). In this vein, Bentham (1996) suggested that we consider the pain (costs) and pleasure (benefits) occasioned by each act on a case-by-case basis (a position known as hedonistic act-utilitarianism). But as many take this to advocate slavery and the torturing of an innocent for the benefit of the whole, Mill (1991) suggested that we abandon act-utilitarianism in favor of rule-utilitarianism. According to this approach, we should judge particular acts and choices not according to their particular consequences, but according to whether they violate a rule that is morally binding because its adoption produces favorable consequences for everyone. Fairly comfortable with this last idea, some ethical thinkers were still bothered by the hedonistic aspect of Bentham's thinking. In the place of a pleasure/pain calculus they suggested that we tally any and all consequences that either satisfy our inclinations (preference utilitarianism) or are intuitively recognized as good or bad (ideal utilitarianism), regardless of the pleasure or pain that they entail (Hare, 1981; Moore, 1903).

DISTILLING OUT A STANDARD FOR TEACHERS

Individually, virtue-based, consequentialist, and duty-based thinkers would find the task of deciding the ethical status of the civic and philanthropic approaches fairly easy. Virtue-based ethicists would look to whether either or both developed the student's virtue (e.g., wisdom, justice, benevolence, rationality), duty-based ethicists would look to which fulfilled their particular list of duties to whichever groups they deemed relevant (e.g., students, society, particular interests), and consequentialists would calculate the benefits and burdens that each approach inflicted upon the individuals and groups that they deemed relevant. The problem for teachers is that all of these come to different conclusions on a regular basis. And as all of these ethical theories enjoy strong proponents to whom teachers must answer, the decisive use of any particular theory is precluded. Consequently, the solution for teachers must lie in deriving a set of normative principles that are seen as having merit by people all along the ethical spectrum just outlined.

At a minimum, then, the following principles must guide the teacher's determination of whether either the civic or philanthropic approach is more or less ethical than the other. First, consider virtue-based ethical approaches. These suggest that at a minimum the teacher must make such choices as develop the virtues of wisdom, temperance, justice, and courage in both the student and the institutions of society. In addition, they suggest that the choice must be rational in the minimal sense of being sufficiently disinterested and open-minded as to (1) not lend preference to one set of attitudes, values, and beliefs without first comparing it to competing beliefs and identifying reasons for accepting it and (2) allow students to think for themselves (West, 1998, p. 805). These virtue-based principles are necessary to allow learning to occur, not only by the student but by the teacher and other interested parties as well.

Next, consider consequentialist theories. Taken together, the theories following this approach suggest that the proper choice is that service-learning experience that redounds to the personal benefit of the teacher, the student, and the society. Under this approach, the primary purpose of an education is to assist the students, the faculty, and the society in discovering and securing both the truths they seek and the best ways of seeking the truth. In other words, the primary activity at an educational institution should be intellectual inquiry (West, 1998, p. 805).

Finally, consider duty-based theories. Taken together, these suggest that we base our choice between the civic and the philanthropic approach upon which of the two does the most to help those in need to pursue their best interests, and to do so in a way that does not harm others. They require that the service-learning approach chosen acknowledge both the student's freedom to choose his or her actions and the student's rights to life, liberty, privacy, conscience, free expression, and safety. To do this, professors have an intellectual obligation to respect the student's auton- omy and rationality by giving them reasons for what we ask them to believe and by ensuring that they have the ability to assess those reasons for themselves (Markie, 1996, p. 297). In addition, to fulfill all of these duties to the student, teachers have a duty to allow free and open discus- sion of all positions they present, to allow students to challenge their views, to listen carefully and to take seriously what students have to say, to avoid intimidation, and to challenge respectfully even those positions with which they agree (West, 1998, p. 805).

In brief, we suggest that people all along the ethical spectrum will see merit in that approach to service-learning that best (1) advances the vir- tues of wisdom, justice, rationality, temperance, and benevolence in both students and social institutions; (2) redounds to the personal benefit of the teacher, the student, and the society primarily by advancing intellec- tual inquiry; (3) helps those in need to pursue their best interests in ways that do not harm others; and (4) respects both the student's autonomy and rationality and the autonomy and rationality of individuals and groups in the society at large, in part by ensuring that they have both the opportunity and the ability to access, challenge, and assess for themselves the strengths and weaknesses of different attitudes, values, and beliefs.

APPLYING THE STANDARD

With regard to the first criterion, the philanthropic approach seems to score above the civic approach. While it might be said that to some extent the civic approach advances the virtue of justice in groups and social institutions, it does so at the expense of tolerance, temperance, rationality, and wisdom. That is, it assumes without argument the justice of social transformation and the consequent training of students to the idea that particular attitudes, values, and beliefs are necessarily more cogent than others. For this reason, those championing the civic approach proclaim that "service-learning pedagogies stand apart from much of traditional . . . education in that these pedagogies do not seek, nor claim, value neu- trality" (Godfrey, 1999, p. 364). Rather, service-learning is an opportunity for affecting the power struggle among multiple and conflicting political interests.

The philanthropist ideal, on the other hand, is neither social transformation nor training in social, political, and economic activism nor developing the sort of indoctrination in particular group interests that those of the civic persuasion hold appropriate to their idea of democracy. Rather, it is in the rational pursuit of knowledge and the growth of character and wisdom within the individual. From this, it is hoped, society in general will benefit as the critical condition widens with the creation of an educated public (Gutmann, 1987). More specifically, the philanthropic approach as opposed to the civic approach favors debate over partisan indoctrination in the classroom so that the understanding of competing interests might be as rich and subtle as possible. At a minimum this dynamic includes putting forward views nonconfrontationally, citing and assembling examples, seeking out and responding to rival views, abstractly modifying one's view to meet exceptions, explaining why a particular vision may remain coherent even after modification, and willingly opening one's mind to distasteful and threatening options. In this way it advances the virtues of tolerance, temperance, justice, and wisdom in as rational a manner as possible.

With regard to the second criterion, and true to the ideals of ethical egoism, the philanthropic approach offers access to both the personal joys of education for its own sake and to the fuller life that it provides through the personal satisfaction, self-realization, intellectual autonomy, and wisdom that come from general learning, open debate, self-critique, and the mastery of sophisticated rational thought. Moreover, given that in our society the allocation of social goods depends to a significant extent upon just such habits of thought and the special skills required to develop and employ that form of thinking, choosing such an approach offers increased chances for enhancing one's income, power, and prestige (Blau & Duncan, 1967; Hauser, 1970; Lenski, 1966).

In contrast, ethical egoism is anathema to proponents of the civic approach. To them, the proper ethical focus of the classroom experience is neither upon the internal benefits to the student nor the externally derived rewards that the student might garner. Rather, the proper focus is external; it is upon how the student might serve society's oppressed and marginalized groups. To this extent it might be said that the civic approach triumphs over the possessive individualism, avarice, and narcissism of the philanthropic approach; unless, of course, one wonders (along with Pufendorf, 1927; and Kant, 1985) exactly how much use an indoctrinated mind is to the downtrodden as compared to a mind that has taken an interest in its own development. Moreover, the ethical altruism of the civic approach appears limited to very narrow groups, seeking the welfare of only those it identifies as subjugated and oppressed. Moreover, as it is the teacher that must identify the downtrodden and as there is an assumption that certain kinds of democratic processes and outcomes are inherently superior, there is a very real danger that the other-regardedness of the approach will be lost as civic pedagogies become mechanisms for giving voice to the political predilections of the professor or the university (Ellsworth, 1989, p. 307).

Be that as it may, philanthropists fulfill not only the requirements of ethical egoism but those of ethical altruism as well, hence scoring once again over those advancing the civic approach. Briefly, philanthropists fulfill the social responsibility required by ethical altruism in two ways: first, by helping people to acquire the intellectual tools demanded by contemporary civilized life and second, by keeping alive the pressure for progress and adaptation that is given force by the opposing visions of the good life and a just society that are generated by thoughtful, open minds. This last benefit is accomplished as the neutrality of educators enriches the wider social debate in which competing visions of what is possible and desirable are developed and deployed by (1) keeping momentarily unpopular or misunderstood or widely unknown visions in play; (2) providing a public space wherein individuals are empowered to participate most fully in social, intellectual, and cultural life; and (3) identifying and keeping alive the range of meanings attributed to such social ideals as justice and the good society so that we might appreciate the complexity and nuance of their meaning, develop their meaning as time and context change, and achieve a cohesive sense of them as we develop them in the conflicting discourses into which they are woven (Gallie, 1962). For this reason philanthropists hold that educational institutions should not discriminate in assisting one doctrine over another but should present doctrines neutrally and abstractly so that they are retained as part of the discourse in their most sophisticated form and not trivialized by the pressures, compromises, and reservations inevitably accompanying political action (Ackerman, 1980; Dworkin, 1985; Feinberg, 1988; Gutmann, 1985, p. 313; Kymlicka, 1989; Larmore, 1987; Lloyd-Thomas, 1988, pp. 1–2; Rawls, 1988; Rosenblum, 1989; Waldron, 1989).

With regard to the third criterion, the civic approach seems to score above the philanthropic approach in being more thoroughly interested in directly helping those in need to pursue their best interests. The philanthropic approach focuses first upon the benefits of its pedagogy to the student and then only indirectly upon the benefits to those in need that might be secured through the efforts of thoughtful, reflective minds that choose to so engage themselves. In contrast, the civic approach focuses exclusively upon the benefits of its pedagogy to others. As a means of promoting antagonism between the dominant and the oppressed and as a means of instilling an oppositional ideology in both students and various subjugated groups in society (Giroux, 1983), both students and teachers are urged to become transformative intellectuals who legitimate the voices of others "in an effort to empower them as critical and active citizens" (Giroux, 1988, p. 32). Furthermore, critical educators "must . . . encourage forms of solidarity rooted in the principles of trust, sharing, and a commitment to improving the quality of human life" (Giroux, 1987, p. 334). This other-regarding dimension of the civic approach seems true to the ideals of a duty-based ethics that holds those in the classroom duty bound to bestow the benefits of an oppositional ideology upon select groups within a society (Giroux, 1983).

However laudable this focus of the civic approach upon the downtrodden, the means of coming to their aid are ethically problematic. The duty-based criterion requires not only that we help those in need, but that we do so in ways that do not harm others as well. The harm in the civic approach is that pointed out by Kant (trans. 1985) when he proffered the single self-evident principle of reason (the categorical imperative) that enjoins us always to act in recognition of the inherent value of each individual by treating people with dignity and never using them as mere instruments for our personal ends. The unfortunate fact is that the civic approach does harm to the dignity of students by explicitly employing them for the ends of others.

Finally, with regard to the fourth criterion, the philanthropic approach seems to score above the civic approach yet again. Education in the philanthropic as opposed to the civic sense involves freeing the mind and enabling autonomous, critical, and dialogical thought that is capable of self-determination and is empowered to act as a source of independent social, political, and economic criticism, should the individual so desire (McMurtry, 1991, p. 209). In this way the fundamental or natural rights to liberty and self-determination are preserved. Philanthropic service-learning grounds itself in an educational philosophy maintaining that when universities are earnest in the disinterested pursuit of knowledge and sound thinking, they lay the necessary foundation for individuals to choose those forms of personal engagement in critical and constructive practices that they decide are most productive. Rather than becoming embroiled in ideological and partisan social conflict and presuming to identify (or to help others to identify), promote, or attack ostensible social goods or evils directly, the philanthropic approach seeks to provide the wherewithal for individuals to make these identifications by themselves and to choose the most individually appropriate form of participation for themselves.

The civic approach, promoting as it does the classroom as the proper venue for nurturing a particular (oppositional) model of democracy and seeking as it does to socialize students into just those values, habits, and dispositions that promote the particular kinds of patriotism, community, and good citizenship this model requires, fails in its duty to respect not only the dignity of the student, but the rights to liberty, conscience, and self-determination as well. Championing a politicized classroom in which dispositions, attitudes, and behaviors are altered so that students will embrace a specific model of democratic politics, the civic approach champions the denial to students of the wherewithal to choose their form of participation in society for themselves.

Considering all, then, the philanthropic approach scores above the civic approach when evaluated according to the principles distilled from virtue-based, duty-based, and consequentialist ethics. Moreover, as the above discussion indicates, each of the representative schools would individually find merit in the philanthropic over the civic approach. The ethical choice thus seems clear.

IN CONCLUSION: A CONSIDERATION OF SOME OTHER ARGUMENTS FOR ADVOCACY

Some argue that avoiding advocacy is impossible as even "balanced presentations depend on a particular formulation of the dispute and the alternatives" (Ernst, 1996, p. 307). Hence advocacy is not a question of normative ethics but simply a fact. However, one can (and should) identify and make one's formulations and biases explicit, thereby revealing them as the professor's predilections and opening them for critique. Now, to give this position its due, we should recognize that there is at the very core of education a commitment to both reasoned inquiry and constant self-critique that expresses a moral, political, and educational bias against both authoritarianism and nihilism. But this is not so much a bias as a *reason d'etre*. Education, that is, exists in contradistinction to training and indoctrination on the one hand and to the complete autonomy to think and believe just anything one wishes on the other, simply because both authoritarianism and nihilism represent a denial that any real learning is possible. Holding that only one correct understanding is admissible or that some minority (or majority) has a corner on the truth or that no answer is any better than any other denies that opinions and understanding can improve, thereby robbing education of a reason for being.

Others argue that neutrality in the classroom leads to relativism and cynicism. Students, it is argued, have a right to expect scholars and experts to come to some approximation of the truth; if all they do is interpret, question, and uncover hidden assumptions, then people will come to believe that no opinion or understanding is better than another and that all reasoning is mere rationalization (Wilder, 1978). However, "the position of neutrality is recommended not in scholarship but in teaching, and this represents a significant distinction between the two activities" (Baumgarten, 1982, p. 289).

One final argument is frequently advanced for incorporating advocacy into the classroom. The critical thinking argument contends that because of "the rise in apathy, the decline in [civic and] political participation, and the decline in [civic and] political literacy that are increasingly evident among students and throughout U.S. society in general . . . advocacy in the . . . classroom is a necessary response to a perceived crisis in democratic culture and citizenship" (Weaver, 1998, pp. 799–802). The critical thinking corrective to this problem argues that classroom advocacy is therefore essential to the maintenance of democracy (Atwater, 1991; Cohen, 1993). According to this corrective, the teacher should be an effective advocate of different ideological perspectives, inviting students to do the same. In this manner, it is thought that critical thinking skills will be developed by forcing students to confront inconvenient facts and to reflect on their assumptions (Love, 1991, p. xix).

However, this approach fails to appreciate fully the unequal power relationship between teacher and student. While those making the critical thinking argument concede that teachers must attempt to avoid using their positions of power in the classroom to advocate their personal ideologies, behaviors, or choices to their students, they fail to recognize the structural and institutional reinforcements of the teacher's power vis-à-vis the students. While lecturing, for example, the professor stands opposite the students, who must remain silent and for the sake of their grades "attend a teacher's course while there is nobody present to oppose him with criticism" (Weber, 1946, p. 146). In such circumstances, it is clearly an act of domination by the teacher to employ his or her status, knowledge, and experience to imprint upon students his or her personal views. However, merely placing chairs into a circle and encouraging students to participate in critical discussions does not eliminate the power relationship "inherent in the grading system and other structural features of contemporary academic institutions" (Weaver, 1998, p. 800). The teacher still grades, still favors subtly certain approaches and values, still holds the status of expert, and still retains the authority to guide the conversation by regulating who speaks when and for how long. Thus, the teacher remains at least first among equals, and "it is, in part, this asymmetry of power that makes advocacy in the classroom . . . so problematic" (Weaver, 1998, p. 800).

All in all, then, there seems little in favor of the civic approach to service-learning given its predilection for advocacy in the classroom. What this ethical analysis points out is simply a reminder that the ends of politics are essentially different from those of classroom teaching and that teachers must keep in mind the clear distinction between advocacy and teaching. The first demands adherence to a designated position and excludes other positions. The second accepts dissent and grants that other positions exist and should be examined. By reason of all of the ethical principles examined above, the ultimate effect of the classroom experience should be not the students' acceptance of any particular view on any topic but an awareness on their part that there are many views, each with some substance and some defects, and that no one (student, teacher, or political activist) has a right to an opinion that is not based upon sound thinking and informed by a solid command of the information and scholarship (normative and empirical) available on the particular issue involved.

REFERENCES

Ackerman, B. (1980). *Social justice in the liberal state*. New Haven, CT: Yale University Press.

Aristotle (1984). Nichomachean ethics (W. D. Ross, Trans.). In J. Barnes (Ed.), *The complete works of Aristotle*. Princeton, NJ: Princeton University Press.

Atwater, T. (1991). Critical thinking in basic U.S. government classes. *PS: Political Science and Politics, 24*, 209–211.

Barber, B. R., & Battistoni, R. (1993). A season of service: Introducing service-learning into the liberal arts curriculum. *PS: Political Science and Politics, 26*, 235–240.

Baumgarten, E. (1982). Ethics in the academic profession: A Socratic view. *Journal of Higher Education, 53*(3), 289.

Bentham, J. (1996). *Introduction to the principles of morals and legislation*. Oxford, UK: Oxford University Press.

Blau, P. M., & Duncan, O. D. (1967). *The American occupational structure*. New York: John Wiley.

Boyte, H. C. (1993). Civic education as public leadership development. *PS: Political Science and Politics, 26*, 763–769.

Chesney, J. D., & Feinstein, O. (1993). Making political activity a requirement in introductory political science courses. *PS: Political Science and Politics, 26*, 535–538.

Cohen, M. (1993). Making critical thinking a classroom reality. *PS: Political Science and Politics, 26*, 241–244.

Dworkin, R. (1985). *Liberalism: A matter of principle*. London: Harvard University Press.

Ehrlich, T. (1997). The legacy of public work: Educating for leadership. *Educational Leadership, 54*, 12–18.

Ellsworth, E. (1989). Why doesn't this feel empowering?: Working through the repressive myths of critical pedagogy. *Harvard Educational Review, 59*, 307.

Ernst, B. (1996). Some implications of the faculty's obligation to encourage student academic freedom for faculty advocacy in the classroom. In P. M. Spacks (Ed.), *Advocacy in the classroom: Problems and possibilities* (p. 307). New York: St. Martin's Press.

Feinberg, J. (1988). *The moral limits of the criminal law*. Oxford, UK: Oxford University Press.

Gallie, W. B. (1962). Essentially contested concepts. In M. Black (Ed.), *The importance of language*. Englewood Cliffs, NJ: Prentice Hall.

Giroux, H. A. (1983). Theories of reproduction and resistance. *Harvard Educational Review, 53*, 257–293.

Giroux, H. A. (1987). Liberal arts, public philosophy and the politics of civic courage. *Curriculum Inquiry, 17,* 334.

Giroux, H. A. (1988). *Schooling and the struggle for public life: Critical pedagogy. The Modern Age.* Minneapolis, MN: University of Minnesota Press.

Godfrey, P. C. (1999). Service-learning and management education: A call to action. *Journal of Management Inquiry, 8*(4), 364.

Gutmann, A. (1985). Communitarian critics of liberalism. *Philosophy and Public Affairs, 15,* 313.

Gutmann, A. (1987). *Democratic education.* Princeton, NJ: Princeton University Press.

Hare, R. M. (1981). *Moral thinking.* Oxford, UK: Clarendon Press.

Hauser, R. M. (1970). Educational stratification. *The United States Sociological Inquiry, 40,* 102–109.

Hobbes, T. (1994). *Leviathan.* Chicago: Hackett.

Kant, I. (1985). *Grounding for the metaphysics of morals* (W. K. Ellington, Trans.). Indianapolis, IN: Hackett.

Kymlicka, W. (1989). *Liberalism, community and culture.* Oxford, UK: Oxford University Press.

Larmore, C. (1987). *Patterns of moral complexity.* Cambridge, UK: Cambridge University Press.

Lenski, G. (1966). *Power and privilege: A theory of social stratification.* New York: McGraw-Hill.

Lloyd-Thomas, D. (1988). *Defense of liberalism.* Oxford, UK: Blackwell.

Locke, J. (1963). *Two treatises* (P. Laslett, Ed.). Cambridge, UK: Cambridge University Press.

Love, N. S. (Ed.). (1991). *Dogmas and dreams: Political ideologies in the modern world.* Chatham, NJ: Chatham House.

MacIntyre, A. (1984). *After virtue.* Notre Dame, IN: University of Notre Dame Press.

Markie, P. (1996). The limits of appropriate advocacy. In P. M. Spacks (Ed.), *Advocacy in the classroom: Problems and possibilities* (p. 297). New York: St. Martin's Press.

McMurtry, J. (1991). Education and the market model. *Journal of Philosophy of Education, 25,* 209.

Mill, J. S. (1991). Utilitarianism. In J. M. Robson (Ed.), *Collected works of John Stuart Mill.* Toronto, Ontario, Canada: University of Toronto Press.

Moore, G. E. (1903). *Principia ethica.* Cambridge, UK: Cambridge University Press.

Plato (1941). *The republic* (F. M. Cornfield, Trans.). London: Oxford University Press.

Pufendorf, S. von (1927). *The two books of the duty of man and citizen according to natural law.* New York: Oxford University Press.

Rawls, J. (1971). *A theory of justice.* Cambridge, MA: Harvard University Press.

Rawls, J. (1988). The priority of the right and ideas of the good. *Philosophy and Public Affairs, 17,* pp. 251–276.

Rosenblum, N. (1989). Introduction. In *Liberalism and the moral life* (pp. 1–18). Cambridge, UK: Cambridge University Press.

Waldron, J. (1989). Autonomy and perfectionism in Raz's *Morality of Freedom. Southern California Law Review, 62,* 1097–1131.

Weaver, M. (1998). Weber's critique of advocacy in the classroom: Critical thinking and civic education. *PS: Political Science & Politics, 31*(4), 799–802.

Weber, M. (1946). Science as a vocation. In H. H. Gerth & C. W. Mills (Eds.), *From Max Weber: Essays in sociology* (p. 146). New York: Oxford University Press.

West, E. M. (1998). Some proposed guidelines for advocacy in the classroom. *PS: Political Science & Politics, 31*(4), 805.

Wilder, H. T. (1978). Tolerance and teaching philosophy. *Metaphilosophy, 9*(3), 11–23.

CHAPTER 11

Service-Learning and Professional Ethics in a Catholic University

Richard L. Henderson

Previous chapters have provided a sound understanding and a solid foundation in history, philosophy, and theoretical perspectives. It may then be appropriate to conclude with a connection to practice and the world of professional employment. This chapter will begin by placing the writing in a specific context that includes an explanation of service-learning requirements at a Catholic university and how this sectarian view fits into the philanthropic approach as described by Dr. Abel in Chapter Three. Additionally, this section will review selected professional ethical codes articulated by the leadership in those fields and examine the expectation leveled at institutions responsible for education and preparation of the human resources for those same professions. Therefore, the focus of this writing is primarily practical rather than philosophical. However, contextual placement is important for clear understanding, and even a cursory review of institutional documents puts the Catholic university philosophically into the philanthropic philosophical view (Giles & Cruz, 1999; Larmore, 1987; Rosenblum, 1989).

In providing a justification of the philanthropic model Abel, in chapter 3, suggests:

Philanthropists hold that universities fulfill their social responsibility in two ways: first, by helping people to acquire the intellectual tools demanded by contemporary civilized life and second, by concerning themselves with the development of epistemological skills and the self-reflective development of moral values.

This, of course, represents conceptual agreement with the mission statement for Catholic universities including that of the University of the

Incarnate Word (UIW). A descriptive statement within the mission document for UIW states:

> The curriculum offers students an integrated program of liberal arts and profes-
> sional studies that includes a global perspective and an emphasis on social justice
> and community service. (University of the Incarnate Word, 1996)

Moreover, the foundational documents that represent the philosophical, or more correctly, the theological birth of the institution present further ideological agreement. A letter to the founding French sisters of the Incarnate Word community in San Antonio from Bishop Dubuis stated: "Our Lord Jesus Christ, suffering in the persons of a multitude of the sick and infirm of every kind, seeks relief at your hands" (UIW, 1866). This statement clearly indicates the *service* orientation of the religious community, its institutions, and the expectations of the people who populate those institutions.

To understand the specifics of current implementation, it may be instructive to review the interviews with Drs. Connelly and Lonchar, who were greatly responsible for the relatively recent formalization of service-learning at the UIW through support from the Lilly Foundation. These professors, from the philosophy and the English departments respectively, indicated that:

> When UIW joined with four other religious-affiliated institutions in 1996 to seek
> funding from the Lilly Foundation to assist our implementation of Service-
> Learning, we did so knowing that such an initiative was inherent within our
> mission. For three years, the Lilly grant supported our Service-Learning imple-
> mentation and Faculty Development efforts. At the close of the Lilly Grant, the
> university had established Service-Learning as an aim in its Vision Document and
> accepted Service-Learning activities as appropriately meeting the Graduation Ser-
> vice Requirement for students. Further, four distinct programs integrated Service-
> Learning Pilots into their course structure; assessments of these pilot courses
> guided the Service-Learning Committee to formulate processes for continued ad-
> dition of Service-Learning courses into the university curriculum. Formal proce-
> dures for official S-L course designation in the college schedule are now in place
> and steps to establish a Service-Learning transcript have begun. Service-Learning
> has also become one aspect of a faculty member's performance criteria. A Service-
> Learning Advisory Council, composed of external community members, serves
> as a vital link between campus programs and the greater San Antonio community.

> But processes, forms, and vision inclusion are not the most laudatory of the
> Service-Learning initiatives at UIW, important as these areas are. The results of
> UIW's Service-Learning initiative are most evident and most significant in the
> actual work of service and learning now occurring in the San Antonio community
> by UIW faculty and students. This work with underserved populations includes:

> The Nursing school now operates a Health Ministry as part of its Service-
> Learning program: Nursing students assist in various health education and moni-

toring tasks, nursing faculty staff a clinic, PE majors assist in supervision of wellness activities, Business majors assist in accounting procedures, and Nutrition majors conduct Nutrition Information sessions. Most of this work is conducted in both English and Spanish. Education majors have added Literacy Workshops/ Children's Play Days as part of their course work. These majors also established a Peter Rabbit Literacy Garden at the San Antonio Botanical Center and have served as advisors/consultants for several non-profit groups who wish to establish and maintain Safe Play Areas for children. (Connelly & Lonchar, 2003)

The formalization of service-learning at UIW has obviously been a long time coming. The founders, the Sisters of Charity of the Incarnate Word, and the institutions that followed were primarily *service* organizations. Moreover, the teaching institutions within those organizations, including Incarnate Word School, Incarnate Word High School for young women, St. Anthony's High School for young men, Incarnate Word College, and finally, the University of the Incarnate Word have long-standing expectations of service-learning, initially in the form of Christian service expectations and now service-learning graduation requirements for the professional schools.

Foremost among the professions served by the graduates of the UIW are teaching, nursing, and business administration. Therefore, the examples chosen for this writing will concentrate in those professional groups. Additionally, each of these groups takes a different approach to professional ethics and thereby requires some variation in its respective model of service-learning.

SERVICE-LEARNING, PROFESSIONAL ETHICS, AND PROFESSIONAL EDUCATORS

One of the largest professional groups in the United States and for that matter in most of the economically advanced nations in the world is that of education. Teachers at the common school level and the postsecondary level constitute a profession that includes more than four million professionals in the United States alone (National Education Association [NEA], 2002).

What does the code of professional ethics say about those four million professionals and what does the profession expect of the newly educated entering population that may have implications for service-learning activity? The most pervasive expectations within the code are found in the *principles*. The second principle, referred to as *commitment to the profession*, states:

The public with a trust and responsibility requiring the highest ideals of professional service vests the education profession in the belief that the quality of the services of the education profession directly influences the nation and its citizens, the educator shall exert every effort to raise professional standards, to promote a climate that encourages the exercise of professional judgment, to achieve conditions that attract persons worthy of the trust to careers in education, and to assist in preventing the practice of the profession by unqualified persons. (NEA Representative Assembly, 1975, p. 2)

In the general field of health care, a large and parallel group is the nursing profession. For the more than 2.5 million active nurses in the United States, the very specific and detailed code of ethics is prefaced with the following statement:

Ethics is an integral part of the foundation of nursing. Nursing has a distinguished history of concern for the welfare of the sick, injured, and vulnerable and for social justice. This concern is embodied in the provision of nursing care to individuals and the community. Nursing encompasses the prevention of illness, the alleviation of suffering, and the protection, promotion, and restoration of health in the care of individuals, families, groups, and communities. Nurses act to change those aspects of social structures that detract from health and well being. Individuals who become nurses are expected not only to adhere to the ideals and moral norms of the profession but also to embrace them as a part of what it means to be a nurse. The ethical tradition of nursing is self-reflective, enduring, and distinctive. A code of ethics makes explicit the primary goals, values and obligations of the profession. (American Nurses Association, 2001)

By the statement of purpose attached to the code, the document is designed, in part, as *an expression of nursing's own understanding of its commitment to society.*

The other profession included here poses an ethical code that seems to be without parallel in length or complexity. The American Institute of Certified Public Accountants accepts voluntary membership by certified public accountants who assume an obligation of self-discipline above and beyond the requirements of law and regulation. The set of principles of the *Code of Professional Conduct of the American Institute of Certified Public Accountants,* according to the organization, expresses the profession's recognition of its responsibilities to the public, to clients, and to colleagues. It guides members in the performance of their professional conduct. The principles call for an unswerving commitment to honorable behavior and the sacrifice of personal advantage (American Institute of Certified Public Accountants, 2003). While this group of highly trained business professionals is significantly smaller in number than the professional educators or nurses, its presence and program prominence in colleges and universities across the United States is certainly equal to the other professional groups described above.

What do these groups have in common, and what are the formal and informal processes that connect aspiring students to the service components of these important example professions represented in universities? And is this education and socialization to professional ethical standards facilitated or at least enhanced through service-learning projects required or offered by the schools? To approach these and other pertinent questions, a review of professional ethics documents, institutional policies, and selected interviews has been instructive.

Prospective teachers typically begin their preparation by capturing at least a general knowledge base in a discipline area. Upon entering a school of education, these students begin a socialization and professional readiness process that includes observations in school settings, working with certified professional educators in a number of contexts, and realizing the possibility of joining professional organizations (as a student member). In their final semesters, they take advanced classes in pedagogy and other professional areas of study and finally, they enter an experience usually referred to as *student teaching*. All of these experiences combine to provide students with socialization toward the teaching profession and the development of an appropriate attitude toward the countless experiences that require varying levels of service and personal altruism.

Historically this predominantly female profession likely relied on the nurturing nature of the female gender and the less than equitable expectations leveled at women to provide for service to the profession and to society that is likely unparalleled, with the possible exception of nurses, who have a similar history. Additionally, the evolution of the common school institution from the Latin grammar school operated by the Roman Church has no doubt provided for a standard of altruistic service that may not be present in most other contexts.

It may be indicative of the circumstances explained above that the student teaching experience is not only unpaid; it is, in fact, a tuition-bearing internship that provides certified teachers and the schools in which they are employed with unpaid interns who are willing to provide nearly any service requested, remembering that the grade they receive for this service course is primarily influenced by the field supervising teacher.

The profession has a long and distinguished history of service to clients and to society in general. It has been stated that those who enter the profession have a disposition toward altruism and service to society. In fact, association (union) leaders inside the profession have expressed the concern that the public has an expectation of exaggerated altruistic service and low pay for teachers. It would appear that service-learning is and has been an integral part of the *normal school* process of teacher training throughout its history in the United States. While it may be helpful to advocates and students of service-learning to review and model at least parts of the teacher preparation process in other fields, it may also be instructive to review the negative results on the profession in terms of remuneration for its professionals, society's expectations with respect to altruistic service, and other results.

Finally, the profession of education provides a practical example for those interested in service-learning to understand the inextricable link between professional socialization and academic preparation. According to professors and administrators in the professional school, this linkage may also help to explain the lack of long-term success of many alternatively certified teachers. The fact that they are attempting a career change to the profession of education sans the socialization and much of the academic preparation process may help to explain the number of failures in this abbreviated albeit necessary process.

SERVICE-LEARNING, PROFESSIONAL ETHICS, AND PROFESSIONAL NURSES

The process for training teachers is similar to the preparation of nurses for the health-care profession, which has a well-established history relative to gender-driven expectations and the process for preparation institutions. Nursing students typically begin their higher education in science and mathematics courses, which constitute foundational knowledge for health-care professionals. Much like education students, when nursing students enter the schools of nursing, they begin the socialization and rigorous academic processes that allow them to join this human-service profession. The clinical experiences, observations, and other practicums that take place in hospitals and other organizational settings allow an increasingly clear understanding of the professional ethical standards and the altruistic nature of the job.

An example of the service-learning experiences demanded of nursing students is depicted in a course syllabus related to service-learning. Pointedly, the example illustrates the fostered connection between personal values and the expectations of professional ethical standards in the profession. In the section of the document entitled "Central Course Objectives" the following expectations are listed:

a. The nursing student demonstrates development of accountability in professional nursing by:
　　I. Examining contemporary issues and problems in nursing.
　　II. Exploring solutions to problems.
　　III. Defending a position on an issue, and evaluating one's development as a professional nurse.
b. The nursing student will clarify one's own values in relation to selected issues in nursing utilizing:
　　I. The Code of Ethics for nurses with Interpretive Statements,
　　II. Models for ethical decision-making, and
　　III. One's philosophy of nursing (UIW, 2003b)

Clearly, these objectives cited above illustrate the foundation of the service-learning experience and expectations for a well-developed service-learning environment. Additionally, when placed in juxtaposition to the professional ethics documentation for the profession of nursing, these course objectives also provide clear evidence of the linkage between professional ethics and service-learning. With a history similar to that of professional educators, this predominantly female endeavor is replete with examples of heroines who have made remarkable personal sacrifices and accomplished seemingly impossible achievements against tremendous odds.

SERVICE-LEARNING, PROFESSIONAL ETHICS, AND PROFESSIONAL ACCOUNTANTS

Professional accounting aspirants begin their preparation like most other students with university core curriculum and then follow that general educational experience with introductory courses in the field of business. During their upper-division years as business school students, they also enter into practicums and other courses with a focus on field practice. The advanced accounting preparation for Certified Public Accountants is, of course, in part accomplished at the graduate level.

This profession, seated in the business world of work, is a significant departure from the previously described teaching and nursing professions. It is, first of all, not predominantly female, currently or historically. Moreover, even though it may be considered a service profession, it is not among the *human-service* professions. This highly skilled and highly paid profession does not necessarily have altruism or social consciousness at its professional core. It is, nonetheless, a profession that hinges on professional ethics for successful practice. This necessity for adherence to professional ethics has been recently illustrated in worldwide media reports related to Enron and other major corporate scandals. Therefore, the need for inculturation and for students to understand and embrace the formal and informal professional ethical standards, through service-learning or some other vehicle, is of obvious and substantial importance.

The *service* in service-learning relative to the accounting profession is not emphasized in the same way as it is in teaching and nursing. The service-learning projects undertaken by prospective accountants are constructed, articulated, and typically result from an adherence to institutional mission, at least in the Catholic university environment. An interview of selected faculty and administration in the School of Business and Applied Arts at a private Catholic university verified that the projects as well as the design for them came from a review of the institutional mission by college faculty and administration. The ethics of the profession as indicated in the above-cited documents are specifically directed at the integrity and reliability of the process and the information used as a data-ase by accounting professionals. The integrity, honesty, and quality of the service provided are, of course, of major importance in the profession of accounting. However, the commitment to the general good or to altruistic behavior by these highly skilled professionals is not based on the same professional ethical foci as that of educators and health-care professionals.

What conclusions can be made then related to the focus of the chapter? And what are the implications for the higher-education practitioners who are making design and implementation decisions about service-learning programs in the university setting?

To capture possible answers to these questions, appropriate additional information was collected through a series of interviews with administra-tors and professorial personnel at a university site. This sample of con-venience included administrators and professors in each of the above-named schools at a private Catholic metropolitan campus. The re-sults add to the information and answers gleaned from the review of professional ethics documentation, articulated professional standards, and school and university policy documents. The experienced opinion, reflective answers, and open-ended responses combined with the docu-ment data provide a practical view of the ideas proffered in the previous chapters.

CONCLUSIONS

Appropriate qualifications must be placed on this final section, as it is from a unique context. The University of the Incarnate Word is a small Catholic university in San Antonio, Texas, with a mission statement that is purposefully tied to service. Moreover, UIW has a relatively well de-veloped organizational emphasis on service-learning. Since 1997, UIW has integrated the concept of academic service-learning into curriculum. Un-der the direction of Drs. Bob Connelly and Pat Lonchar and with initial funding from a Lilly grant, UIW has seen the Schools of Nursing, Edu-cation, and Business Administration and Applied Arts, and the Depart-ments of Nutrition, Psychology, Information Systems, Wellness, English, and Computer Literacy integrate service-learning into courses. In addi-tion, students may use their service-learning experiences as part of their service requirements. As of next semester, schedules will list courses with a service-learning component by an "SL" designation. A Service-Learning Advisory Council has been established as well as a special faculty award recognizing service-learning contributions (UIW, 2003a).

It suffices to say that in the above-described context, service-learning is not only linked to professional preparation but also to the entire academic process. However, it is frequently through ideal or exaggerated circumstances that new ideas may be best understood.

In the School of Education, according to the administrators and professors interviewed, aspiring teachers enter into service-learning enthusiastically. In many cases, it is not so much because it is service-learning but because it is practical experience in the school settings and an opportunity to actually work with children. This, of course, represents a significant departure from the university classroom setting and the ethereal nature of many of the classes. The students are also, by disposition, in most cases likely to embrace the possibility of service-learning due to their philosophy, theology, or predisposition toward teaching as a helping profession. Clearly, most of these preteachers have established their professional preferences before or at the time they enter a school of education.

As to the focus or the ideals operationalized through the service-learning process, for education students the notion of confidentiality of client conversation, records, and the success of students is an immediate learned behavior, important to the profession. Student observers, helpers, and student teachers all experience the importance of the right to privacy and of sharing student information only on a need-to-know basis. Additionally, the notion of equity in educational opportunity and in the treatment of children hopefully becomes a part of the expected and manifest behavior of all students aspiring to the profession of education.

As a matter of practical application, the service-learning of education students provides not only for the enthusiasm of students but also for the necessary inculturation to professional standards. University students involved in classroom observation, service-learning projects, and the student-teaching process have the advantage of working alongside seasoned professionals who understand and manifest behavior indicative of professional expectations. In fact, the administrators and teacher leaders in the receiving institutions have indicated their enthusiastic approval of not only the service-learning projects but of all of the experiences that provide aspiring teachers with guided practice and field experience.

The university nursing candidates have, as previously mentioned, a more refined service-learning curriculum and a tighter link between the professional code of ethics and their service-learning experiences. In the health-care environment, an adherence to professional ethics and a specific standard may be interpreted as even more critical. Moreover the inculturation to a profession that requires precision in behavior adds to the seriousness of modeling professional behavior and learning specific approaches and procedures. Additionally, in this health-care service environment, the professional ethical standards and the mission of a Catholic institution established by an order of nuns by whom hospitals are also operated are not only linked but in many respects entwined.

For the aspiring professional accountants, the environment, the professional ethical standards, and the focus of the service-learning represent a significant departure from the nature of these things in the fields of education and nursing. As indicated in the professional ethics document cited above, the standards and the focus of ethics are on integrity, honesty, and specific procedures within the general practice of accounting. The service, rather than directed at society in general or at issues related to general welfare, is specific to business concerns. While tax accounting may indeed have service implications for nearly every member of our society, these service concerns are specific to individuals and are not among those considered to be a part of the human-service profession.

The service-learning projects designed for accounting and business students were described differently by the administrators and faculty interviewed as coming from the institutional mission at least as much as from professional ethical standards. While it is evident that any accounting practice would reflect professional standards, the university mission was described as the source and inspiration for service-learning projects. Moreover, the service-learning projects come directly from the professors. Sometimes the community will come forward with short-term projects, but more frequently the projects come from the professor, who also typically sets the performance standards on a project-by-project basis.

Specifically, in the institution studied, accounting and other school of business students are required to enter into service-learning projects just as those in human-service professional preparation. However, to focus the projects on segments of the community with heightened need or who normally are without the means to acquire such services, poor minority members and recent immigrants with limited understanding of the language were targeted. This specific segment of the community was then scheduled and served through service-learning projects. The focus on this specifically targeted population segment allowed the service-learning students to carry out the institutional mission and to practice the ethical standards required by their profession in the context of an altruistic act requiring considerable knowledge and expertise. A frequently used design is the constructing and filing of tax returns for minorities and recent immigrants who are without means or sufficient knowledge to do so on their own.

Professors interviewed had the following to say about the student attitudes: "Before the service experience, the students expressed nervousness and general shyness about their skill. After the service-learning experience, the students were enthusiastic and expressed fulfillment. Additionally, the students acknowledge how much they have gained from the service experience, not only in terms of knowledge, but also in terms of understanding of the needs of the community" (Tiggeman, 2003).

Most of the service-learning students were described by faculty and administration as enthusiastic and appropriately helpful. However, the student attitudes may very well be influenced by the fact that the expectation for service-learning is, for the most part, institutionalized at UIW. Careful planning and organization and positive attitudes from the professors are reflected in the students' acceptance of out-of-classroom assignments. While the students are participating in a service-learning experience, the professor is actually involved in an extension of the classroom, acting as the primary supervisor throughout the service-learning projects.

Institutional leadership, both administrative and academic, is believed to be extremely important for success in planning, organizing, and implementing service-learning. The creation of a climate of service must be, at least in part, based on institutional mission and the policies, procedures, and leadership behavior that follow. The human-service professions and the schools that serve them should take a lead role in the development of service-learning. Moreover, a close working relationship with the professions through their respective organizations is critical in formulating and maintaining a critical and inextricable link between professional ethics and the service-learning and other practical application experiences for aspiring student professionals.

In fact, the service-learning is described as "highly appreciated by the field professionals" (Tiggeman, 2003). Frequently, the service-learning project is an additional and vital part of the letters of recommendation that are written for graduate school and employment.

Finally, it is of major importance that the professionals who will continue to manifest social leadership in our society understand and practice social justice, the ethics of their chosen profession, and the principles of a chosen theology as well as those required by a functioning multicultural democratic society.

REFERENCES

American Institute of Certified Public Accountants. (2003). *Code of professional conduct.* New York: author.

American Nurses Association. (2002). *Code of ethics for nurses with interpretive statements.* Washington, DC: American Nurses Publishing.

Connelly, R., & Lonchar, P. (2003). *Personal interviews related to the service-learning program at the University of the Incarnate Word.* Unpublished manuscript, University of the Incarnate Word Faculty. San Antonio, TX.

Giles, D. E., Jr., & Eyler, J. (1998). A service learning research agenda for the next five years. In R. A. Rhoads & J. P. F. Howard (Eds.), *Academic service-learning.* New Directions for Teaching and Learning, 73. San Francisco: Jossey-Bass.

Larmore, C. (1987). *Patterns of moral complexity.* Cambridge, UK: Cambridge University Press.

National Education Association. (2002). *Rankings & estimates: Rankings of the states 2001 and estimates of school statistics.* Annapolis Junction, MD: author.

National Education Association [NEA] Representative Assembly. (1975). *Code of ethics of the education profession.* (Principle II Commitment to the profession) Washington, DC: National Education Association.

Rosenblum, N. (1989). *Liberalism and the moral life.* Cambridge, UK: Cambridge University Press.

Tiggeman, T. (2003, February). *Interview about service learning in the College of Business and Applied Arts, University of the Incarnate Word.* Personal interview released with permission. University of the Incarnate Word, San Antonio, TX.

University of the Incarnate Word. (1866). *Letter by Bishop Dubuis for the sisters to serve in Texas.* San Antonio, TX: Archives of the Mother House of the Sisters of the Incarnate Word.

University of the Incarnate Word. (1996). *Mission statement of the University of the Incarnate Word.* San Antonio, TX: author.

University of the Incarnate Word. (2003a). *Focus on faculty. Service-learning update.* San Antonio, TX: author.

University of the Incarnate Word. (2003b). *School of nursing syllabus: Issues in nursing: Health disparities (SL).* San Antonio, TX: author.

Selected Sources on Service-Learning

Bruce W. Speck

INTRODUCTION

The burgeoning literature on service-learning continues to grow, particularly as those in higher education seek to understand more about how to help students learn and how to integrate theory and practice in the curriculum. Although the previous chapters in this book provide a wealth of information about service-learning, the literature on service-learning is so extensive that a bibliography of that literature, even one that makes no claim to being exhaustive, is a useful supplement for those who want to investigate more fully the topic of this volume.

The bibliography is divided into four sections. The first lists various sources. The second lists books, collected works, and guides. The third lists journal articles. The fourth lists articles from the *Michigan Journal of Community Service-Learning,* arguably the single most significant source of journal articles on service-learning.

VARIOUS SOURCES

Interest in service-learning has produced special issues devoted to service-learning in a spate of journals, including *Journal of Nursing Education* (2002), 41(10); *Educational Horizons* (2002), 80(4); *Educational Gerontology* (2001), 27(1); *PS: Political Science and Politics* (2000), 33(4); *Academe* (2000), 86(4); *Metropolitan Universities: An International Forum* (2000), 11(1); *School Administrator* (2000), 57(7); and *Phi Delta Kappan* (2000), 81(9). An online bibliography of service-learning literature—Eyler, J. S., Giles, D. E., Jr., Stenson, C. M., & Gray, C. J. (2001). *At a glance: What we know about the effects of service-learning on college students, faculty, institutions and communities, 1993–2000* (3rd ed.)—can be found at www.compact.org/resource/aag.pdf, a section of the National Service-Learning Clearinghouse. In addition, several organizations have Web sites that provide information on service-learning, including Campus Compact. Service-learning links, including one for Campus Compact, can be found at www.nsl exchange.org/exchange/links.cfm.

BOOKS, COLLECTED WORKS, AND GUIDES

Albert, G. et al., (Eds.). (1994). *Service-learning reader: Reflections and perspectives on service.* Raleigh, NC: National Society for Experiential Education.

Anderson, J. B. (2000). *Service-learning and preservice teacher education.* Denver, CO: Education Commission of the States. (ERIC database: No. ED445988)

Anderson, J. B., Swick, K. J., & Yff, J. (Eds.). (2001). *Service-learning in teacher education: Enhancing the growth of new teachers, their students, and communities.* Washington, DC: American Association of Colleges for Teacher Education (AACTE). (ERIC database: No. ED451167)

Babcock, B. (Ed.). (2000). *Learning from experience: A collection of service-learning projects linking academic standards to curriculum.* Milwaukee: Wisconsin Department of Public Instruction. (ERIC database: No. ED444920)

Barber, B. R., & Battistoni, R. (Eds.). (1993). *Education for democracy.* Dubuque, IA: Kendall/Hunt.

Bhaerman, R., Cordell, K., & Gomez, B. (1998). *The role of service-learning in educational reform.* Needham Heights, MA: Simon & Schuster.

Boyle-Baise, M. (2002). *Multicultural service-learning: Educating teachers in diverse communities.* New York: Teachers College Press.

Canada, M., & Speck, B. (Eds.). (2001). *Developing and implementing service-learning programs.* New Directions for Higher Education, 114. San Francisco: Jossey-Bass.

Cantor, J. A. (1995). *Experiential learning in higher education: Linking classroom and community* (ASHE-ERIC Higher Education Report No. 7). Washington, DC: George Washington University, Graduate School of Education and Human Development.

Deans, T. (2000). *Writing partnerships: Service-learning in composition.* Urbana, IL: National Council of Teachers of English. (ERIC database: No. ED445338)

Devine, R., Favazza, J. A., & McLain, F. M. (Eds.). (2002). *From cloister to commons: Concepts and models for service-learning in religious studies.* Merrifield, VA: American Association of Higher Education.

Eyler, J., & Giles, D. E., Jr. (1999). *Where's the learning in service-learning?* San Francisco: Jossey-Bass.

Fein, S., & Melnick, S. (2001). *Linking service-learning and school-to-work: Policy, partnerships, and practice to help all students succeed.* (ERIC database: No. ED458441)

Furco, A., & Billig, S. (Eds.). (2002). *Service-learning: The essence of the pedagogy. Advances in service-learning research.* Greenwich, CT: Information Age.

Halpern, D. F., & Associates. (Eds.). (1994). *Changing college classrooms: New teaching and learning strategies for an increasingly complex world.* San Francisco: Jossey-Bass.

Howard, J. (Ed.). (2001). *Service-learning course design workbook.* Ann Arbor: Edward Ginsberg Center for Community Service, University of Michigan.

Jacoby, B., & Associates. (1996). *Service-learning in higher education: Concepts and practices.* San Francisco: Jossey-Bass.

Keeton, M. T., & Associates. (Eds.). (1976). *Experiential learning.* San Francisco: Jossey-Bass.

Kendall, J., & Associates. (Eds.). (1990). *Combining service and learning: A resource book for community and public service.* Raleigh, NC: National Society for Internships and Experiential Education.

Klopp, C., Toole, P., & Toole, J. (2001). *Pondering learning: Connecting multiple intelligences and service-learning.* Clemson, SC: National Dropout Prevention Center, College of Health, Education, and Human Development, Clemson University. (ERIC database: No. ED457123)

Kolb, D. A. (1984). *Experiential learning: Experience as the source of learning and development.* Englewood Cliffs, NJ: Prentice Hall.

Kuh, G. D., Douglas, K. B., Lund, J. P., & Ramin-Gyurnek, J. (1994). *Student learning outside the classroom: Transcending artificial boundaries* (ASHE-ERIC Higher Education Report, Vol. 23, No. 8). Washington, DC: George Washington University, Graduate School of Education and Human Development.

Mann, S., & Patrick, J. J. (Eds.). (2000). *Education for civic engagement in democracy: Service-learning and other promising practices.* Bloomington, IL: ERIC Clearinghouse for Social Studies/Social Science Education. (ERIC database: No. ED447065)

Morse, S. W. (1989). *Renewing civic capacity: Preparing college students for service and citizenship* (ASHE-ERIC Higher Education Report No. 8). Washington, DC: School of Education and Human Development, George Washington University.

Pace, J. (2002). *Cornerstones: Building rural America through service-learning.* South Carolina: Kellogg Foundation. (ERIC database: No. ED466335)

Payne, D. A. (2000). *Evaluating service-learning activities and programs.* Lanham, MD: Scarecrow Press.

Pearson, S. S. (2002). *Finding common ground: Service-learning and education reform. A survey of 28 leading school reform models.* Washington, DC: American Youth Policy Forum. (ERIC database: No. ED466334)

Reidy, P. J. (2001). *To build a civilization of love: Catholic education and service-learning.* Washington DC: National Catholic Education Association (NCEA). (ERIC database: No. ED454125)

Rhoads, R. A., & Howard, J. P. F. (1998). *Academic service-learning.* New Directions for Teaching and Learning, 73. San Francisco: Jossey-Bass.

Rimmerman, C. A. (2001). *The new citizenship: Unconventional politics, activism, and service* (2nd ed.). Boulder, CO: Westview Press.

Runkel, P. J., Harrison, R., & Runkel, M. (Eds.). (1969). *The changing college classroom.* San Francisco: Jossey-Bass.

Sims, R. R., & Sims, S. J. (1995). *The importance of learning styles: Understanding the implications for learning, course design, and education.* Westport, CT: Greenwood Press.

Stanton, T. K., Giles, D. E., Jr., & Cruz, N. I. (1999). *Service-learning: A movement's pioneers reflect on its origins, practice, and future.* San Francisco: Jossey-Bass.

Swick, K. J., Winecoff, L., Nesbit, B., Kemper, R., Rowls, M., Freeman, N. K., et al. (2000). *Service-learning and character education: Walking the talk.* Washington, DC: Corporation for National Service.

Wade, R. C. (Ed.). (2000). *Building bridges: Connecting classroom and community through service-learning in social studies.* Washington, DC: National Council for the Social Studies. (ERIC database: No. ED446008)

Weatherford, C. G. (2000). *Tales that teach: Children's literature and service-learning. Linking learning with life.* Clemson, SC: National Dropout Prevention Center, College of Health, Education, and Human Development, Clemson University.

Zlotkowski, E. (Ed.). (1998). *Successful service-learning programs: New models of excellence in higher education.* Bolton, MA: Anker.

Zlotkowski, E. (Ed.). (2000). *AAHE's series on service-learning in the disciplines.* Washington, DC: American Association for Higher Education.

ARTICLES

Abernathy, T. V., & Obenchain, K. M. (2001). Student ownership of service-learning projects: Including ourselves in our community. *Intervention in School and Clinic, 37*(2), 86–95.

Agha-Jaffar, T. (2000). From theory to praxis in women's studies: Guest speakers and service-learning as pedagogy. *Feminist Teacher, 13*(1), 1–11.

Amtmann, J., Evans, R., & Powers, J. (2002). Case study of a service-learning partnership: Montana Tech and the Montana State Prison. *Journal of Correctional Education, 53*(1), 23–27.

Anderson, J. B., & Pickeral, T. (2000). Challenges and strategies for success with service-learning in preservice teacher education. *National Society of Experimental Education Quarterly, 25*(3), 7–22.

Anderson, J. D. (1995). Students' reflections on community service-learning. *Equity and Excellence in Education, 28*(3), 38–41.

Arman, J. F., & Scherer, D. (2002). Service-learning in school counselor preparation: A qualitative analysis. *Journal of Humanistic Counseling, Education and Development, 41*(1), 69–86.

Astin, A. W. (1995, March–April). The role of service in higher education. *About Campus,* pp. 14–19.

Astin, A. W. (1997). Liberal education and democracy: The case for pragmatism. *Liberal Education, 83*(4), 4–15.

Astin, A. W., & Sax, L. J. (1998) How undergraduates are affected by service participation. *Journal of College Student Development, 39*(3), 251–263.

Astin, A. W., Vogelgesang, L. J., Ikeda, E. K., & Yee, J. A. (2000). How service-learning affects students. (ERIC database: No. ED445577)

Bailey, D., DeVinny, G., Gordon, C., & Schadewald, J. P. (2000). AIDS and American history: Four perspectives on experiential learning. *Journal of American History, 86*(4), 1721–1733.

Ball, K., & Goodburn, A. M. (2000). Composition studies and service-learning: Appealing to communities? *Composition Studies/Freshman English News, 28*(1), 79–94.

Barber, B. R., & Battistoni, R. (1993). A season of learning: Introducing service-learning into the liberal arts curriculum. *PS: Political Science and Politics, 26*(2), 235–240.

Barner, J. C. (2000a). First-year pharmacy students' perceptions of their service-learning experience. *American Journal of Pharmaceutical Education, 64*(3), 266–271.

Barner, J. C. (2000b). Implementing service-learning in the pharmacy curriculum. *American Journal of Pharmaceutical Education, 64*(3), 260–265.

Barnett, L. (1996). Service-learning: Why community colleges? *New Directions for Community Colleges, 93*, 7–15.

Barton, A. C. (2000). Crafting multicultural science education with preservice teachers through service-learning. *Journal of Curriculum Studies, 32*(6), 797–820.

Bassis, M. (1997). One college's compact for individual and social responsibility. *Educational Record, 78*(3–4), 43–44.

Battistoni, R. (1995). Service-learning, diversity, and the liberal arts curriculum. *Liberal Education, 81*(1), 30–35.

Battistoni, R. (1997). Service-learning and democratic citizenship. *Theory into Practice, 36*(3), 150–156.

Beamer, G. (1998). Service-learning: What's a political scientist doing in Yonkers? *PS: Political Science and Politics, 31*(3), 557–561.

Beckman, M. (1997). Learning in action: Courses that complement community service. *College Teaching, 45*(2), 72–75.

Beisser, S. R. (2002, April). *An electronic resource for service-learning: A collaborative project between higher education and a state department of education.* Paper presented at the annual meeting of the American Educational Research Association, New Orleans, LA. (ERIC database: No. ED467597)

Berman, S., Bailey, S., Collins, R., Kinsley, D., & Holman, E. (2000). Service-learning: an administrator's tool for improving schools and connecting with the community. (ERIC database: No. ED445995)

Berry, H. A. (1985). Experiential education: The neglected dimension of international/intercultural studies. *International Programs Quarterly, 1*(3–4), 23–27.

Billig, S. H. (2002). Service-learning. *Research Roundup, 19*(1), 1–6.

Bittle, M., Duggleby, W., & Ellison, P. (2002). Implementation of the essential elements of service-learning in three nursing courses. *Journal of Nursing Education, 41*(3), 129–132.

Bordelon, S. (2002, March). *Service-learning and multiculturalism: Integrating cultural knowledge of native elders into the writing classroom.* Paper presented at the annual meeting of the Conference on College Composition and Communication, Chicago, IL. (ERIC database: No. ED464355)

Boyle-Baise, M., Epler, B., McCoy, W., Paulk, G., Clark, J., Slough, N., et al. (2001). Shared control: Community voices in multicultural service-learning. *Educational Forum, 65*(4), 344–353.

Boyle-Baise, M., & Sleeter, C. E. (2000). Community-based service-learning for multicultural teacher education. *Educational Foundations, 14*(2), 33–50.

Bringle, R. G., & Hatcher, J. A. (1996). Implementing service-learning in higher education. *Journal of Higher Education, 67*(2), 221–237.

Bringle, R. G., & Hatcher, J. A. (1999). Reflection in service-learning: Making meaning of experience. *Educational Horizons, 77*(4), 179–185.

Bringle, R. G., & Hatcher, J. A. (2000). Institutionalization of service-learning in higher education. *Journal of Higher Education, 71*(3), 273–291.

Brown, S. L., & Lashley, T. L. (2002, April). *Appalachian rural systemic initiative: An account of a service-learning collaboration of two science educators.* Paper presented at the annual meeting of the American Educational Research Association, New Orleans, LA. (ERIC database: No. ED466333)

Brotherton, P. (2002). Connecting the classroom and the community. *Black Issues in Higher Education, 19*(5), 20–24.

Buchanan, A. M., Baldwin, S. C., & Rudisill, M. E. (2002). Service-learning as scholarship in teacher education. *Educational Researcher, 31*(5), 28–34.

Burns, M., Storey, K., & Certo, N. J. (1999). Effect of service-learning on attitudes towards students with severe disabilities. *Education and Training in Mental Retardation and Developmental Disabilities, 34*(1), 58–65.

Burr, K. (2001). Building for hope: Progressive service-learning enhances education. *Journal of Industrial Teacher Education, 38*(4), 84–93.

Burr, K. L. (2001). Progressive service-learning: Four examples in construction education. *Journal of Construction Education, 6*(1), 6–19.

Bush-Bacelis, J. L. (1998). Innovative pedagogy: Academic service-learning for business communication. *Business Communication Quarterly, 61*(3), 20–34.

Buttleman-Malcolm, D. (2002). Literacy projects: An ideal service-learning genre for scholastic journalists. *Quill and Scroll, 76*(2), 10–11.

Calleson, D. C., Serow, R. C., & Parker, L. G. (1998). Institutional perspectives on integrating service and learning. *Journal of Research and Development in Education, 31*(3), 147–154.

Callister, L. C., & Hobbins-Garbett, D. (2000). Enter to learn, go forth to serve: Service-learning in nursing education. *Journal of Professional Nursing, 16*(3), 177–183.

Carr, K. (2002). Building bridges and crossing borders: Using service-learning to overcome cultural barriers to collaboration between science and education departments. *School Science and Mathematics, 102*(6), 285–298.

Carpenter, B. W., & Jacobs, J. S. (1994). Service-learning: A new approach in higher education. *Education, 115*(1), 97–99.

Carver, R. L. (1997). Theoretical underpinnings of service-learning. *Theory into Practice, 36*(3), 144–149.

Chapin, J. R. (1999). Missing pieces in the service-learning puzzle. *Educational Horizons, 77*(4), 202–207.

Checkoway, B. (1996). Combining service and learning on campus and in the community. *Phi Delta Kappan, 77*(9), 600–606.

Chickering, A. W., & O'Connor, J. (1996). The university learning center: A driving force for collaboration. *About Campus, 1*(4), 16–21.

Clabaugh, G. K. (1999). Service-learning: The right thing for the wrong reasons? *Educational Horizons, 77*(4), 163–165.

Clark, C. (2003). Unfolding narratives of service-learning: Reflections in teaching, learning, literacy, and positioning in service-learning. *Journal of Adolescent and Adult Literacy, 46*(4), 288–297.

Clark, T., Croddy, M., Hayes, W., & Philips, S. (1997). Service-learning as civic participation. *Theory into Practice, 36*(3), 164–169.

Cleary, C. (1998). Steps to incorporate service-learning into an undergraduate course. *Journal of Experiential Education, 21*(3), 130–133.

Cleary, C., & Benson, D. E. (1998). The service integration project: Institutionalizing university service-learning. *Journal of Experiential Education, 21*(3), 124–129.

Conderman, G. J., & Patryla, V. (1996). Service-learning: The past, the present, and the promise. *Kappa Delta Pi Record, 32*(4), 122–125.

Covan, E. K. (2001). Employing service-learning to teach research methods to gerontology students. *Educational Gerontology, 27*(7), 623–627.

Cromwell, R. R., & Curran, J. M. (2002). Service-learning integrated into a conceptual framework improves a teacher education program. (ERIC database: ED464072)

Cross, D. (1974). The pedagogy of participation. *Teachers College Record, 76*(2), 316–334.

Cruz, A. M. (2002). Civic responsibility, ethics and integrity. *Community College Journal, 72*(3), 33–35.

Cushman, E. (1999). The public intellectual, service-learning, and activist research. *College English, 61*(3), 328–336.

Cushman, E. (2002). Sustainable service-learning programs. *College Composition and Communication, 54*(1), 40–65.

Dalton, J. C., & Petrie, A. M. (1997). The power of peer culture. *Educational Record, 78*(3–4), 18–24.

Degelman, C. (Ed.). (2000). Fostering civic responsibility through service-learning. *Service-Learning Network, 8*(1).

Degelman, C. (Ed.). (2000). Linking service-learning and standards. *Service-Learning Network, 8*(2).

Degelman, C. (Ed.). (2001). Breaking the age barrier: Multi-generational service-learning. *Service-Learning Network, 8*(4).

Deruosi, P., & Sherwood, C. S. (1997). Community service scholarships: Combining cooperative education with service-learning. *Journal of Cooperative Education, 33*(1), 46–54.

DeSchiffart, C. (2000). Community service-learning with unemployed young Nova Scotians. *Canadian Journal of Counseling, 34*(3), 186–192.

Dickson, A. (1979). Altruism and action. *Journal of Moral Action, 8*(3), 147–155.

Dickson, A. (1979, Winter). Matching curriculum and social needs. *Synergist, 31*(3), 16–18.

Dinkelman, T. (2000, April). *Service-learning in student teaching: "What's social studies for?"* Paper presented at the annual meeting of the American Educational Research Association, New Orleans, LA. (ERIC database: No. ED444971)

Drake, B. (2001). Service as a feature of quality education. *International School Journal, 20*(2), 46–53.

Dubinsky, J. M. (2001, March). *Service-learning and civic engagement: Bridging school and community through professional writing projects.* Paper presented at the annual meeting of the Warwick Writing Programme, Department of English and Comparative Literary Studies, University of Warwick, Coventry, England. (ERIC database: No. ED459462)

Duke, J. I. (1999). Service-learning: Taking mathematics into the real world. *The Mathematics Teacher, 92*(9) 794–796, 799.

Dundon, B. L. (2000). My voice: An advocacy approach to service-learning. *Educational Leadership, 57*(4), 34–37.

Dunlap, M. R. (1998a). Adjustment and development outcomes of students engaged in service-learning. *Journal of Experiential Education, 21*(3), 147–153.

Dunlap, M. R. (1998b). Methods of supporting students' critical reflection in courses incorporating service-learning. *Teaching of Psychology, 25*(3), 208–210.

Eddy, G., & Carducci, J. (1997). Service with a smile: Class and community in advanced composition. *Writing Instructor, 16*(2), 78–90.

Edwards, S. K. (2001). Bridging the gap: Connecting school and community with service-learning. *English Journal, 90*(5), 39–44.

Ehrlich, T. (1997). Civic learning: Democracy and education revisited. *Educational Record, 78*(3–4), 57–65.

Ehrlich, T. (1998). Reinventing John Dewey's 'Pedagogy as a university discipline.' *Elementary School Journal, 98*(5), 489–509.

Elliott, P. G. (1997). To improve service-learning experiences. *Planning for Higher Education, 25*(4), 48–49.

Elwell, M. D., & Bean, M. S. (2001). The efficacy of service-learning for community college ESL students. *Community College Review, 28*(4), 47–61.

Ender, M. G., Martin, L., Cotter, D. A., Kowalewski, B. M., & DeFiore, J. (2000). Given an opportunity to reach out: Heterogeneous participation in optional service-learning projects. *Teaching Sociology, 28*(3), 206–219.

Estes, C. A., Wilson, S., & Toupence, R. (2001). Methods of conducting complex service-learning projects in recreation, parks, and leisure services curricula. *SCHOLE: A Journal of Leisure Studies and Recreation Education, 16*, 49–69.

Everett, K. D. (1998). Understanding social inequality through service-learning. *Teaching Sociology, 26*(4), 199–307.

Exley, R. J., Gottlieb, K. L., & Young, J. B. (2000). Citizenship and community building. *Community College Journal, 70*(3), 16–20.

Fearn, M. L. (2001). Service-learning in geography: Fertile ground for student involvement in local environmental problems. *Journal of College Science Teaching, 30*(7), 470–473.

Fenzel, L. M. (2001, April). *Enhancing the benefits of service-learning in undergraduate psychology courses.* Paper presented at the annual meeting of the American Educational Research Association, Seattle, WA. (ERIC database: No. ED452756)

Ferrari, J. R., & Jason, L. A. (1996). Integrating research and community service: Incorporating research skills into service-learning experiences. *College Student Journal, 30*(4), 444–451.

Fertman, C. I. (2000, April). *Contributions of adolescent development research to service-learning research.* Paper presented at the annual meeting of the American Educational Research Association, New Orleans, LA. (ERIC database: No. ED443771)

Fleckenstein, M. P. (1997). Service-learning in business ethics. *Journal of Business Ethics, 16,* 12–13, 137–141.

Flower, L. (2002). Intercultural inquiry and the transformation of service. *College English, 65*(2), 181–201.

Forman, S. G., & Wilkinson, L. C. (1997). Educational policy through service-learning: Preparation for citizenship and civic participation. *Innovative Higher Education, 21*(4), 275–285.

Franco, R. W. (2000). The community college conscience: Service-learning and training tomorrow's teachers. (ERIC database: No. ED452890)

Fredericksen, P. J. (2000). Does service-learning make a difference in student performance? *Journal of Experiential Education, 23*(2), 64–74.

Frimannsson, G. H. (2001). Civic education and the good. *Studies in Philosophy and Education, 20*(4), 303–315.

Gallagher, J. J., & Hogan, K. (2000). Intergenerational, community-based learning and science education. *Journal of Research in Science Teaching, 37*(2), 107–108.

Gamson, Z., Hollander, E., & Kiang, P. N. (1998). The university in engagement with society. *Liberal Education, 84*(2), 20–25.

Garavaglia-Maiorano, J. S., & Pile, J. (2001). Service-learning: Making the camp connection. Camp programming that integrates learning through community service. *Camping Magazine, 74*(5), 38–39.

Garbus, J. (2002). Service-learning, 1902. *College English, 64*(5), 547–565.

Gaudiani, C. L. (1997). Catalyzing community: The college as a model of civil society. *Educational Record, 78*(3–4), 81–86.

Gelmon, S. B. (2000). How do we know that our work makes a difference? Assessment strategies for service-learning and civic engagement. *Metropolitan Universities: An International Forum, 11*(2), 28–39.

Gent, P. J., & Gurecka, L. E. (1998). Service-learning: A creative strategy for inclusive classrooms. *Journal of the Association for Persons with Severe Handicaps, 23*(3), 261–271.

Glaser, H. F., & Radliff, A. J. (2000). Integrating service-learning into the communication capstone course. (ERIC database: No. ED444199)

Glenn. J. M. L. (2002). Building bridges between school and community: Service-learning in business education. *Business Education Forum, 56*(4), 6–28.

Gonzales, K. (2000). Reflections on the birth and first year of Bienvenidos, Nuevos Amigos! A service-learning project in Eldorado, Texas, 1999–2000. (ERIC database: No. ED446436)

Gordon, R. (1999). Problem-based service-learning. *Academic Exchange Quarterly, 3*(4), 16–27.

Gorelick, R. P. (2002, March). *Service-learning's flaw: What's community got to do with it?* Paper presented at the annual meeting of the Conference on College Composition and Communication, Chicago, IL. (ERIC database: No. 464339)

Graham, R. (1973). Voluntary action and experiential education. *Journal of Voluntary Action Research, 2*(4), 186–193.

Graves, R. (2001). Responses to student writing from service-learning clients. *Business Communication Quarterly, 64*(4), 55–62.

Grusky, S. (2000). International service-learning—A critical guide from an impassioned advocate. *The American Behavioral Scientist, 43*(5), 858–867.

Gujarathi, M. R., & McQuade, R. J. (2002). Service-learning in business school: A case study in an intermediate accounting course. *Journal of Education for Business, 77*(3), 144–150.

Hamner, J. B., Wilder, B., Avery, G., & Byrd, L. (2002). Community-based service-learning in the engaged university. *Nursing Outlook, 50*(2), 67–71.

Hardy, M. S., & Schaen, E. B. (2000). Integrating the classroom and community service: Everyone benefits. *Teaching of Psychology, 27*(1), 47–49.

Harkavy, I., & Romer, D. (1999). Service-learning as an integrated strategy. *Liberal Education, 85*(3), 14–19.

Hatcher, J. A., & Bringle, R. G. (1997). Reflection: Bridging the gap between service and learning. *College Teaching, 45*(4), 153–158.

Hatcher-Skeers, M., & Aragon, E. (2002). Combining active learning with service-learning: A student-driven demonstration project. *Journal of Chemical Education, 79*(4), 462–464.

Hayward, P. (2000, November). *Service-learning in the public relations course and its impact on students, faculty, and the community.* Paper presented at the annual meeting of the National Communication Association, Seattle, WA. (ERIC database: No. ED465976)

Heffernan, K. (2001). Campus Compact: developing partnerships for community service. *Community and Junior College Libraries, 10*(2), 55–59.

Hellman, S. (2000). Distant service-learning in first-year composition: A grant writing unit. *Teaching English in the Two Year College, 28*(1), 11–20.

Henson, L., & Sutliff, K. (1998). A service-learning approach to business and technical writing instruction. *Journal of Technical Writing and Communication, 28*(2), 189–205.

Hepburn, M. A. (1997). Service-learning in civic education: A concept with long, sturdy roots. *Theory into Practice, 36*(3), 136–142.

Herzberg, B. (2000). Service-learning and public discourse. *JAC: A Journal of Composition Theory, 20*(2), 391–404.

Hilosky, A., Moore, M. E., & Reynolds, P. (1999). Service-learning: Brochure writing for basic level college students. *College Teaching, 47*(4), 143–147.

Hubbert, K. N. (2001, February). *Small group communication and service-learning.* Paper presented at the annual meeting of the Western States Communication Association, Coeur d'Alene, ID. (ERIC database: No. ED452574)

Hubbert, K. (2002). Service-learning and learning communities. (ERIC database: No. 466259)

Huckin, T. N. (1997). Technical writing and community service. *Journal of Business and Technical Communication, 11*(1), 49–59.

Hunt, J. B. (2002, February). *Service-learning delivers real-world accountability.* Paper presented at the annual meeting of the American Association of Colleges for Teacher Education, New York, NY. (ERIC database: No. ED468747)

Hurst, C. P., & Osban, L. B. (2000). Service-learning on wheels: The Nightingale Mobile Clinic. *Nursing and Health Care Perspectives, 21*(4), 184–187.

Ikeda, E. K. (2000, April). *How reflection enhances learning in service-learning courses.* Paper presented at the annual meeting of the American Educational Research Association, New Orleans, LA. (ERIC database: No. ED442436)

Inman, J. O. (2002, March). *Ending the turf wars: Connecting service-learning and cultural studies composition.* Paper presented at the annual meeting of the

Conference on College Composition and Communication, Chicago, IL. (ERIC database: No. ED462728)

Jacoby, B., & Bringle, R. C. (1997). Service-learning in higher education: Concepts and practices. *Journal of Higher Education, 68*(6), 715–717.

Jarosz, L., & Johnson-Bogert, K. (1996). New concepts of the relationship between college and community: The potential of service-learning. *College Teaching, 44*(3), 83–88.

Jennings, M. (2001). Two very special service-learning projects. *Phi Delta Kappan, 9*(4), 474–475.

Joiner, L. L. (2000). Learning to serve: Community service meets curriculum objectives. *American School Board Journal, 187*(11), 32–34.

Jones, B. L., Maloy, R. W., & Steen, C. M. (1996). Learning through community service is political. *Equity and Excellence in Education, 29*(2), 37–45.

Jones, S. R. (2002). The underside of service-learning. *About Campus, 7*(4), 10–15.

Jones, S. R., & Hill, K. (2001). Crossing high street: Understanding diversity through community service-learning. *Journal of College Student Development, 42*(3), 204–216.

Jurgens, J. C., & Schwitzer, A. M. (2002). Designing, implementing, and evaluating a service-learning component in human services education. *Human Service Education: A Journal of the National Organization for Human Service Education, 22*(1), 35–45.

Jutras, P. (2000). How service-learning projects can be a catalyst for faculty learning. *Academic Exchange Quarterly, 4*(1), 54–58.

Kahne, J., & Westheimer, J. (1996). In the service of what?: The politics of service-learning. *Phi Delta Kappan, 77*(9), 593–599.

Kaplan, A. (1997). Public life: A contribution to democratic education. *Journal of Curriculum Studies, 29*(4), 431–453.

Keith, J. F. (1995). Introducing a campus to service-learning. *Journal of Career Development, 22*(2), 135–139.

Kezar, A. (2002). Assessing community service-learning: Are we identifying the right outcome? *About Campus, 7*(2), 14–20.

Kezar, A., & Rhoads, R. A. (2001). The dynamic tensions of service-learning in higher education: A philosophical perspective. *Journal of Higher Education, 72*(2), 148–171.

King, P. M. (1997). Character and civic education: What does it take? *Educational Record, 78*(3–4), 87–93.

Knapp, J. L., & Stubblefield, P. (2000). Changing students' perceptions of aging: The impact of an intergenerational service-learning course. *Educational Gerontology, 26*(7), 611–621.

Kohlmoos, J. (1995). Thoughts on community service-learning. *Equity and Excellence in Education, 28*(3), 42–44.

Kohls, J. (1996). Student experiences with service-learning in a business ethics class. *Journal of Business Ethics, 15*(1), 45–57.

Kolenko, T. A., Porter, G., Wheatley, W., & Colby, M. (1996). A critique of service-learning projects in management education: Pedagogical foundations, barriers, and guidelines. *Journal of Business Ethics, 15*(1), 133–142.

Koliba, C. J. (2000). Moral language and networks of engagement: Service-learning and civic education. *The American Behavioral Scientist, 43*(5), 825–838.

Koulish, R. (1998). Citizenship service-learning: Becoming citizens by assisting immigrants. *PS: Political Science and Politics, 31*(3), 562–567.

Kozeracki, C. A. (2000). Service-learning in the community college. *Community College Review, 27*(4), 54–70.

Kraft, R. J. (1996). Service-learning: An introduction to its theory, practice, and effects. *Education and Urban Society, 28*(2), 131–159.

Kretchmar, M. D. (2001). Service-learning in a general psychology class: Description, preliminary evaluation, and recommendations. *Teaching of Psychology, 28*(1), 5–10.

LaMaster, K. J. (2001). Enhancing preservice teachers' field experience through the addition of a service-learning component. *Journal of Experiential Education, 24*(1), 27–33.

Lamb, C. H., Swinth, R. L., Vinton, K. L., & Lee, J. B. (1998). Integrating service-learning into a business school curriculum. *Journal of Management Education, 22*(5), 637–654.

LeSourd, S. J. (1997). Community service in a multicultural nation. *Theory into Practice, 36*(3), 157–163.

Lewis, M. (2002). Service-learning and older adults. *Educational Gerontology, 28*(8), 655–667.

Lott, C. E. (1997). Learning through service: A faculty perspective. *Liberal Education, 83*(1), 40–45.

Malone, D., Jones, B. D., & Stallings, D. T. (2002). Perspective transformation: Effects of a service-learning tutoring experience on prospective teachers. *Teacher Education Quarterly, 29*(1), 61–81.

Maring, G. H., Wiseman, B. J., & Boxie, P. (2000, October). *Integrating content literacy, critical literacy, and service-learning: A line of research during a decade-long odyssey.* Paper presented at the Research Colloquium of the Department of Teaching and Learning, Washington State University, Pullman, WA. (ERIC database: No. ED455731)

Markus, G. B., Howard, J. P. F., & King, D. C. (1993). Integrating community service and classroom instruction enhances learning: Results from an experiment. *Educational Evaluation and Policy Analysis, 15*(4), 410–419.

Maser, J. A. (2001). Collaborative development and benefits of a science inquiry service-learning course. *Metropolitan Universities: An International Forum, 12*(4), 107–115.

Masucci, M., & Renner, A. (2001). The evolution of critical service-learning for education: Four problematics. (ERIC database: No. ED456962)

Mathews, D. (1997). Character for what?: Higher education and public life. *Educational Record, 78*(3–4), 10–17.

Mayhew, J. (2000). Service-learning in preservice special education: A comparison of two approaches. (ERIC database: No. ED439883)

Mayhew, J., & Welch, M. (2001). A call to service: Service-learning as a pedagogy in special education programs. *Teacher Education and Special Education, 24*(3), 208–219.

McCarthy, A. M., & Tucker, M. L. (2002). Encouraging community service through service-learning. *Journal of Management Education, 26*(6), 629–647.

McEachern, R. W. (2001). Problems in service-learning and technical/professional writing: Incorporating the perspective of nonprofit management. *Technical Communication Quarterly, 10*(2), 211–224.

McKinney, K. G. (2002). Engagement in community service among college students: Is it affected by significant attachment relationships? *Journal of Adolescence, 25*(2), 139–154.

Meister, R. J. (1998). Engagement with society at DePaul University. *Liberal Education, 84*(4), 56–61.

Mendel-Reyes, M. (1998). A pedagogy for citizenship: Service-learning and democratic education. *New Directions for Teaching and Learning, 73,* 31–38.

Mettetal, G., & Bryant, D. (1996). Service-learning research projects: Empowerment in students, faculty, and communities. *College Teaching, 44*(1), 24–28.

Michael, K. Y. (2001). Technology education students make a difference through service-learning. *Technology Teacher, 61*(3), 30–32.

Miller, M. P., & Swanson, E. (2002). Service-learning and community health nursing: A natural fit. *Nursing Education Perspectives, 23*(1), 30–33.

Mogk, D. W., & King, J. L. (1995). Service-learning in geology classes. *Journal of Geological Education, 43*(5), 461–465.

Mohan, J. (1995). Thinking local: Service-learning, education for citizenship and geography. *Journal of Geography in Higher Education, 19*(2), 129–143.

Moore, D. (1981). Discovering the pedagogy of experience. *Harvard Educational Review, 51*(2), 286–300.

Morrill, R. L. (1982). Educating for democratic values. *Liberal Education, 68*(4), 365–376.

Morris, F. A. (2001). Serving the community and learning a foreign language: Evaluating a service-learning programme. *Language, Culture and Curriculum, 14*(3), 244–255.

Morris, P. V., Pomery, J., & Murray, K. E. (2002). Service-learning: Going beyond traditional extension activities. *Journal of Extension, 40*(2). Retrieved from http://www.joe.org/joe/2002april/iw2.html

Muscott, H. S. (2000). A review and analysis of service-learning programs involving students with behavioral disorders. *Education and Treatment of Children, 23*(3), 346–368.

Myers-Lipton, S. (1998). Effect of a comprehensive service-learning program on college students' civic responsibility. *Teaching Sociology, 26*(4), 243–258.

Neururer, J., & Rhoads. R. A. (1998). Community service: Panacea, paradox, or potentiation. *Journal of College Student Development, 39*(4), 321–330.

Novak, C. C., & Goodman, L. J. (1997). Safer contact zones: The call of service-learning. *The Writing Instructor, 16*(2), 65–77.

Novek, E. M. (2000, November). *Tourists in the land of service-learning: Helping middle-class students move from curiosity to commitment.* Paper presented at the annual meeting of the National Communication Association, Seattle, WA. (ERIC database: No. ED448486)

Nunn, M. (2002). Volunteering as a tool for building social capital. *Journal of Volunteer Administration, 20*(4), 14–20.

O'Halloran, J. (2000). The story of a service-learning project: Mathematics in the park. *Humanistic Mathematics Network Journal, 23,* 17–21.

Palmer, P. J. (1987, September/October). Community, conflict, and ways of knowing: Ways to deepen our educational agenda. *Change, 19*(5), 20–25.

Panici, D., & Lasky, K. (2002). Service-learning's foothold in communication schol-arship. *Journalism and Mass Communication Educator, 57*(2), 113–125.

Parker-Gwin, R. (1996). Connecting service to learning: How students and com-munities matter. *Teaching Sociology, 24*(1), 97–101.

Parker-Gwin, R., & Mabry, J. B. Service-learning as pedagogy and civic education: Comparing outcomes for three models. *Teaching Sociology, 26*(4), 276–291.

Pascarella, E. T. (1997). College's influence on principled moral reasoning. *Educational Record, 78*(3–4), 47–55.

Perreault, G. E. (1997). Citizen leader: A community service option for college students. *NASPA Journal, 34*(2), 147–156.

Piper, B., DeYoung, M., & Lamsam, G. D. (2000). Student perceptions of a service-learning experience. *American Journal of Pharmaceutical Education, 64*(2), 159–165.

Plann, S. J. (2002). Latinos and literacy: An upper-division Spanish course with service-learning. *Hispania, 85*(2), 330–338.

Powell, G. M. (2001). Learning through community service. *Camping Magazine, 74*(5), 12–13, 15.

Prentice, M. (2000, October). Service-learning programs on community college campuses. *ERIC Digest*, pp. 1–14. (ERIC database: No. ED451857)

Prentice, M. (2002). Institutionalizing service-learning in community college. (ERIC database: No. ED465399)

Prentice, M., & Garcia, R. M. (2000). Service-learning: The next generation in edu-cation. *Community College Journal of Research and Practice, 24*(1), 19–26.

Prince, G. S., Jr. (1997). Are we graduating good citizens? *Educational Record, 78*(3–4), 34–42.

Pritchard, I. A. (2001). Raising standards in community service-learning. *About Campus, 6*(4), 18–24.

Ramsey, J. (1997). Tanya settles in: 'America Reads' as service-learning. *Liberal Education, 83*(3), 51–54.

Regan, A. E., & Zuern, J. D. (2000). Community-service-learning and computer-mediated advanced composition: The going to class, getting online, and giving back project. *Computers and Composition, 17*(2), 177–195.

Rehling, L. (2000). Doing good while doing well: Service-learning internships. *Business Communication Quarterly, 63*(1), 76–89.

Rhoads, R. A. (1998). In the service of citizenship: A study of student involvement in community service. *Journal of Higher Education, 69*(3), 277–297.

Rhoads, R. A. (2000). Democratic citizenship and service-learning: Advancing the caring self. *New Directions for Teaching and Learning, 82*, 37–44.

Rhodes, N. J., & Davis, J. M. (2001). Using service-learning to get positive reactions in the library. *Computers in the Library, 21*(1), 32–35.

Rice, K. L., & Brown, J. R. (1998). Transforming educational curriculum and service-learning. *Journal of Experiential Education, 21*(3), 140–146.

Robb, C., & Swearer, H. (1985). Community service and higher education: A na-tional agenda. *AAHE Bulletin, 37*(10), 3–8.

Robinson, G. (2000). Stepping into our destiny: Service-learning in community colleges. *Community College Journal, 70*(3), 8–12.

Robinson, G. (2001). Community colleges broadening horizons through service-learning, 2003–2004. (ERIC database: No. ED465405)

Rosenberg, L. (2000). Becoming the change we wish to see in the world: Combating through service-learning learned passivity. *Academic Exchange Quarterly*, 4(1), 6–11.

Rubin, S. (2000). Developing community through experiential education. *New Directions for Higher Education, 109*, 43–50.

Saltmarsh, J. (1997). Ethics, reflection, purpose, and compassion: Community service-learning. *New Directions for Student Services, 77*, 81–93.

Sax, L. J., & Astin, A. W. (1997). The benefits of service: Evidence from undergraduates. *Educational Record, 78*(3–4), 25–33.

Schaeffer, M. A., & Peterson, S. (1998). Service-learning as a strategy for teaching undergraduate research. *Journal of Experiential Education, 21*(3), 154–161.

Schaffer, E., Berman, S., Pickeral, T., & Holman, E. (2001). Service-learning and character education: One plus one is more than two. (ERIC database: No. ED457100)

Schwartzman, R., & Phelps, G. A. (2001, November). *In loco communitas: Service-learning and the liberal arts*. Paper presented at the annual meeting of the National Communication Association, Atlanta, GA. (ERIC database: No. ED458654)

Schnaubelt, T., & Watson, J. L. (1999). Connecting service and leadership in the classroom. *Academic Exchange Quarterly, 3*(4), 7–15.

Schumann, M. F. (2001). An experiment in service-learning: Pairing students with older adults in a lifespan development course. *Inquiry, 6*(1), 61–65.

Schutz, A., & Gere, A. R. (1998). Service-learning and English studies: Rethinking 'public' service. *College English, 60*(2), 129–149.

Sellnow, T. L., & Oster, L. K. (1997). The frequency, form, and perceived benefits of service-learning in speech communication departments. *Journal of the Association for Communication Administration, 3*, 190–197.

Shastri, A. (2001, March). *Examining the impact of service-learning among preservice teachers*. Paper presented at the annual meeting of the American Association of Colleges for Teacher Education, Dallas, TX. (ERIC database: No. ED453241)

Shumer, R. (1987). Taking community service seriously. *Community Education Journal, 15*(1), 15–17.

Shumer, R., & Belbas, B. (1996). What we know about service-learning. *Education and Urban Society, 28*(2), 208–223.

Silcox, H. C., & Leek, T. E. (1997). International service-learning: Its time has come. *Phi Delta Kappan, 78*(8), 615–618.

Sipe, R. B. (2001). Academic service-learning: More than just "doing time." *English Journal, 90*(5), 33–38.

St. John, P. (2000). A team approach to service-learning. *NSEE Quarterly, 26*(1), 12–15.

Stachowski, L. L., & Mahan, J. M. (1998). Cross-cultural field placements: student teachers learning from schools and communities. *Theory into Practice, 37*(2), 155–162.

Stevens, B. (2001). Cross-cultural service-learning: American and Russian students learn applied organizational communication. *Business Communication Quarterly, 64*(3), 59–69.

Stone, E. (2000). Service-learning in the introductory technical writing class: A perfect match? *Journal of Technical Writing and Communication, 30*(4), 385–398.

Stukas, A. A., Snyder, M., & Clary, E. G. (1999). The effects of "mandatory volunteerism" on intentions to volunteer. *Educational Horizons, 77*(4), 194–201.

Swick, K. J. (2001). Service-learning in teacher education: Building learning communities. *Clearing House, 74*(5), 261–264.

Tai-Seale, T. (2001). Liberating service-learning and applying the new practice. *College Teaching, 49*(1), 14–18.

Ternzini, P. T. (1994). Educating for citizenship: Freeing the mind and elevating the spirit. *Innovative Higher Education, 19*(1), 7–21.

Thompson, G. D., Lyman, S., Childres, K., & Taylor, P. (2002). Strategy for alcohol abuse education: A service-learning model within a course curriculum. *American Journal of Health Education, 33*(2), 88–93.

Thompson, J. C., Jr. (1999). Enhancing school-community partnerships: Service-learning can have an impact. *Educational Horizons, 77*(4), 159–162.

Tucker, M. L., McCarthy, A. M., Hoxmeier, J. A., & Lenk, M. M. (1998). Community service-learning increases communication skills across the business curriculum. *Business Communication Quarterly, 61*(2), 88–99.

Varlotta, L. E. (1997). Confronting consensus: Investigating the philosophies that have informed service-learning's communities. *Educational Theory, 47*(4), 453–476.

Wade, R. C. (2000a). Beyond charity: Service-learning for social justice. *Social Studies and the Young Leader, 12*(4), 6–9.

Wade, R. C. (2000b). Service-learning for multicultural teaching competency: Insights from the literature for teacher educators. *Equity and Excellence in Education, 33*(3), 21–29.

Wagner, J. (1987). Teaching and research as student responsibilities: Integrating community and academic work. *Change, 19*(5), 26–35.

Waldstein, F. A., & Reiher, T. C. (2001). Service-learning and students' personal and civic development. *Journal of Experiential Education, 24*(1), 7–13.

Wang, W. (2000, April). *Service-learning: Is it good for you?* Paper presented at the annual meeting of the American Educational Research Association, New Orleans, LA. (ERIC database: No. ED442439)

Ward, S. (2000, April). *Transforming the instructor: Service-learning integrated into a community college curriculum.* Paper presented at the annual meeting of the American Educational Research Association, New Orleans, LA. (ERIC database: No. ED441531)

Warren, K. (1998). Educating students for social justice in service-learning. *Journal of Experiential Education, 21*(3), 134–139.

Washington, P. A. (2000). From college classroom to community action. *Feminist Teacher, 13*(1), 12–34.

Watson, D. L., Crandall, J., Hueglin, S., & Eisenman, P. (2002). Incorporating service-learning into physical education teacher education programs. *Journal of Physical Education, Recreation and Dance, 73*(5), 50–54.

Weglarz, S. G. (2000). *Johnson County Community College service-learning student survey, Spring 2000.* (ERIC database: No. ED454902)

Williams, K., & Kovacs, C. (2001). Balance and mobility training for older adults: An undergraduate service-learning experience. *Journal of Physical Education, Recreation and Dance, 72*(3), 54–58.

Windham, P. W. (2001). *Connecting to the community: Service-learning, partnerships and public service.* (ERIC database: No. ED467301)

Woods, M. (2002). Research on service-learning. *Agricultural Education Magazine, 75*(2), 24–25.

Yob, I. M. (2000). A feeling for others: Music education and service-learning. *Philosophy of Music Education Review, 8*(2), 67–78.

Zlotkowski, E. (1997). Service-learning and the process of academic renewal. *Journal of Public Service & Outreach, 21*(1), 80–87.

Zlotkowski, E. (2001). Mapping new terrain: Service-learning across the disciplines. *Change, 33*(1), 24–33.

Zukergood, D., & Lucy-Allen, D. (2000). Utilizing service-learning to incite student passion for learning. *Academic Exchange Quarterly, 4*(1), 12–15.

MICHIGAN JOURNAL OF COMMUNITY SERVICE-LEARNING

1994, Volume 1

Barber, B. R. A proposal for mandatory citizen education and community service. 86–93.

Cohen, J. Matching university mission with service motivation: Do the accomplishments of community service match the claims? 98–104.

Fox, H. Teaching empowerment. 55–61.

Giles, D. E., Jr., & Eyler, J. The theoretical roots of service-learning in John Dewey: Toward a theory of service-learning. 77–85.

Hammond, C. Integrating service and academic study: Faculty motivation and satisfaction in Michigan higher education. 21–28.

Levine, M. A. Seven steps to getting faculty involved in service-learning: How a traditional faculty member came to teach a course on 'voluntarism, community, and citizenship.' 110–114.

Miller, J. Linking traditional and service-learning courses: Outcome evaluations utilizing two pedagogically distinct models. 29–36.

Moon, A. Teaching excellence: The role of service-learning. 115–120.

Motiff, J. P., & Roehling, P. V. Learning while serving in a psychology internship. 70–76.

Reardon, K. M. Undergraduate research in distressed urban communities: An undervalued form of service-learning. 44–54.

Root, S. Service-learning in teacher education: A third rationale. 94–97.

Smith, M. W. Community service-learning: Striking the chord of citizenship. 37–43.

Stanton, T. K. The experience of faculty participants in an instructional development seminar on service-learning. 7–20.

Tice, C. H. Forging university-community collaboration: The agency perspective on national service. 105–109.

Yelsma, P. Combining small group problem solving with service-learning. 62–69.

1995, Volume 2

Aparicio, F. R., & José-Kampfner, C. Language, culture, and violence in the educational crisis of U.S. Latino/as: Two courses for intervention. 95–104.

Bringle, R. G., & Hatcher, J. A. A service-learning curriculum for faculty. 112–122.

Conniff, B., & Youngkin, B. R. The literary paradox: Service-learning and the traditional English department. 86–94.

Connor-Linton, J. An indirect model of service-learning: Integrating research, teaching, and community service. 105–111.

Cooper, D. D., & Julier, L. Writing the ties that bind: Service-learning in the writing classroom. 72–82.

De Acosta, M. Journal in writing in service-learning: Lessons from a mentoring project. 141–149.

Greene, D., & Diehm, G. Educational and service outcomes of a service integration effort. 54–62.

Hesser, G. Faculty assessment of student learning: Outcomes attributed to service-learning and evidence of changes in faculty attitudes about experiential education. 33–42.

Hudson, W. E., & Trudeau, R. H. An essay on the institutionalization of service-learning: The genesis of the Feinstein Institute for Public Service. 150–158.

Jeavons, T. H. Service-learning and liberal learning: A marriage of convenience. 134–140.

Liu, G. Knowledge, foundations, and discourse: Philosophical support for service-learning. 5–18.

Morton, K. The irony of service: Charity, project and social change in service-learning. 19–32.

Olney, C., & Grande, S. Validation of a scale to measure development of social responsibility. 43–53.

Schmiede, A. E. Using focus groups in service-learning: Implications for practice and research. 63–71.

Zlotkowski, E. Does service-learning have a future? 123–133.

1996, Volume 3

Cone, D., & Harris, S. Service-learning practice: A theoretical framework. 31–43.

Connors, K., Seifer, S., Sebastian, J., Cora-Bramble, D., & Hart, R. Interdisciplinary collaboration in service-learning: Lessons from the health professions. 113–127.

Driscoll, A., Holland, B., Gelmon, S., & Kerrigan, S. An assessment model for service-learning: Comprehensive case studies of impact on faculty, students, community and institution. 66–71.

Herman, L., & Shortell, J. W. Learning peace? Creating a class on creating community. 128–138.

Hudson, W. E. Combining community service and the study of American public policy. 82–91.

Kendrick, J. R., Jr. Outcomes of service-learning in an introduction to sociology course. 72–81.

Mendel-Reyes, M., & Weinstein, J. Community service-learning as democratic education in South Africa and the United States. 103–112.

Minter, D. W., & Schweingruber, H. The instructional challenge of community service-learning. 92–102.

Myers-Lipton, S. J. Effect of a comprehensive service-learning program on college students' level of modern racism. 44–54.

Richman, K. A. Epistemology, communities, and experts: A response to Goodwin Liu. 5–12.

Saltmarsh, J. Education for critical citizenship: John Dewey's contribution to the pedagogy of community service-learning. 13–21.

Varlotta, L. E. Service-learning: A catalyst for constructing democratic progressive communities. 22–30.

Ward, K. Service-learning and student volunteerism: Reflections on institutional commitment. 55–65.

1997, Volume 4

Althaus, J. Service-learning and leadership development: Posing questions not answers. 122–129.

Bullard, J., & Maloney, J. Curious Minds after-school program: A creative solution to a community need. 116–121.

Coyle, E. J., Jamieson, L. H., & Sommers, L. S. EPICS: A model for integrating service-learning into the engineering curriculum. 81–89.

Dunlap, M. R. The role of the personal fable in adolescent service-learning and critical reflection. 56–63.

Eyler, J., Giles, D. E., Jr., & Braxton, J. The impact of service-learning on college students. 5–15.

Frazier, D. A multicultural reading and writing experience: Read aloud as service-learning in English class. 98–103.

Hatcher, J. A. The moral dimensions of John Dewey's philosophy: Implications for undergraduate education. 22–29.

Hayes, E., & Cuban, S. Border pedagogy: A critical framework for service-learning. 72–80.

Holland, B. Analyzing institutional commitment to service: A model of key organizational factors. 30–41.

Lenk, M. M. Discipline-specific knowledge in service-learning: A strategic alliance amongst universities, professional associations, and non-profit organizations. 104–108.

Miller, J. The impact of service-learning experiences on students' sense of power. 16–21.

Morton, K., & Saltmarsh, J. Addams, Day, and Dewey: The emergence of community service in American culture. 137–149.

Raskoff, S. Group dynamics in service-learning: Guiding student relations. 109–115.

Reardon, K. M. Institutionalizing community service-learning at a major research university: The case of the East St. Louis Action Research Project. 130–136.

Rice, D., & Stacey, K. Small group dynamics as a catalyst for change: A faculty development model for academic service-learning. 64–71.

Wade, R. C., & Yarbrough, D. B. Community service-learning in student teaching: Toward the development of an active citizenry. 42–55.

Williams, D. D., & Eiserman, W. D. Expanding the dialogue: Service-learning in Costa Rica and Indonesia. 90–97.

1998, Volume 5

Buchanan, R. L. Integrating service-learning into the mainstream: A case study. 114–119.

Dunlap, M. R. Voices of students in multicultural service-learning settings. 58–67.

Foos, C. L. The 'different voice' of service. 14–21.

Gelmon, S. B., Holland, B. A., Seifer, S. D., Shinnamon, A., & Connors, K. Community-university partnerships for mutual learning. 97–107.

Keith, N. Z. Community service for community building: The school-based service corps as border crossers. 86–96.

Koliba, C. Lessons in citizen forums and democratic decision-making: A service-learning case study. 75–85.

Mabry, J. B. Pedagogical variations in service-learning and student outcomes: How time, contact, and reflection matter. 32–47.

Mattson, K. Can service-learning transform the modern university?: A lesson from history. 108–113.

Ogburn, F., & Wallace, B. Freshman composition, the Internet, and service-learning. 68–74.

Osborne, R. E., Hammerich, S., & Hensley, C. Student effects of service-learning: Tracking change across a semester. 5–13.

Reeb, R. N., Katsuyama, R. M., Sammon, J. A., & Yoder, D. S. The community service self-efficacy scale: Evidence of reliability, construct validity, and pragmatic utility. 48–57.

Wolfson, L., & Wilinsky, J. What service-learning can learn from situated learning. 22–31.

1999, Volume 6

Bacon, N. The trouble with transfer: Lessons from a study of community service writing. 53–62.

Coles, R. L. Race-focused service-learning courses: Issues and recommendations. 97–105.

Cumbo, K. B., & Vadeboncoeur, J. A. What are students learning?: Assessing cognitive outcomes in K-12 service-learning. 84–96.

Deans, T. Service-learning in two keys: Paulo Freire's critical pedagogy in relation to John Dewey's pragmatism. 15–29.

Howard, V. A. The humanities and service-learning: Whence and whither? 123–132.

Kellogg, W. A. Toward more transformative service-learning: Experiences from an urban environmental problem-solving class. 63–73.

Korfmacher, K. S. Alumni perspectives on environmental service-learning: Implications for instructors. 38–52.

Sherman, M. A. Teaching grassroots democracy through service-learning: Lessons from the collaborative teaching/lawyering method of clinical legal education. 74–83.

Tucker, R. E. Biting the pragmatist bullet: Why service-learning can do without epistemology. 5–14.

Vernon, A., & Ward, K. Campus and community partnerships: Assessing impacts and strengthening connections. 30–37.

Whitfield, T. S. Connecting service- and classroom-based learning: The use of problem-based learning. 106–111.

2000, Volume 7

Boyle-Baise, M., & Kilbane, J. What really happens? A look inside service-learning for multicultural teacher education. 54–64.

Cummings, C. K. John Dewey and the rebuilding of urban community: Engaging undergraduates as neighborhood organizers. 97–108.

Ferrari, J. R., & Worrall, L. Assessments by community agencies: How "the other side" sees service-learning. 35–40.

Godar, S. H. Live cases: Service-learning consulting projects in business courses. 126–132.

Jeffers, C. S. Between school and community: Situating service-learning in university art galleries. 109–116.

Payne, C. A. Changes in involvement preferences as measured by the community service involvement preference inventory. 41–45.

Robinson, T. Dare the school build a new social order? 142–157.

Rockquemore, K. A., & Schaffer, R. H. Toward a theory of engagement: A cognitive mapping of service-learning experiences. 14–24.

Strage, A. A. Service-learning: Enhancing student learning outcomes in a college-level lecture course. 5–13.

Subramony, M. The relationship between performance feedback and service-learning. 46–53.

Varlotta, L. Service as text: Making the metaphor meaningful. 76–84.

Vogelgesang, L. J., & Astin, A. W. Comparing the effects of community service and service-learning. 25–34.

Wallace, J. The problem of time: Enabling students to make long-term commitments to community-based learning. 133–141.

Werner, C. M., & McVaugh, N. Service-learning "rules" that encourage or discourage long-term service: Implications for practice and research. 117–125.

Williams, D. R. Participants in, not spectators to, democracy: The discourse on civic responsibility in higher education. 158–164.

2000, Special Issue

Astin, A. W. Conceptualizing service-learning research using Ken Wilber's integral framework. 98–104.

Bringle, R. G., & Hatcher, J. A. Meaningful measurement of theory-based service-learning outcomes: Making the case with quantitative research. 68–75.

Chesler, M., & Scalera, C. V. Race and gender issues related to service-learning research. 18–27.

Cruz, N. I., & Giles, D. E., Jr. Where's the community in service-learning research? 18–34.

Driscoll, A. Studying faculty and service-learning: Directions for inquiry and development. 35–41.

Eyler, J. S. What do we most need to know about the impact of service-learning on student learning? 11–17.

Furco, A. Establishing a national center for research to systematize the study of service-learning. 129–134.

Gelmon, S. B. Challenges in assessing service-learning. 84–90.

Harvaky, I., Puckett, J., & Romer, D. Action research: Bridging service and research. 113–118.

Holland, B. Institutional impacts and organizational issues related to service-learning. 52–60.

Howard, J. P. F., Gelmon, S. B., & Giles, D. E., Jr. From yesterday to tomorrow: Strategic directions for service-learning research. 5–10.

Kahne, J., Westheimer, J., & Rogers, B. Service-learning and citizenship: Directions for research. 42–51.

Moore, D. T. The relationship between experiential learning research and service-learning research. 124–128.

Pollack, S. The role of research and policy in constituting the service-learning field. 105–112.

Ramaley, J. A. Strategic directions for service-learning research: A presidential perspective. 91–97.

Shumer, R. Science or storytelling: How should we conduct and report service-learning research? 76–83.

Stanton, T. K. Bringing reciprocity to service-learning research and practice. 119–123.

Zlotkowski, E. Service-learning in the disciplines. 61–67.

Fall 2001, Volume 8 Number 1

Gent, P. J., and Gurecka, L. E. Service-learning: A disservice to people with disabilities? 36–43.

Green, A. E. "But you aren't white": Racial perceptions and service-learning. 18–26.

Handley, G. B. The humanities and citizenship: A challenge for service-learning. 52–61.

Kinnevy, S. C., & Boddie, S. C. Developing community partnerships through service-learning: Universities, coalitions, and congregations. 44–51.

Mills, S. D. Electronic journaling: Using the web-based, group journal for service-learning reflection. 27–35.

Porter, M., and Monard, K. *Ayni* in the global village: Building relationships of reciprocity through international service-learning. 5–17.

Spring 2002, Volume 8 Number 2

Dubinsky, J. M. Service-learning as a path to virtue: The ideal orator in professional communication. 61–74.

Litke, R. A. Do all students 'get it'?: Comparing students' reflections to course performance. 27–34.

Moely, B. E., Mercer, S. H., Ilustre, V., Miron, D., & McFarland, M. Students' attitudes related to service-learning. 15–26.

Prins, E. S. The relationship between institutional mission, service, and service-learning at community colleges in New York State. 35–49.

Root, S., Callahan, J., & Sepanski, J. Building teaching dispositions and service-learning practice: A multi-site study. 50–60.

Steinke, P., & Buresh, S. Cognitive outcomes of service-learning: Reviewing the past and glimpsing the future. 5–14.

Fall 2002, Volume 9 Number 1

Abes, E. S., Jackson, G., & Jones, S. R. Factors that motivate and deter faculty use of service-learning. 5–17.

Bacon, N. Differences in faculty and community partners' theories of learning. 34–44.

Curry, J. M., Heffner, G., & Warners, D. Environmental service-learning: Social transformation through caring for a particular place. 58–66.

Moely, B. E., McFarland, M., Miron, D., Mercer, S., & Ilustre, V. Changes in college students' attitudes and intentions for civic involvement as a function of service-learning experiences. 18–26.

Pompa, L. Service-learning as crucible: Reflections on immersion, context, power, and transformation. 67–76.

Winter 2003, Volume 9 Number 2

Anderson, D. D. Students and service staff learning and researching together on a college campus. 47–58.

Chesler, M. A., Kellman-Fritz, J., & Knife-Gould, A. Training peer facilitators for community service-learning leadership. 59–76.

Evangelopoulos, N., Sidorova, A., & Riolli, L. Can service-learning help students appreciate an unpopular course?: A theoretical framework. 15–24.

Sperling, R., Wang, V. O., Kelly, J. M., & Hritsuk, B. Does one size fit all? The challenge of social cognitive development. 5–14.

Stevens, C. S. Unrecognized roots of service-learning in African American social thought and action, 1890–1930. 25–34.

Stoecker, R. Community-based research: From practice to theory and back again. 35–46.

Summer 2003, Volume 9 Number 3

Marulla, S., Cooke, D., Rollins, A., Burke, J., Bonilla, P., & Waldref, V. Community-based research assessments: Some principles and practices. 57–68.

Polanyi, M., & Cockburn, L. Opportunities and pitfalls of community-based research: A case study. 16–25.

Stoecker, R., Ambler, S. H., Cutforth, N., Donohue, P., Dougherty, D., Marulla, S., et al. Community-based research networks: Development and lessons learned in an emerging field. 44–56.

Strand, K., Marulla, S., Cutforth, N., Stoeker, R., & Donohue, P. Principles of best
    practice for community-based research. 5–15.
Weinberg, A. S. Negotiating community-based research: A case study of the 'Life's
    Work' project. 26–35.
Willis, J., Peresie, J., Waldref, V., & Stockmann, D. The student's role in community-
    based research. 1–4.

Index

About the Editors and the Contributors

C. D. ABEL is an associate professor at Stephen F. Austin State University. She teaches both graduate and undergraduate teacher candidates in the areas of literacy and assessment and has worked with many preservice teachers in the field. Last year's publications include a book chapter on internationalizing higher education and an article she coauthored on high-stakes testing and teacher preparation in the National Council of Teachers of English *Language Arts* journal.

C. F. ABEL is an assistant professor of political science and director of the Knowledge Factory, a center for basic and applied research at Stephen F. Austin State University in Nacogdoches, Texas.

FRANK CODISPOTI is an assistant professor of political science at Stephen F. Austin State University. His interest in service-learning stems from a more basic interest in ethics and politics. He is currently working on a study of sources of authority in justifications of civil disobedience.

ROBERT J. EXLEY serves as vice president for academic affairs at Iowa Western Community College, Council Bluffs, Iowa. He served as the founding director for the Miami-Dade Community College Partners in Action and Learning service-learning program. He also serves as an adjunct instructor for Iowa State University in education policy and leadership. He has been an active member of Broadening Horizons through

Service-learning, a national service-learning project of the American Association of Community Colleges.

RICHARD L. HENDERSON is a professor of education and coordinator of the organizational leadership Ph.D. program at the University of the Incarnate Word in San Antonio, Texas, where he currently holds the Theophane Power Chair in Education. He has teaching and administrative experience in private as well as public education and as a consultant for a variety of human service institutions and private corporations. He has more than 25 publications to his credit and has been a presenter at numerous national and international conferences.

SHERRY L. HOPPE has more than 17 years as a college president in the Tennessee Board of Regents system and currently serves as president of Austin Peay State University.

J. G. LACINA received her Ph.D. in Curriculum and Instruction/TESOL from the University of Kansas in 1999. She is currently an assistant professor in the Department of Elementary Education at Stephen F. Austin State University. She coordinates a Web-based postbaccalaureate and ESL program, and she teaches and publishes in the areas of TESOL, teacher education, and writing methods. Dr. Lacina serves as the column editor for "Technology in the Classroom" for the journal *Childhood Education*, and she serves on the advisory board for the Higher Education Collaborative with the Texas Center for Reading/Language Arts at the University of Texas at Austin.

CHRISTINA MURPHY is the dean of the College of Liberal Arts and professor of English at Marshall University in Huntington, West Virginia. Dr. Murphy has published extensively on writing centers and writing program administration. She is the author of seven books, including *The St. Martin's Sourcebook for Writing Tutors* and *Writing Centers: An Annotated Bibliography*, and has won national awards for her scholarly publications. She is recognized as a leading scholar in writing center theory and has also received national recognition for her work as editor of the scholarly journals *Composition Studies* and *Studies in Psychoanalytic Theory*.

JORDY ROCHELEAU is an assistant professor of philosophy at Austin Peay State University, where he teaches courses in ethics, including educational ethics, and nineteenth- and twentieth-century philosophy. He recently completed his dissertation on the political ethic of Habermas, titled "Universalism and Its Critics: A Defense of Discourse Ethics," at Michigan State University. His current research interests are in democratic theory, international politics, and human rights.

ARTHUR SEMENTELLI is an assistant professor of public administration at Florida Atlantic University and a member of the editorial board of *Administrative Theory and Praxis*. Dr. Sementelli has a Ph.D. from Cleveland State University's Levin College of Urban Affairs, an M.P.A. from Gannon University, and an undergraduate degree from Carnegie Mellon. He is the author of articles on environmental policy, critical theory, and discourse theory.

BRUCE W. SPECK is professor of English and vice president for academic affairs at Austin Peay State University. He has held faculty appointments at Indiana University, Purdue University at Fort Wayne, and the University of Memphis. He was associate vice chancellor for academic affairs and dean of the College of Arts and Sciences at the University of North Carolina at Pembroke. He has published two books on writing, six annotated bibliographies, and coedited volumes on assessing online classes, internationalizing higher education, grading students' classroom performance, establishing service-learning opportunities for students, and teaching nonnative English speakers. He has also published poems and a book of poetry.

PETER H. STODDARD is associate professor of social work at Austin Peay State University. He received his Ph.D. from Case Western Reserve University.

J. B. WATSON, JR., serves as associate professor of sociology and gerontology coordinator at Stephen F. Austin State University, Nacogdoches, Texas. Two service-learning projects he directed (in 1994 and 1997) were recognized as Make A Difference Day Top 50 Honorable Mention events by *USA Weekend* magazine. His research interests include the long-term impact of disasters and intergenerational service-learning.

GREGORY R. ZIEREN is an associate professor of history at Austin Peay State University, where he has taught since 1991. He received a B.A. from the University of Michigan, an M.A. from the University of London, and a Ph.D. from the University of Delaware. He taught history for three years at the University of Iowa and held a Fulbright Fellowship to teach in Germany at the University of Kassel and the University of Erlangen. He is working on a book about the image of the United States in Germany in the pre–World War I era. He also directs an oral history service-learning project for students conducting interviews with World War II and Korean War veterans.

3